The Dick Van Dyke Show

The Dick Van Dyke Show

GINNY WEISSMAN and COYNE STEVEN SANDERS

ST. MARTIN'S PRESS
New York

Library of Congress Cataloging in Publication Data

Weissman, Ginny.
    The Dick Van Dyke show book / Ginny Weissman
and Coyne Steven Sanders.
      p.   cm.
    Rev. ed. of: The Dick Van Dyke show. 1st ed. © 1983.
    "A Thomas Dunne book."
    ISBN 0-312-08766-7 (pbk.)
    1. Dick Van Dyke show (Television program)
I. Sanders, Coyne Steven.   II. Weissman, Ginny.
Dick Van Dyke show.   III. Title.
   PN1992.77.D5W4   1993
    791.45′72—dc20
                                      92-44034
                                           CIP

FIRST REVISED EDITION

10 9 8 7 6 5 4 3 2 1

For
Carl Reiner,
who made *The Dick Van Dyke Show* possible
and
our parents
Josephine and Edwin Komos
and
Marge Sanders,
who made *us* possible

Contents

Acknowledgments

WE WISH TO EXPRESS our sincere appreciation to the following people who graciously shared both time and memories with us: Dick Van Dyke, Mary Tyler Moore, Sheldon Leonard, Danny Thomas, Bill Persky, and Marge Mullen; a special thank you to Carl Reiner, Richard Deacon, Rose Marie, Morey Amsterdam, Sam Denoff, Ann Guilbert, Jerry Paris, John Rich, Larry Mathews, Jane Dulo, and Frank Adamo who, in addition, loaned to us irreplaceable photographs and materials from their own collections.

Our gratitude to Dick Jordan and Maureen McMaster; Patricia Newcomb and Jacqueline Becher; Gail Plautz and Sallie Jones at CBS; Judi Nagy; Bill Wills; George Shapiro; Jackie Koch; Norman Lear; Barbara Scher, Carl Reiner's assistant; Stuart Shostak of Shokus Video; William McNeil, Randy Pursley and Tom Gilbert; Nikki Biers; Lynette Cimini; Sol Leon of the William Morris Agency; and Larry Jones, Scott Webb, and Donna Friedman of Nick at Nite.

A personal note of thanks to John R. Powers, Don Azars, Larry Townsend, Michael Miller, Reiva Lesonsky, our agent, Dominick Abel (for believing in us and the project from the start), our editor, Tom Dunne, and his assistants, Sharon Rudd, Pamela Dorman, and Peter Wolverton.

And finally, a very special thank you to a very special man, Ron Jacobs, who gave most generously of his knowledge and the resources of Calvada Productions, providing us with a wealth of photographs and reference materials. Mr. Jacobs has been invaluable in the preparation of this book, and we are most grateful.

Foreword

WHENEVER ASKED what I consider my best effort of all the things I've ever done in show business, I answer, unhesitatingly, *The Dick Van Dyke Show*.

I'm happy to find that someone feels strongly enough to write a book about the show. Why else would they bother to write a book called *The Dick Van Dyke Show: Anatomy of a Classic* if they didn't feel that way? For the money? Impossible.

I might argue about the title calling *The Dick Van Dyke Show* a classic. I think the word "classic" should be reserved for a work that endures longer than thirty years, but I won't quibble. Perhaps *The Dick Van Dyke Show: Anatomy of a Classy Bunch* would be better, because this *was* a classy bunch of people. Maybe you need classy people to *make* a classic. In that context, I would accept the word "classic."

That the show was a collaborative effort has been said so many times, but it's absolutely true. *The Dick Van Dyke Show* was a totally nourishing experience.

Carl Reiner

Introduction

THERE EXISTS in the history of television a handful of programs that truly can be deemed "classics." Within that group, only a cluster of series are populated by characters that are appealing, warm, vulnerable, human, and funny.

The ensemble of *The Dick Van Dyke Show* generated a near-unparalleled amount of loyalty, making it one of the most beloved series of all time. The added ingredients of consistently fine writing and direction resulted in critical acclaim and numerous accolades.

Initially, few realized its potential and none predicted its phenomenal success. Three decades later, this literate, sophisticated series has weathered the mercurial tastes of the American public. Never off the air since its network premiere on October 3, 1961, this timeless situation comedy continues to be discovered by new generations.

Its popularity has earned *The Dick Van Dyke Show* a special place in broadcasting history and a permanent place in our hearts.

This book is a tribute to the creativity, talent, imagination, and humanity of an extraordinary group of people.

We invite you to join us in a fond celebration of America's continuing love affair with Rob, Laura, Buddy, and Sally.

Ginny Weissman
Coyne Steven Sanders
August 1992

The
Dick Van Dyke
Show

☆ 1 ☆

Anatomy of a Classic

"I remember exactly where it happened—it was on 96th Street by the East River in New York. I was driving my car downtown from New Rochelle, wondering what ground do I stand on that no one else stands on? I thought, I am an actor and writer who worked on the Sid Caesar shows. That's a different milieu: the home life of a television show writer."

—CARL REINER

It was 1959. Carl Reiner had just ended an illustrious nine-year association with Sid Ceasar on *Your Show of Shows, Caesar's Hour,* and *Sid Caesar Invites You.* As resident member of a sterling company that included Imogene Coca, Howard Morris, Mel Brooks, Neil Simon, Larry Gelbart, Joe Stein, Mel Tolkin, Lucille Kallen, and Tony Webster, Reiner won Emmy Awards in 1956 and 1957 as "Best Supporting Actor."

Although billed as a performer, Reiner was also an uncredited writer who was always in the writer's room—"the most interesting room I'd ever been in," claims Reiner. Gradually he began thinking of himself as more of a writer than a performer. During his summer vacations, he wrote his autobiographical novel, *Enter Laughing,* published in 1958.

At the conclusion of his television association with Sid Caesar, Reiner felt that the revue form (comedy/variety) was dying and that situation comedy would come into its own. Besieged with offers, he was inundated with scripts that by his estimation—and that of his wife, Estelle—were not very good. Discouraged by inferior material, Reiner didn't know what to do. Estelle Reiner read some of the scripts offered to her husband and told him, "You can write better scripts than these."

The challenge appealed to Reiner, who had never written a situation comedy. "That little nub stayed in my head—I kept asking myself, 'What do I know about that's different from anything else?' "

Reiner spent the summer of 1959 on Fire Island, where he worked on the concept. He would star in a situation comedy as Robert Petrie—a name he

Starring
CARL REINER

1

thought sounded like a television writer's name. (Robert was also the name of Reiner's twelve-year-old son—who would eventually costar in *All in the Family*.)

Petrie would be head writer for a weekly variety series, *The Alan Sturdy Show*. Reiner chose the name Alan Sturdy because "it was metaphoric, a poetic name—a name that was strong," he says. (Later the name would be changed to Alan *Brady* after Sheldon Leonard and Morey Amsterdam both remarked that Alan Sturdy sounds like "Alan's dirty.")

Sturdy surrounded himself with a first-rate, disparate writing staff. Under Petrie were Sally Rogers—modeled after two TV writers, Selma Diamond and Lucille Kallen, with whom Reiner had previously worked—and Buddy Sorrell.

The producer of *The Alan Sturdy Show* was Calvin Cooley (later renamed Melvin Cooley), who not-so-coincidentally was the star's brother-in-law.

Petrie had a home at 448 Bonnie Meadow Road in New Rochelle, New York—Reiner simply added one number to his own address "so nobody would come visit me." The Petrie family consisted of Rob, his wife, Laura—"a name romantic to me somehow," Reiner says—and their only child, Ritchie. Rob met Laura Meehan when he was a sergeant in the Army, stationed at Camp Crowder in Joplin, Missouri, and she was a dancer in the USO. Laura willingly had given up her career to become Mrs. Robert Petrie.

"It was actually what my wife and I were doing.

She was an artist who decided she wanted to be a mother. She had three children, and gave up her own career for that," explains Reiner.

At first glance those ingredients might seem mundane. What propelled the story out of the ordinary was Reiner's execution of the work/home relationship. He had conceived a first in television history. "What I was doing was examining my life and putting it down on paper," recalls Reiner. In doing so he would create what in essence was "the first situation comedy where you saw where the man worked *before* he walked in and said, 'Hi, honey, I'm home!'"

Danny Thomas had followed that formula to some extent in his series, but, as Reiner points out, Thomas's series focused on his home life and only occasionally showed him in his nightclub.

In no time, Reiner wrote a pilot script that he titled *Head of the Family*. After completing the draft, he decided he needed several scripts to illustrate the emphasis and the kind of behavior and relationships he was striving for. "I didn't want to leave it to anybody else," he recalls.

Completely absorbed in *Head of the Family*, Reiner wrote, by his estimation, a complete script every three or four days. At first he thought he'd write four to eight scripts before showing them to anybody; the total mushroomed to thirteen. "This would be a nucleus, a bible, for anybody who would help write it after that," recalls Reiner. "It would guard against supposition; everything would be spelled out."

He did not submit any of the scripts until all thirteen had been completed. Reiner's agent, Harry Kalcheim of the William Morris Agency, was astounded that someone would write thirteen scripts for a series that had neither a sponsor nor a network.

Academy Award–winning writer Frank Tarloff (who would later write three *Dick Van Dyke Show* scripts) recalls being "aghast" during a conversation with his prolific friend. "I said to Carl, 'Did you write the pilot?' and he said, 'No, I wrote all thir-

The original Petrie family: Laura (Barbara Britton), Ritchie (Gary Morgan), and Rob (Carl Reiner).
CARL REINER

teen of them.' As an old, experienced person in the business, I said, 'Carl, you don't do it that way. You don't write number two until they've bought number one.' "

Kalcheim sent the scripts to Peter Lawford, who had expressed an interest in producing a television series. Lawford, at that time the husband of Pat Kennedy (sister of the soon-to-be-President), gave the scripts to his father-in-law Joseph Kennedy because, as Reiner discloses, "Everything the Kennedy money went into had to be approved by him." Kennedy okayed Reiner's material and subsequently financed the pilot with Lawford.

The pilot then was cast and filmed in New York as a one-camera show, that is, it was shot out of sequence without an audience.

The storyline: Rob Petrie—originally pronounced PEE-TREE not PET-REE—(Carl Reiner), and wife Laura (Barbara Britton) attempt to convince their son Ritchie (Gary Morgan) that Petrie's occupation as a television writer is as important as those of the fathers of his classmates. Rob brings his son to the office to show him how valuable he is to his colleagues, Sally Rogers (Sylvia Miles) and Buddy Sorrell (Morty Gunty), and to the star, Alan Sturdy (Jack Wakefield).

Reiner contends that the pilot, which was aired on July 19, 1960, on *Comedy Spot*, was very well received by the sponsors. Yet, he recalls, only one situation comedy sold that year—*Love and Marriage*. (It was canceled at midseason.) The sponsors opted, in Reiner's words, "to go with horses and guns." Westerns were riding high that season. (*Gunsmoke*, *Wagon Train*, and *Have Gun, Will*

Carl Reiner: "There's no way I could ever have brought to this part what Dick Van Dyke did. He was masterful. I think he's the best light situation comedy performer who ever lived. There's no question about it. Dick made everything I wrote twice as good as I could have, just by his presence and the way he performed it. It became much better than I could ever have done it."
CALVADA PRODUCTIONS

Travel were the three top-rated shows of the 1959–60 and 1960–61 seasons).

But Kalcheim continued to remind Reiner that *Head of the Family* was too good to let atrophy. He insisted the scripts be submitted once again in the hopes of reviving the idea as a possible series. "He hounded me, week after week," says Reiner, who was opposed to the idea. He told Kalcheim, "I don't want to fail twice with the same material. They don't understand it or they would have bought it in a second. If they don't want it, they don't want it."

Undaunted by Reiner's protests, Kalcheim persisted. He then conspired to bring Reiner together with another client: Sheldon Leonard.

"I consider myself lucky to have been a television pioneer."

—SHELDON LEONARD

In 1953, Leonard had begun an extremely successful association with Danny Thomas. In the first season of *Make Room for Daddy*, he was signed as executive producer and director. With Thomas he had created, by 1960, *The Andy Griffith Show* and *The Real McCoys*. In fact, Leonard had never produced a pilot that didn't sell. That perfect record, coupled with his keen perception of what was salable, salvageable material, made him, in Kalcheim's opinion, the ideal candidate to resurrect *Head of the Family*.

Kalcheim arranged for Reiner, who was eager to learn more about situation comedy, to meet with the veteran Leonard, who offered him free access to observe and "audit" any productions he wished. During his visit, Carl spoke of his aborted venture. Leonard expressed an interest in screening the pilot to judge for himself, and Reiner agreed.

Leonard vividly remembers the day: "The lights went up, and I was torn between a desire to be helpfully honest and a desire to be tactful."

When Carl asked his opinion, Leonard answered, "I believe that if recast, the show would have every chance of making it."

Misunderstanding his carefully worded response, Reiner replied, "No, I don't want to do it again."

"The only honest thing I could say was, 'Carl, you're not right for what you wrote for yourself!' "

Chita Rivera (left), *Kay Medford* (center), *and Dick Van Dyke in the Broadway production* Bye Bye Birdie.
FRANK ADAMO

recalls Leonard, who then asked to read the remaining twelve scripts.

"It was a tremendous body of material. For unrevised drafts, [it was] the best material I have ever read," states Leonard. Believing in the strength and quality of the scripts, he told Reiner, "This series deserves another shot. Do you mind if I try to rewrap the package?" Reiner accepted. The characters would be recast, Leonard would direct the pilot, and Reiner would produce and continue to write.

That would not be the last time Sheldon Leonard would save Rob Petrie from extinction.

Faced with the recasting of the crucial role of Rob Petrie, it no longer was enough for Sheldon Leonard to feel intuitively that Reiner wasn't right for the part: he had to find the actor who *was*.

A seemingly endless string of candidates was eventually narrowed to two actors: Dick Van Dyke and Johnny Carson. Van Dyke was the suggestion of Leonard, who remembered him from a 1958 Broadway revue, *The Girls Against the Boys* (also featuring Bert Lahr, Shelley Berman, and Nancy Walker). Previously the young performer had made several unsold TV pilots, had served as emcee on various daytime programs, and had been a frequent variety show guest. Back on Broadway, Van Dyke was in a leading role in *Bye Bye Birdie* (with Chita Rivera and Kay Medford), for which he won a Tony Award.

Although Carson was perhaps more well-known at the time, Leonard believed Van Dyke the ideal choice for the role of Rob Petrie. He also defied the trend of showcasing film stars, such as Robert Taylor and Dick Powell, who were, as Leonard believed, "too glamorous to be sharing your living room. Dick's [Van Dyke] jaw was a little too long, his walk a little too gangly—assets, not liabilities, on TV," explains Leonard. The part of Rob Petrie, Reiner contended, "required a performer who doesn't want to get up in front of an audience, but who can perform in a room at a party."

On Leonard's recommendation, Carl Reiner traveled to New York to see *Bye Bye Birdie* and meet with Van Dyke. As he watched him perform, Reiner remembers thinking, "He is the perfect choice. I was very impressed." Backstage he offered Dick the role of Rob Petrie and asked him to return to California. Van Dyke was reluctant to relinquish the security of a hit show, but Reiner's enthusiasm was so persuasive Dick agreed to star in the pilot and would arrange to get one week off from *Birdie* for rehearsal and filming, never imagining those seven days would be the turning point of his career.

Script supervisor Marge Mullen recalls the very first time Dick came into the office: "Carl and Sheldon were wondering how many people would be in the entourage to protect him and talk about script ideas. Dick just walked in all by himself. I thought, here's somebody who just trusts them. He can talk to them on a man-to-man basis and not have an agent over his shoulder talking for him. He was secure enough in his own knowledge and talent to talk for himself. And that's the way it worked right from the beginning."

Van Dyke agreed to a five-year contract (if the pilot became a series) with a first-season salary, according to him, of $1500 weekly. (He states his top salary for the series was $2500 weekly.)

With Van Dyke signed as the lead the search was underway for a new supporting cast.

Unlike Van Dyke, Rose Marie had enjoyed a successful career in television prior to being cast as Sally Rogers, Rob Petrie's glib, perennially single coworker.

"I had done," Rose Marie flatly states, "almost every guest shot on television there was to do." In addition to a recurring role on *The Bob Cummings Show* she was a regular on *My Sister Eileen*, a short-lived series of the 1960–61 season.

Having begun performing at age three as "Baby Rose Marie"—and holding the distinction of starring in her own NBC network radio series at the age of seven—Rose Marie was unquestionably a show business veteran. Her lifelong career had reaped many benefits, including longstanding friendships with both Danny Thomas and Sheldon Leonard.

Yet those friendships had never resulted in her being cast by them. She recalls, "I always teased Danny and Sheldon by saying, 'Why can't I do your show? You put everyone else on but me!'"

At one point, Leonard flew to Las Vegas to see her nightclub act, and as Rose Marie remembers, said to her, "Don't you ever do badly?" She retorted, "Yeah, I *must* because I can't get a shot on your show!" He promised, "Your time will come."

It did a short time later when Rose Marie received a call from the casting office at Desilu–Cahuenga Studios. She was pleased Leonard had kept his promise and assumed he wanted her for a guest shot on *The Danny Thomas Show*. To her surprise she was told it was a continuing role in a series to star Dick Van Dyke. She hadn't seen him in *Bye Bye Birdie*, but the name registered since she had appeared with him on a game show, *Pantomime Quiz*, a year or so earlier.

When she met Carl Reiner he greeted her by saying, "I don't know that much about you, but Sheldon said, 'If you want the best, get Rose Marie!'" She was cast on the spot.

Rose Marie was curious to know who they had chosen to play the third writer, Buddy Sorrell. They hadn't decided, so she suggested Morey Amsterdam, whom she says she had known "for thousands of years"—they met when both appeared on Al Pearce's radio program when Rose Marie was only twelve years old.

Reiner jumped at the suggestion. Rose Marie quickly contacted Morey, who was living in New York, explained the concept of the series, and told him to expect Reiner's call. Morey warmed to the promise of the show as well as the opportunity to move to California. At the time Reiner phoned, Amsterdam remembers he was, "digging himself out of the snow in Yonkers."

Morey Amsterdam had had a show business ca-

Dick Van Dyke and personal assistant Frank Adamo in Dick's dressing room.
FRANK ADAMO

Rose Marie, 1961
CALVADA PRODUCTIONS

8

Morey Amsterdam, 1961
CALVADA PRODUCTIONS

9

reer as durable as Rose Marie's, having begun performing at the age of ten as a boy soprano on radio. Known as "the human joke machine," he had established himself as a nightclub performer, comedian, and comedy writer—all perfect credentials for the role.

Reiner asked Morey to catch a plane to Califor-

part." He was scheduled among the first to read that day and recalls speaking to Carl Reiner, who promptly told him, "You're exactly what I had in mind."

Although Reiner knew Deacon socially, having met him at a party at Imogene Coca's, Deacon recalls, "He knew nothing of any past credits I had,"

The Alan Brady Show *staff at work*
CALVADA PRODUCTIONS

nia the next day. He didn't hesitate and soon was cast as Buddy Sorrell.

As the book *Watching TV* notes, "In a stroke of genius, veteran comics Morey Amsterdam and Rose Marie were cast as the new Buddy and Sally. Both brought a much needed sharp comic edge to their characters."

The next role cast was the blustering producer of *The Alan Sturdy Show.* Richard Deacon answered a casting call and remembers: "Twenty-two character actors—the best in town—auditioned for the

which included supporting roles in the films *Good Morning, Miss Dove, The Blackboard Jungle,* and *The Solid Gold Cadillac* and hundreds of appearances on radio and television, on programs such as *The Life of Riley, I Love Lucy, Leave it to Beaver, The Gale Storm Show,* and *Burns and Allen.*

Deacon remembers Reiner telling him, "I don't want you to read anything—you probably could write your own script. The sad part of it is, I am morally and duty bound to see the rest of the actors out there, but you're it." A man of his word, Reiner

Richard Deacon, 1961
JANE DULO

11

Larry Mathews, age four and a half
CALVADA PRODUCTIONS

cast Deacon only after auditioning the remaining hopefuls.

Only one controversy surrounded Richard Deacon's character—naming him Mel Cooley. In his original script starring himself, Reiner had named the producer *Calvin* Cooley. According to Deacon it was Sheldon Leonard who thought Calvin Cooley sounded too much like President Calvin Coolidge and might "get a bad response." In Deacon's opinion, "It was Sheldon's only mistake in judgment. The name 'Mel' didn't ring true with me, I'd much rather it have been Calvin or Cal."

"Danny Thomas lives up the street from me. He comes over a couple of times a week to borrow a cup of jokes."

—MOREY AMSTERDAM

Whatever the name, Richard Deacon would provide Morey Amsterdam with the perfect foil for his deprecating one-liners. "I got a little paranoid about Morey always throwing a line at me," says Deacon. "I guess I was beginning to take it personally, although I knew he didn't mean it. So I told Carl. He tried about three lines, but none of them fit me, somehow. He asked, 'What's your reaction [to Buddy]?' I simply said, 'Yecch!' Carl said, 'That's it!' It became part of the show and it had only come out of my own frustration."

The casting of Ritchie, Rob and Laura's only child, was due indirectly to the efforts of a mailman.

While on his route in Burbank, California, the postman noticed the constant efforts of one of the Mazzeo family's seven children to get attention. "I was always doing mimicry and small skits," recalls Larry. The mailman's own son had won a talent contest, and he offered to introduce four and a half-year-old Larry Mazzeo to the boy's acting coach, Lois Auer, who specialized in training child actors. As a result, Larry signed with a management agency known for handling child performers.

As Larry recalls, "Not too long after I signed with them, Carl Reiner phoned, saying he needed a boy for the Dick Van Dyke pilot. I was the only one they sent."

Larry recounts being ushered into Mr. Reiner's office and being instructed by Carl "to be very sick and to lie on the couch and say, 'Oh, Mommy, my stomach hurts!' Next thing I knew, Mr. Reiner took me over to the stage and told me to do the same thing all over again."

Reiner introduced Larry to Sheldon Leonard, who agreed he was not a typical child actor but the All-American "normal boy they were looking for," as the CBS press release announcing Larry's signing put it.

Larry Mazzeo had become Larry Mathews because, as he put it, "Ethnic wasn't in at the time." But Larry was, and what remained was finding a mother for young Ritchie Petrie.

"The search for Laura Petrie was a tough one," confesses Carl Reiner, who by his own estimation saw well over sixty actresses for the part.

At one point while auditioning, Sheldon Leonard and Carl met with Leonard's business partner Danny Thomas, and told him they were on the verge of signing a New York actress. Thomas shrugged, saying, "Fine. If you like her, hire her. I'm going to get my hair done!" He left the morose pair to contemplate the compromise they were about to make in casting this very vital role. According to producer Ron Jacobs the actress was "the best of everyone we auditioned but still lacked that special spark we were looking for."

Thomas recalls that while he was in the barber chair "two heads popped through the door, one on top of the other, just like in the movies." Sheldon and Carl had tracked down Danny Thomas to tell him, "We sent her back to New York." "Why?" Danny asked. "Because you didn't like her!" Danny threw his hands up in the air, while the barber continued to snip away. "It's two against one, and I'm not even *against* you!" cried Danny.

Thomas then pictured a girl who a year earlier had auditioned to replace Sherry Jackson as Danny's daughter in his series. The actress lost the role to Penney Parker because, as Danny points out, "She was too sophisticated to be in our family." Besides, her physiognomy was against her. "She had the kind of nose that went the other way," explains Thomas.

After that cryptic description, Danny asked Sheldon and Carl if either of them could identify the actress. "Wasn't she in a detective show or something, showing her legs?" queried Leonard.

"What's her name?" "I don't know, she's got three," offered Thomas. "John Charles Thomas?" volunteered Leonard.

While Reiner continued auditioning other actresses, Sheldon searched for the name of this memorable but obscure actress who had impressed him during her audition for *The Danny Thomas Show*. "I thought longingly of that girl," sighs Leonard. "If only I could find her."

Leonard assimilated the fragments of information and concluded the girl with the three names had played the part of David Janssen's secretary, Sam, in the television series, *Richard Diamond, Private Detective* in 1959. The role was unusual—her legs were seen and her voice was heard but that was it. The performance was provocative to viewers, but it was frustrating for the actress (who left the series for those very reasons). The show's casting file provided the three names: Mary Tyler Moore.

Discouraged by her stagnant (albeit brief) career, Mary Tyler Moore contemplated not even bothering to answer the call to audition for Carl Reiner.

By the age of twenty-two, Moore claimed the dis-

Mary Tyler Moore as "Happy Hotpoint."
SHOKUS VIDEO

tinction of debuting as "Happy Hotpoint," merrily dancing atop kitchen appliances. After the unsatisfactory role of "Sam" she languished for two years as a dramatic actress in television series such as *77 Sunset Strip, Hawaiian Eye, The Deputy,* and *Bourbon Street Beat*.

Indelible is the moment her agent telephoned: "I was angry, having been on an interview that morning for a job I knew I wasn't going to get." Still disappointed over a series of unsuccessful interviews several days earlier for pilots and commercials, Mary was "having coffee with a girl friend when my agent called telling me, 'Get over to Carl Reiner's office. He wants to talk to you about playing Dick Van Dyke's wife.' I said to him, 'No, I'm not going. I may just as well stay home. I'm not going to get it. It's just not in the cards.' "

Despite her pessimism, Mary did, of course, agree to audition for two reasons: "I knew that it was potentially a very important interview. And I had been madly in love with Carl Reiner since he had been on the Sid Caesar show. I thought he was the funniest, most handsome thing ever."

Reiner recalls, "She said one line: 'Hello Rob, are you home?' or something. I grabbed her by the hair . . . [I think] she thought I was going to rape her!" Moore continues, "Carl commanded, 'Come with me!' and he took me by the arm and *dragged* me into Sheldon's office." Reiner gleefully exclaimed, "Here she is! She says 'hello' like a real person!" Sheldon listened to Mary read and concurred.

Sheldon and Carl then ran to Danny Thomas to announce their discovery and, as Thomas laughs, "Bow to the great genius who couldn't even think of one of her three names."

As Leonard, Reiner, and associate producer Ronald Jacobs remember it Mary was hired on the spot. Yet the one person who was doubtful was Moore herself. "I knew they were very excited but I don't think they were quite that specific, because I went through two days of agony waiting to hear from my agent."

Regardless of when Mary won the role, everyone concerned was joyous. They had found the perfect Laura Petrie, "filling the gaping hole in the middle," as Leonard puts it.

Moore feels she was "damned lucky" to have got-

Newsweek, August 6, 1966:
"Mary Tyler Moore is more than the girl next door—she is the fantasy girl of the American Dream."
CALVADA PRODUCTIONS

14

ten the role, although she was a little apprehensive at first. "I was going into a show that was essentially a comedy, surrounded by incredibly gifted comedians—and that made me quite nervous."

When introducing Mary to Dick, Reiner joked, "The chemistry between you two is very important, so I would appreciate it if you would go spend the weekend together somewhere!"

Associate producer Ron Jacobs describes Mary as "an unknown who became marvelous." Despite her ever-blossoming talents Mary seemed unaware of her potential and according to Sheldon Leonard once said during the series "that all she really hoped to get out of it was enough money for new drapes."

Regarded as one of the best and brightest in the business, Sheldon Leonard, who was in the enviable position of having an unspoiled record for producing pilots that went on the air, admits he had "the unquestioning support of two very powerful sponsors: Procter & Gamble and General Foods.

"Sponsors then were more powerful than the networks," he explains. "It was the sponsors who controlled the programing of a given time period." (This was a practice begun in radio that decreased as the cost of television advertising increased.) "General Foods, for example, owned nine o'clock Mondays on CBS, and put in whatever they wanted. If CBS president Jim Aubrey didn't like it, General Foods would take their daytime business elsewhere"—which by even the most conservative estimates would have been an enormous loss of revenue to the network.

"I was at that time doing three shows for General Foods and as a result had a very good relationship with Lee Rich, head of television at the Benton & Bowles agency, which represented both Procter & Gamble and General Foods. Benton & Bowles wanted to strengthen its hold on Procter & Gamble's business."

Lee Rich, who would go on to become president of Lorimar, producer of many successful TV series, including *The Waltons* and *Dallas*, arranged a meeting between Leonard and P&G, who, says

Mary Tyler Moore and Dick Van Dyke
CALVADA PRODUCTIONS

Leonard, "gave me what amounted to a blank check. They said they would back any pilot I chose in return for first refusal"—an option that would allow P&G to accept or reject the pilot before any other sponsor or advertising agency could view the property.

Leonard informed Procter & Gamble, Lee Rich, and the William Morris Agency (which represented him) he intended to produce *The Dick Van Dyke Show*. According to Leonard, "The William Morris Agency did an about-face and became hostile to the whole idea of *The Dick Van Dyke Show*." His perfect record was a "very valuable asset, not only to me but to the Morris Agency as well," explains Leonard. "They didn't want to see me spoil my batting average by producing a pilot [they felt] was destined to be a failure. But Procter & Gamble backed me up."

Leonard then faced interference from his protectors again: "The William Morris Agency said I was giving away too much in allowing Procter & Gamble first refusal on the Van Dyke pilot. Get last refusal, they said. If P&G, who pays for it, turns it down, who do you think will buy it? They said I didn't need Procter & Gamble's money. So I went to Danny Thomas, who funded the pilot for sixty thousand dollars."

Thomas recalls Leonard's offer: "'You finance it and I'll give my time.' I always worked with Sheldon like that. I would guarantee the money and he would get in there and pitch!"

Despite his success, Thomas admits, "I wasn't so wealthy at the time that I could afford to gamble. The money was right out of my own pocket. But I was perfectly willing to do it because I had great faith in it."

It was agreed the pilot would not have the same storyline as the version starring Reiner. Rather, another of his scripts was chosen, "The Sick Boy and the Sitter."

Marjorie Mullen, script supervisor for the series, conjectures that script was selected because it allowed Dick, Rose Marie, and Morey to perform in solo spots at a party at Alan Brady's. Mullen feels that device was important in quickly acquainting the audience with the characters of Rob Petrie, Sally Rogers, and Buddy Sorrell while showcasing the versatility of Dick Van Dyke, Rose Marie, and Morey Amsterdam.

"Sick Boy and the Sitter" had a simple plot: Head writer Bob Petrie is requested—tacitly commanded—by his boss, the star of *The Alan Brady Show,* to appear at a party at his penthouse that night along with his coworkers, Sally and Buddy, and Rob's wife, Laura.

Rob arrives home to tell Laura, "We've been invited to Alan Brady's penthouse to mingle with rich people."

LAURA: When?
ROB: Tonight! C'mon, better start doing those things you do to your face. I'll see if I have . . .
LAURA: Rob, we can't go tonight.
ROB: Why not?
LAURA: Ritchie isn't feeling well.
ROB: What's wrong with him?
LAURA: Nothing yet, but he was playing with Ellen and she suddenly came down with a temperature.

Dick Van Dyke: "The show would never have been that good without that cast."

ROB: Did Dr. Miller see him?
LAURA: Yes. He says we'd better keep an eye on him.
ROB: Then he's not really sick.
LAURA: Well, if you mean has he collapsed—no.
ROB: Well, is he in pain?
LAURA: Well, no . . .
ROB: Then how do you know he's sick?
LAURA: There are symptoms . . .
ROB: What symptoms?
LAURA: Well . . .
ROB: Come on, tell me, I'm the boy's father.
LAURA: He turned down his cupcake!

Laura refuses to leave Ritchie to attend the party, feeling Rob was invited to entertain Brady's guests. Adamant, Rob insists they attend.

LAURA: Then I think you should go . . . I really do. There's no sense in both our staying home. After all, you do have a responsibility to your work and I know how you feel.
ROB: You do?
LAURA: I do.
ROB: And you won't mind if I go alone?
LAURA: Not at all, darling.

Rob starts to go.

LAURA: *(cont'd):* It's just that *I* couldn't go to a party knowing that my son was on the verge of getting sick . . . I couldn't enjoy *myself.*

Rob manages to convince his wife to reluctantly leave Ritchie with a sitter, fifteen-year-old Janie, arguing that their son's temperature is only one-tenth of a degree higher than normal.
Woman's intuition warns Laura that: "Something is going to happen if I leave the house tonight."

Laura gives Janie her sitting instructions.

LAURA: Now here's the number. You be sure to call if he should get up and complain about anything.

Rob enters.

LAURA: And here's Dr. Miller's number. If he seems very sick, you can call Dr. Miller after you call

In "Sick Boy and the Sitter," a disgruntled Rob Petrie looks on as his frenetic wife Laura gives last-minute instructions to Ritchie's sitter Janie (Mary Lou Dearing).
CALVADA PRODUCTIONS

us. First call us, though, so we can start out right away.

ROB: Laura, it's getting late . . .

LAURA: Please, darling! Now do you understand what you're to do, Janie?

JANIE *(looking at pad)*: I'm to call this number if Ritchie gets sick and then call this number after I call this number.

LAURA: That's right. But you be sure to call and if the number is busy just keep trying. There'll be a lot of people there . . .

ROB: Laura, please can we get started?

LAURA *(she starts out and starts back)*: Oh, and if anything unusual happens, call your mother, she lives next door.

ROB: She knows where her mother lives.

LAURA: Oh, that's right. I'm sorry. Now . . . *(She takes pad back from Janie and starts writing.)* Here's your mother's phone number . . .

ROB: Honey, she *knows* her own number.

LAURA *(to Rob)*: I'm not myself. You see why I shouldn't be going to this party?

ROB: The drive will clear your head. *(Taking Laura's arm and leading her out)* C'mon honey.

LAURA *(who is now almost out of the room, shouts back)*: Oh Janie, there are some cupcakes in the breadbox and some milk in the refrigerator. There's a bottle that's been started on the door . . .

ROB: Honey, Washington said farewell to his troops in less time.

LAURA *(speaking rapidly)*: There's some orange soda-pop in the cupboard next to the sink. The ice cubes are in the freezer.

ROB *(with a cry in his voice; he is going slightly crazy)*: Laura, one more instruction and I'm going to pick you up and carry you out.

LAURA: I'm ready dear . . .

ROB: *(exasperated and sarcastic)*: Are you sure? Don't you want to tell Janie what TV program to watch?

LAURA *(to Janie)*: There's a special on juvenile delinquency. I don't know the time or the channel but there's a program guide in Ritchie's room . . .

Rob scoops her up on his shoulder in a fireman's carry, and starts out.

LAURA *(cont'd)*: My purse.

He bends over to allow her to grab her purse. And he starts for the door . . .

LAURA: Don't go into Ritchie's room. You may wake him. The TV program listings are in the paper. The newspaper is in the waste basket. Fresh pears and apples in the fruit bowl . . . bottom shelf of the refrigerator.

Rob has reached door.

JANIE: What did you say was in the bowl on the bottom shelf of the refrigerator?

ROB: What's the difference? If it's food eat it. If it's a telephone number, call it!

Rob exits.

As Laura predicted, Rob, Buddy, and Sally are

requested by *The Alan Brady Show* producer, Mel Cooley, to entertain the party guests while "Alan is tied up on a long-distance phone call." Laura, certain something has happened at home, wants to leave the party but before she can get Rob out of the room the command performance begins. While Rob impersonates his uncle coming home from an office party after a little too much to drink, Laura

Sally and Rob entertaining guests at Alan Brady's party in "Sick Boy and the Sitter."
CALVADA PRODUCTIONS

watches nervously from the back of the room. Sally sings a tribute to Jimmy Durante and Buddy plays his cello before the trio unites for a big finish leaving the guests cheering for more.

Rob and Laura return home only to discover a doctor's black bag in the kitchen along with neighbors Sam and Dotty. As they begin to explain, Janie enters along with Dr. Miller saying it was she who had the accident, hitting her head on the freezer door. Dr. Miller leaves along with the neighbors.

ROB: You and your woman's intuition.
LAURA: How about that? I'm sorry I was such a nag, dear.
ROB *(very tenderly)*: Aw, sweetheart . . . you're not a nag . . . *(Laura starts to smile.)* You're a worrier. *(Laura gets sad again.)* And I'm glad you are . . . *I* don't worry enough and you worry too much and together we worry just about right *(kiss)*. You know you're pretty amazing. You really did expect something to happen here tonight, didn't you?
LAURA: Yes, but I didn't expect Janie to bang her head on the freezer.
ROB: But you did expect *something*.
LAURA: Uh-huh.
ROB: How did you know?
LAURA: Darling . . . *(pecks him on the cheek and strides sexily to the door)* I'm a woman.
ROB *(ogles her as she goes)*: Yeah!

Fade out.

According to Danny Thomas, he learned during dress rehearsal for the pilot that Procter & Gamble had agreed to sponsor the series.

Rose Marie remembers the enthusiastic response from the representatives of P&G who reassured the cast verbally. As far as Reiner, Leonard, and associate producer Ron Jacobs were concerned, though, the deal wasn't firm until the contracts were signed.

The pilot was filmed and sent to the lab. Leonard, rushing to catch a plane for New York, where he would screen the pilot for various agencies and network executives, stopped at the lab and was told that George Giroux of Procter & Gamble's West Coast office had picked up the print and was waiting for him at the airport.

"I said, 'It's not his print, it's *my* print!' The lab said Giroux told them he was my associate from P&G. I went to the airport and there was Giroux with canary feathers all around his mouth, holding my print! They got first look at the damned thing and bought it. Procter & Gamble had first refusal without paying a dime!"

Now Carl Reiner, Sheldon Leonard, Danny Thomas, and Dick Van Dyke were faced with finding a suitable title for their series. Carl's original choice, *Head of the Family*, had given way to *Dou-*

ble Trouble, subsequently replaced by *All in a Day's Work.*

According to Van Dyke, "We searched and searched for a title and couldn't find anything that really pleased everybody. Somebody pointed out how *Make Room for Daddy* eventually became known as *The Danny Thomas Show* just out of common usage. So they decided to start out that way, since it probably would be called *The Dick Van Dyke Show* anyway."

It was a logical argument but not a popular one. Dick recalls, "It was an uphill battle, because my name meant nothing." Sheldon Leonard remembers the question around Madison Avenue was "What is a Dick Van Dyke?"

The quartet also devised a name for their production company: Calvada, CA for Carl Reiner, L for Sheldon Leonard, VA for Van Dyke, and DA for Danny Thomas. It was agreed that each partner would receive a certain percentage of profits from

From left: Dick Van Dyke, Mary Tyler Moore, executive producer Sheldon Leonard, Carl Reiner (seated), Rose Marie, Morey Amsterdam, and associate producer Ron Jacobs after filming "Sick Boy and the Sitter" pilot, January 1961.
CALVADA PRODUCTIONS

The presiding geniuses of The Dick Van Dyke Show: *Carl Reiner* (left), *Danny Thomas* (center), *and Sheldon Leonard.*
CBS PHOTOS

'You know, this is a very sad moment. Do you realize this is the last time we will ever be able to gather as a group on a public street? Once the series is on the air, people will mob you.' "

The Dick Van Dyke Show premiered October 3, 1961, nearly a year after the pilot was shot in January. Five months elapsed between the filming of the season opener and the next episodes, which were not broadcast in the same order as they were filmed.

The second show aired was "My Blonde-Haired Brunette," actually the ninth show filmed. The refinement that occurred between January and August, when "Brunette" was shot, was noticeable. The Petries' living room was a regular part of the set but the neighbors (Dotty, Sam and Janie, featured in "Sick Boy and the Sitter") were replaced by Dentist Jerry Helper and his wife Millie, based on the real-life friends of Carl and Estelle Reiner.

"Jerry Paris is one of the sweetest people in the world," says Dick Van Dyke. "He's outgoing, gregarious, and loves to talk."
CALVADA PRODUCTIONS

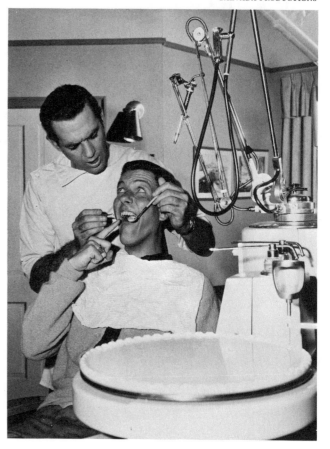

the weekly series as well as monies derived from any daytime or syndication sales.

Most others connected with the series signed the then-common six-play contract. This meant the actor would be paid on a downward sliding-scale basis for the first six times each episode in which the performer appeared aired. After the sixth rebroadcast the actors would receive no further payment. "Everybody thinks we're all still making money on the show. People think I'm filling mattresses with money. And I'm not!" laments Rose Marie.

The time immediately prior to the network premiere of *The Dick Van Dyke Show* was one of great anticipation and excitement. But to director John Rich it was also bittersweet: "We filmed six or seven shows before we went on the air, which was a customary lead time. We used to go out after every filming and have dinner together. The night before the show was to premiere, Morey had invited us to see a friend at a nightclub on the Sunset Strip. We had a wonderful time. It was two in the morning and we were standing on the street waiting for the valet to bring our cars around. I said to the others,

The Petrie living room
CALVADA PRODUCTIONS

The role of Dr. Jerry Helper was cast during the seventh-inning stretch of a baseball game. Sheldon Leonard spotted Jerry Paris eating a hot dog while watching the Dodgers.

Unbeknownst to his "old acting buddy" Leonard, Paris was about to leave California and television to try his luck on Broadway. Sheldon approached him, told him of his involvement in *The Dick Van Dyke Show,* and asked if he was interested in playing the part of Petrie's neighbor.

" 'No!' I told him. 'I've had it with TV. I don't want to work on another series.' " But Leonard suggested he meet with Reiner before leaving for New York.

"Carl Reiner?" a suddenly enthusiastic Jerry Paris asked. "From *Your Show of Shows?* I love Carl Reiner!"

He agreed to delay his flight to the East Coast and meet with Reiner. "I walked in Carl's office with Sheldon, and there sat a bald man with a stack of scripts towering over his head. Sheldon said to Carl, 'I think he ought to play Dick's next-door neighbor. They're both built the same and he's a good actor.' "

They negotiated briefly and the part was offered to Jerry. Paris then asked the pair who had been cast as his wife. "We haven't found her yet," Reiner moaned, "and we need her within a week."

"I've got the girl!" exclaimed Paris. "My best friend is married to an actress named Ann Morgan Guilbert. She'd be perfect!"

Paris brought Guilbert to the studio and recalls Leonard and Reiner pulling him aside whispering, "She's not pretty enough."

Jerry argued, "That's just a stereotype that the next-door neighbor has to be great-looking. She's marvelous! Watch her. She'll knock you out!"

"They liked me," remembers Guilbert, "but I know Jerry pushed for me a lot."

Paris was protective of Guilbert, often acting as her agent. "I had an agent," she laughs, "but Jerry would always say, 'I'll get you more money!' And he would go to them and get me a little more."

Guilbert decided not to accept Reiner's offer for a contract after her first few appearances. "I told Carl I'd prefer to do it as it comes."

As with Jerry Paris another chance meeting resulted in a talented addition to *The Dick Van Dyke Show.*

One day Sheldon Leonard happened to run into John Rich at a board of directors' meeting at the Director's Guild. Rich was a highly respected television veteran who recently had begun directing westerns instead of situation comedies because he was "bored with them." Leonard approached Rich at the Guild meeting and told him about the new series starring Dick Van Dyke. Again Reiner's name

Jerry Paris and Ann Morgan Guilbert as neighbors Jerry and Millie Helper.
ANN MORGAN GUILBERT

sparked interest. "I didn't know Carl Reiner but I certainly admired him. I thought he was a genius," says Rich. Leonard capped the conversation with an offer to direct the series. Rich unhesitatingly accepted the offer.

A meeting was arranged that week at Reiner's home. Despite a brief moment of embarrassment when Rich complimented Dick Van Dyke on his performance in a TV production called *Vintage 60* (the actor he was thinking of was actually Dick Patterson), the meeting went very well. Rich signed on as director of *The Dick Van Dyke Show,* freeing Leonard from his dual role of executive producer and director after the first three episodes.

Rich had a difficult task, as he explained to Rose Marie: "The ensemble must learn to trust me, to know that I am looking out for their best interests."

Rich soon accomplished just that. Rose Marie describes him as "the greatest comedy director there is," and the rest of the company shared her high respect for him.

In *Life* magazine José M. Ferrer III wrote, "The actors never jump out of character for the sake of a laugh. They stay real amidst the plot twists."

The role of Rob Petrie was monitored by Carl Reiner to ensure the character would stay within the realm of realism and plausibility. "The show was like an overcoat," Reiner explains. "I used to try on everything Rob Petrie would do, say, or feel while I was writing."

Van Dyke's association with his character is clear. "Rob Petrie is me," he declares, adding with delight, "Whatever faults I have, I gave to Rob Petrie!"

Van Dyke also had free rein to improvise scenes involving visual comedy. "I think better on my feet," he explains. "If they had an episode in which I had to do visual comedy, the writers would just leave it blank, saying Dick does five minutes or whatever, letting me play with it myself."

Rose Marie recalls watching Van Dyke create:

Ladies' Home Journal, *October 1963: "Dick's body is concave, as lank and limber as a reed. He seems not so much born whole as wired together. Where muscles ought to be, there are springs . . . in repose, he might be mistaken for a bent exclamation point."*
CALVADA PRODUCTIONS

"He would fall into a bit when we would read the scripts and just do something that was crazy or nutty. We'd laugh, saying, 'That's wonderful.' He'd say, 'Is it funny?' Dick has so much talent, he doesn't even realize it. He's like a rubberband. He's unbelievable."

Commenting on her own performance, Rose Marie admits: "I play me in almost everything I do. I play a part to the best of my ability to get a joke out, to sell it, and to do it best."

To director John Rich, "Rose Marie is the epit-ome of the fast-talking straight woman. The most important thing about a joke is the delivery of the straight line, and Rose Marie was brilliant at it. She could lay out a line with the best of them."

Her skill as a comedienne added immeasurably to her portrayal of a television rarity: a successful, mature, respected career woman.

Morey Amsterdam echoes Van Dyke in his approach to his character, Buddy Sorrell. "I am Buddy," he confirms. "Buddy is not only a comic, but an experienced writer, a fellow who knows tim-

Watching TV: *"The office scenes were bits of inspired brilliance that gave the show its drive."*
CALVADA PRODUCTIONS

ing and funny situations." John Rich describes Morey as "always full of energy, hysterically funny."

Assesses Rose Marie, "Morey is a consummate performer," whose seemingly limitless supply of jokes added enormously to the show.

Amsterdam concludes: "I learned a great deal. When you surround yourself with happy people, it's much easier to do the show. We had fun."

Larry Mathews was an exception among child performers: He was neither pushed in front of the camera nor treated to a spoiled, pampered existence.

Larry adapted easily to his schedule: performing interspersed with three hours of schoolwork with a tutor each day on the set. He developed a close relationship with his on-screen parents and friends. "They treated me like their own kid," he says of the cast, who frequently included him in off-camera socializing. "After the filming, everybody would usually go out and have drinks. I would go along with them and have a sundae."

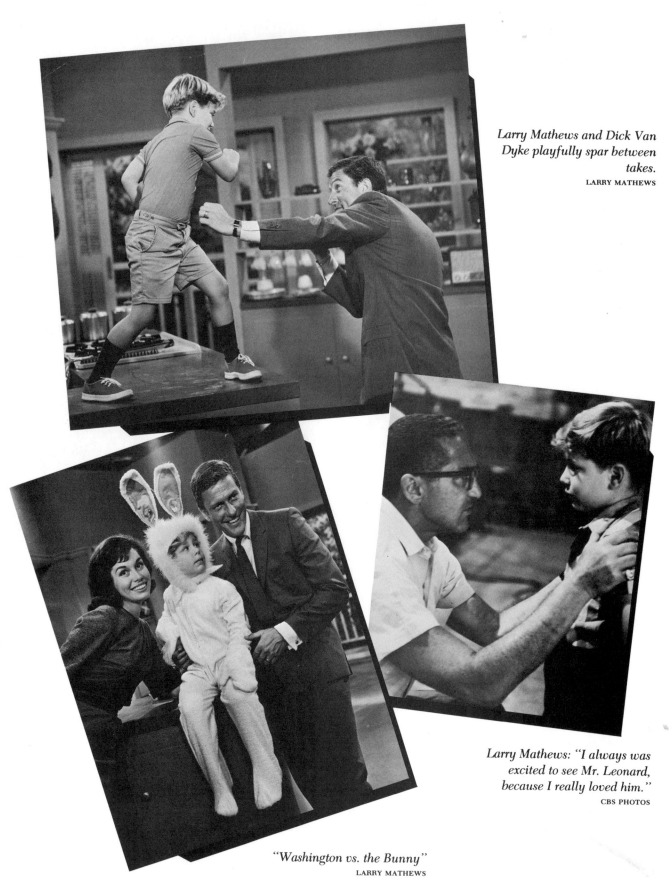

Larry Mathews and Dick Van Dyke playfully spar between takes.
LARRY MATHEWS

Larry Mathews: "I always was excited to see Mr. Leonard, because I really loved him."
CBS PHOTOS

"Washington vs. the Bunny"
LARRY MATHEWS

An experienced actor before he came to *The Dick Van Dyke Show*, Richard Deacon finally received national recognition as Mel Cooley, the butt of Buddy's barbs. "I was glad to do two or three one-liners and get off. I could come in, make a statement, and leave. I never felt that I didn't have enough to do."

As for their on-camera "antagonism," Amsterdam explains, "I didn't dislike Mel, I disliked what he stood for—nepotism. It got to the point that when he walked into the office I'd just look at him and the audience would break up. The audience loved it."

Unlike her experienced costars, Mary Tyler Moore was a mere twenty-three years old at the onset of *The Dick Van Dyke Show* and had no background in comedy. Yet as Van Dyke enthuses, "She picked it up in no time at all."

Director John Rich theorizes that it was Mary's burgeoning talent as a comedienne that resulted in greater emphasis on Rob Petrie's home life. "Mary was first hired as an 'ear'—she was there to listen to Dick talking about his troubles at work. She was there (at first) to do very little."

But "My Blonde-Haired Brunette," changed the direction of Laura Petrie's role. It remains Mary's favorite. In that show, Laura feels Rob is taking her for granted and is convinced by neighbor Millie that she can spice up her marriage by becoming a blonde. Laura's plans to surprise Rob backfire when he calls asking his "favorite brunette" out to dinner. As Millie frantically tries to redye Laura's hair brown, Rob arrives home early only to discover his wife with a head of half-blond, half-brown hair. John Rich, who directed "Brunette" states: "Mary made a hysterically wonderful episode out of it. She was brilliant."

Following that show, as Mary recalls, "Carl then began writing episodes in which I could not only be the straight man—which is essentially what I was as Laura Petrie—but a straight man who gets laughs."

Another script nearly four years later would reflect Moore's growth in comedy. Carl Reiner touted "Never Bathe on Saturday," Mary says, "as one of the greatest episodes I would ever be a part of." She remembers him proclaiming, "I've written the second scene . . . the fourth scene . . . I can't wait for you to see it!" "It had such a buildup, I was expecting *the* perfect script for me," laughs Mary.

"I read it and indeed it was a brilliant script, very

"Yecch!"
RICHARD DEACON

29

funny, but I was off camera the whole time! [Laura's toe is caught in the bathtub faucet and she is heard but not seen.] I was crushed. I cannot [describe] my disappointment. I was so angry it was the only time in my life I stormed off the set. I

different. It is the only show on the air that edits scripts properly."

Executive producer Sheldon Leonard made it a point to attend the script sessions of each show he produced. He interlocked the schedules of each

Laura's dilemma in "Never Bathe on Saturday": the consequences of "playing with a drip."
CARL REINER

remained in my dressing room for about ten minutes, then stormed back on stage and got through the show."

Moore concludes, "It was just a case of my having been bitterly disappointed by a script that turned out to be wonderful."

One writer told *Life* magazine, "On most shows some producer with no right to put a pencil on paper carves you up. *The Dick Van Dyke Show* is

Thomas–Leonard production so he could be involved in what to him was "its vital process."

Bill Persky, one of the writers, remembers, "Sheldon would sit behind me in a high chair as I sat at the table. As the reading progressed and the script got progressively worse, Sheldon's breathing would become deeper and deeper. I sometimes didn't hear the readings, all I heard was Sheldon's breathing! Leonard would then declare, 'This script

Mary Tyler Moore, TV Guide,
September 1970: "It was my
childhood in the business, my
growing up time, the happiest
period of my life."

up and *down* more.' I did and I haven't had any
trouble since. So much for my training."

He further explains, "We had the perfect balance
and combination of talent. Carl was daring and
innovative but Sheldon always held us to what
worked. They would get into philosophical clashes
in our writing meetings, but Carl would always get
through with some new ideas."

Leonard also influenced the decision to film the
Van Dyke series in the same manner as *The Danny
Thomas Show*—using the three-camera, studio au-
dience method refined in 1951 for *I Love Lucy*.

In Reiner's opinion, "Sheldon Leonard was a brilliant teacher as well as being a brilliant executive
producer. In two short sessions in his home, he
taught me how to make my thirteen one-camera
shows into three-camera shows and how to extend
scenes and make them more like plays."

Mary Tyler Moore describes the three-camera

A terror-filled night in a haunted
cabin gives not "The Ghost of A.
Chantz."
CALVADA PRODUCTIONS

is a disaster,' opening the rewrite session. 'OK, who
wants to jump in first?' We'd start on page one and
fix it—nobody left."

"Sheldon would come in for the final reading and
would critique the entire script," says Frank Adamo, Van Dyke's stand-in, secretary, and frequent
bit player on the series. "Everybody took down
notes, and then would look up and say, 'Sheldon,
that was wonderful'—and he'd be gone. Rose Marie
dubbed him 'Lamont Cranston, the Shadow,' here
one minute, gone the next. The cast even gave him
a floor mat one Christmas embossed with "Lamont
Cranston," remembers Rose Marie.

"We worked with the best teacher," praises Van
Dyke, who also credits Leonard with giving him his
one and only acting lesson. "After the first two or
three shows of the first season, Sheldon said, 'Dick,
you're talking in a monotone. Make your voice go

*Deac gets his just desserts . . . and
so does Dick.*
CALVADA PRODUCTIONS

33

style as an advantage in that "it combines the best of theater and film. You have the adrenalin going because of the audience, but you also have the protection of film. If you make a mistake, forget a line or discover something doesn't play the way you wanted it to, you can go back and do it again."

Leonard and Thomas also continued a practice begun on *Make Room for Daddy*—"analyzing and dissecting scripts around the table with the entire cast. We stayed and fixed a script until we thought it worked. We kept polishing until the patina of the script could not be duplicated," Leonard revealed.

Leonard had a concise philosophy regarding scripts: "Analyze and understand your strengths and weaknesses and write to emphasize one and minimize the other." Supporting Leonard's view, Thomas reveals, "We would stay up all night,

*Script supervisor Marge Mullen,
November 1981*
C. S. SANDERS

Sheldon and I, and get no sleep because of one scene. And this was just a simple teleplay—we treated it like it was opening night." Or as one cynic remarked to the bleary-eyed pair, very late one night, "Are you guys still worrying about one lousy line? You're not writing *Gone With the Wind.*"

Yet worry they did. And care. "You have to care," confesses Thomas, "or you won't have a good show."

Each week the creative process would begin at the table sessions. On Wednesday mornings you could find the cast, writers, director, and producers of *The Dick Van Dyke Show* at the Desilu-Cahuenga Studios assembled around the table in what they dubbed "The Christian Science Reading Room."

"It just wasn't work," Van Dyke declares. "We were due in by ten, but we never got started before eleven. After coffee, doughnuts, and horsing around we'd finally get into it. We were like a bunch of otters—very hard to control."

"We'd get two scripts to read," explains script supervisor Marge Mullen. "One would be pink—which would be the following week's script—and the current week's would be white. We would always read the following week's script first and get a rough timing on it. People would have an hour or so of input on what they felt was wrong with the script or how they could make it better."

And better is what everybody, not just the writers, was determined to make it.

"Some writers couldn't handle this at all," continues Mullen. "They felt they handed in a script and nobody changed it. Well, they shouldn't have written for our show, because there were some scripts that by the time we did it, every word had been excised [from the original draft]."

Rose Marie recounts a time when Marge Mullen saved an impromptu rewrite session: "The first scene of the "Twizzle" show was a big, long scene that wasn't working. Something was wrong and we didn't know what it was. After the rehearsal on shooting day [Tuesday] Carl said, 'We'll talk about it at dinner.' So in the commissary, we went over the scene. Morey would say, 'How about . . .' and Carl would say, 'Yeah, that's good!' and someone would say something else. Carl said, 'My god, did anybody write this down?' And Marge, who was [sitting] in the corner, wrote it all down on the napkin! And she typed it up very fast and handed it out before the filming."

As script supervisor, Mullen's duties were primarily to work with the director. Mullen attended script and rewrite sessions, timed the length of scenes and individual camera shots, recorded block-

Danny Thomas and Mary Tyler Moore at the cast party after filming of "The Twizzle" episode, January 9, 1962
CBS PHOTOS

ing, then provided these notations to the film editor, Bud Molin, who subsequently would assemble the footage.

Mullen often displayed an uncanny knack for choosing the best material. "I can recognize a good joke," concedes Mullen. "As I'd be writing them down, if I would nod my head or start to laugh, they'd say, 'That's the one!'"

She also invented the "SOS File." During rehearsal the cast would come up with good material that they couldn't fit into the episode they were working on so at the back of her script, Marge kept a notebook labeled "SOS—Some Other Show." Van Dyke explains, "She wrote *everything* down, and when we'd be stuck for something, she'd throw those ideas back at us."

"We had great comraderie," says Morey Amsterdam, who explains that "nobody counted lines the way some actors do." As Dick remembers, no one was "ever made to do a line or anything they felt uncomfortable with." In fact, they often traded lines. Morey offers an example: "Dick would say, 'Hey, I shouldn't do that line, Morey should do it.'"

Associate producer Ron Jacobs describes the script sessions as "fruit on the table, creative differences, and always love." Ann Morgan Guilbert admits, "The part of the show I always enjoyed the most was not the acting, but sitting around the table going over the scripts because it was such fun. All the people were so bright and tremendously witty. And Carl is so funny. I never felt insecure or put down in making my own suggestions. Everybody could create. I don't think there was a script that came out that didn't have a contribution from somebody in it."

Suggestions and contributions made, the writers of the next week's script were dispatched to do rewrites and further work. Van Dyke reveals, "We only threw out one script in the whole five years. I can't remember what it was about, but when we finished reading it and closed it, you saw ten scripts go up in the air." Richard Deacon adds, "Carl then picked it up as if it were a piece of *filth* and dropped it into the wastebasket. We never saw it again."

"Dick and Mary were incredibly fast studies. They could hear a line once and have it locked in immediately. When they couldn't learn it quickly they knew something was wrong," explains Mullen.

Frank Adamo, Dick's stand-in and secretary, emphasizes her point: "The littlest guy who swept up the floor—if he didn't like a line then it was out!" The remark may be an exaggeration, but it was

prompted, no doubt, by the company's obvious commitment to teamwork.

Wednesday afternoon the current week's script would have a run-through. "Carl would come down and look at it," continues Mullen. "I would retype the changes at night and we'd get them back in the morning." Besides forbidding contemporary slang, which Reiner felt would date the show in reruns, he insisted on proper grammar and sentence structure, and Mullen often made these corrections as she typed the scripts.

On Friday the cast would run through the entire script without makeup or audience. A revised script would be delivered to the actors at their homes on Saturday so they could learn their lines over the weekend. On Monday morning the director would block the camera shots with stand-ins, then the actors would go through their moves in front of the camera.

Carl Reiner warms up the studio audience before filming.
CBS PHOTOS

Dick Van Dyke: "If Deac was going to forget a line, he'd telegraph it ahead of time. First his eyes would glaze over, then beads of perspiration would pop out on his forehead like water in a skillet. Every time I'd see that happen, he never got the chance to blow his line, because I became hysterical."

Jose M. Ferrer III, Life magazine: "Lean, rubber-faced and impossibly double-jointed, he still manages to look like a tall, narrow Boy Scout."
MOREY AMSTERDAM

37

"It was a great way to start directors—three-camera shows," says Ron Jacobs. "They could be creative, we'd see a run-through and whatever was wrong—you'd sit around with pencil and paper and fix it."

And fix it they did, right through the day of filming.

"On Tuesday, we'd come in at noon," says Mullen, "and during the afternoon, people would come in and out of makeup and go through every scene twice with the camera. At four-thirty we'd have another run-through for the producers." The final polishing continued, as Mullen explains. "Very often after our dress rehearsal, they'd write things, as the final makeup was done. We'd have dinner and around seven, they'd start the warmup. [In three-camera shows, it is customary for the cast to be introduced to the studio audience. Occasionally, Danny Thomas would join Rose Marie and Morey Amsterdam in priming the audience for the comedy to follow.]

"The show would start at seven-thirty," Mullen

Richard Deacon: "Danny Thomas once came in and said, 'How can you people expect to do a show when you're laughing and carrying on? Don't you know comedy is a very serious business!' "

continues. "We'd go straight through like a stage show. Very rarely would we do any retakes in front of the audience, unless somebody broke down and the audience was laughing. Then we'd go back and show them how it should have been done. After the audience left, we'd do pickups [close-ups or insert shots] and usually we were done by ten or ten-thirty."

The pieces of the puzzle were now in the hands of the film editor, who would fit them into a twenty-four-minute teleplay; it was not a simple task, for the audience's laughter often had lengthened a show. "We were always accused of using canned laughter, but we never did," declares Van Dyke. "The only time we would 'sweeten' was when we had a big cut, because we had to take out something and they cut right into the laugh," adds Mullen.

The episode was "in the can," to be broadcast in six to eight weeks, and the weekly creative process would begin anew.

Rehearsing "The Masterpiece" episode and filming of the same scene.
CBS PHOTOS

"Every show has one source from which everything clearly emanates—very often it's the star, but in this case, it was clearly Carl."

—BILL PERSKY

"Where Did I Come From?" the inevitable question asked by the Petrie's son, was an exceptional script by Carl Reiner that sparked tremendous controversy.

"We censored ourselves, and when the networks or sponsors tried to censor us, we got very angry," states Carl Reiner, who was vitriolic at the network's proclamation that the following dialogue in his script be altered:

RITCHIE: I was inside Mommy, wasn't I?

Laura and Rob exchange glances. Ritchie watches for a moment.

RITCHIE (cont'd): Why are you and Mommy looking like that?
ROB: Uh, we just didn't know you knew about . . .
RITCHIE: Everybody knows that!

LAURA (*smiles*): Well, not *everybody*.

ROB: Ritchie, why did you ask where you came from, if you knew?

RITCHIE: I *don't* know.

ROB: But you said you came from Mommy.

RITCHIE: Oh, I know that. I meant where do I come from . . . like Freddie came from New Jersey?

ROB (*laughs*): Oh well, you came from New York.

Reiner continues, "They said, 'You can't say that.' I said, 'What do you mean? That's where he came from! It's not an *opinion* like saying Republicans are better than Democrats. It's true!' "

Not convinced, the network was adamant, forcing Reiner to rewrite the dialogue:

RITCHIE: Daddy, where did I come from?

ROB: What did you say, Ritch?

RITCHIE: I said, where did I come from?

ROB (*laughs nervously*): That's what I thought you said, Ritch. (*to Laura*) Did you hear what Ritchie asked?

LAURA: I did, darling.

RITCHIE: Where *did* I come from, Daddy?

ROB: Well, Ritch, that's kind of complicated . . . well, ah, let's see . . . (*pauses*) Where's Doctor Spock? (*takes book from bookshelf behind the sofa*) Ritch, where do you think you came from?

RITCHIE: Same place Freddie Helper did—New Jersey.

ROB: (*looks at book*): He's not ready for this . . . Ritchie, you didn't come from New Jersey, you came from New York, don't you remember?

RITCHIE: Oh yeah, I forgot . . . were you there, Mommy?

LAURA: Yes, I was there.

RITCHIE: Good.

"It hurt me a lot to do that [Dr. Spock] joke," concedes Reiner. "But at least I was suggesting that there was a scientific way of being born."

Also cause for considerable controversy and censorship was Mary Tyler Moore's wardrobe.

"I suggested to Carl that when I vacuum the rug, I wear pants," recounts Mary. "I couldn't imagine putting on a little dress." Thus the Capri slacks became Laura Petrie's trademark.

According to Moore, "In the second year, they

Time magazine, April 9, 1965: "She helped make Capri slacks the biggest trend in U.S. casual attire."
CALVADA PRODUCTIONS

did a survey and found that most women couldn't identify with that and made me go back to wearing dresses—which I did, gritting my teeth. That lasted about three months. Then they started getting a lot of mail saying, 'Wait a minute! We liked her better in pants. Put them back!' "

A compromise was reached: Mary was allowed one scene, of her choice, each show to wear slacks.

But the wardrobe battle wasn't over yet. Reiner vividly remembers a sponsor representative advising him, "You've got to watch the undercupping." Reiner was puzzled. "I didn't know what he was

Rob once again explains the facts of life to son Ritchie in "Go Tell the Birds and the Bees."

Bottoms up!
CBS PHOTOS

Dick Van Dyke and Mary Tyler Moore won top honors in a national polling of TV editors asking them to name "Television's Most Glamorous Couple." The pair received 75 percent of the votes cast by 147 newsmen.

talking about. He said, 'When she wears a tight dress, her behind is sculptured too well!' I said, 'I'm not watching any undercupping, you watch it.' Those were the things they worried about," sighs Reiner.

Reiner was more concerned with the character dimensions of Laura Petrie. "I was a little better

43

than most in treating Laura. She had a high level of intelligence and was Rob's worthy adversary—which hadn't been done before."

In her own evaluation of the character, Moore says, "I wanted to establish her as a woman who had her own point of view and who would fight with her husband—a good fight, if necessary. She wasn't a 'yes' wife, nor did she focus everything on him. But that's about as liberated as Laura Petrie was. I think she truly believed that her only choice was to be a wife and mother and couldn't combine [that with] a career."

Van Dyke concludes, "The marriage was believable. It worked."

The electricity that Van Dyke and Moore generated was unmistakable from the start. Richard Deacon offers this tribute: "They had a very special rapport. Dick and Mary working together was magic!"

Despite the customary twin beds, Rob and Laura displayed an obvious physical attraction and were, as Sheldon Leonard describes, "the first pair [on TV] that may be having some fun in the hay."

While twin beds may not have been common in the homes of most viewers, the situations Rob and Laura found themselves in usually were.

The book *Watching TV* observes: "The series presented a range of characters living out exaggerated views of everyday life in a world not very different from the one most viewers faced. Rob and Laura lived in a real middle-class town in which real people commuted to and from real jobs. He was a decent, intelligent, hard-working father and she was a helpful and clever wife who was neither wacky, gorgeous, nor conniving. The program effectively replaced the interchangeable blandness of the fifties with a generally real view of the successful middle-class life of the early sixties."

The real-life situations were the result of Carl Reiner listening as well as contributing. Jerry Paris explains, "Carl took real stories from all of us."

Every writer as well as every cast member who contributed a story idea or shooting script was

greeted with a firm dictum from Reiner. "Tell me about yourself, *not* about other television shows you've seen. *That's* how we'll get a story."

Bill Persky revealed to *Look* magazine during the course of the series just how pervasive Reiner's philosophy was. "You can't have an experience without trying to relate it to the show. I had a flat tire on a deserted Mexican highway not long ago; all the time I was scared to death, but I was thinking, how can I put this into the show?"

Many of the scripts Reiner himself wrote were derived from real-life incidents, a logical evolution in that the characters were based on his family and friends.

It was his neighbor, the "real" Millie, who gave Reiner the idea for "A Bird in the Head Hurts!" Her son had been continually assaulted by a woodpecker intent on using the boy's hair for a nest. As Reiner recalls, the advice given to distraught mother Laura, "Let him wear a pith helmet!" was quoted verbatim from an ASPCA official. Reiner

The Petries and Helpers discover a giant rock in the basement of "Your Sweet Home Is My Home."
CBS PHOTOS

Mary Tyler Moore: "You could hang clothes on my hair, there's so much spray!"
CBS PHOTOS

"The Cat Burglar"
CALVADA PRODUCTIONS

Sorrell's canine, who Rob agrees to care for over a weekend. "I eyed my German shepherd," recalls Reiner, "and said, 'I'm going to write a script for you!' "

"Empress Carlotta's Necklace"—an episode about a piece of ugly jewelry given by well-meaning Rob to his wife—was a result of Reiner's confession that his "gypsylike tastes" often clashed with those of his wife. Similarly, his admission that "I can't handle money, which is *still* a problem," resulted in "My Husband Is a Check Grabber," which took "two and a half years to write. I kept putting it aside and coming back to it, because I couldn't throw it away. It had too much good stuff in it."

Reiner delighted in "Gezundheit, Darling!" because he got to do a show about his allergy. He transferred his sneezing to Rob, who is alarmed that he may be allergic to his wife, his son, and his neighbors. Rob is relieved to discover, as Carl had been, that the cause of his affliction is a hidden cat.

"Never Name a Duck," was a poignant, funny tale of Ritchie's attachment to a duckling who quickly outgrows its home in the Petrie's kitchen sink. The script was a slight variation on the experience of Reiner's two young children when they adopted a pair of ducklings. Laura's concern that her son's duck is not adapting to domesticity was actually expressed by Reiner's wife, Estelle, who lamented about their sick duck, "He looks pale!"

"The show where Rob went to court with the case of the pillows that smelled like ducks happened to me," confesses Bill Persky. He and Sam Denoff would write "The Case of the Pillows" ten years after the incident.

"October Eve" was based on Persky's experience of spotting a painting in a gallery that bore a striking resemblance to his wife. As he told the story, Jerry Paris revealed that his wife had had a similar experience. He and his wife, Ruth, had visited a prison where an inmate sketched Mrs. Paris. The prisoner, using his imagination, painted her nude and sent the present to Paris's home.

Serge Carpetna (Carl Reiner) unveils a painting with Laura's face on another model's nude body.
CALVADA PRODUCTIONS

embellished only slightly: "I put sunglasses on Ritchie to make him look funny."

Reiner's neighbor received a story credit and idea fee of $200.

"Your Home Sweet Home Is My Home," a flashback episode featuring a giant rock in the basement of a home for sale offered to both the Petries and the Helpers, was modeled after Reiner's own California home. "The house was on a hill," he explains, "but the rock was all right because it never rained in the basement."

The Reiner family dog was the inspiration for "The Unwelcome House Guest," featuring Buddy

*Brothers Dick and Jerry Van Dyke
as brothers Rob and Stacey Petrie.*
FRANK ADAMO

When Dick Van Dyke and writer Jerry Belson traded stories they discovered they both had worked as shoe salesmen. The conversation resulted in "Young Man with a Shoehorn."

"The Cat Burglar" is credited to Dick Van Dyke: "My wife had taken the bullets out of the gun I had and put them in her jewelry box that played 'The Blue Danube.' I tried to get the bullets out before it started to play!"

During the first season, Dick showed an article to Carl written about his younger brother Jerry, who was a comedian on the Playboy Club circuit. "What if I wrote a show for him?" Reiner offered.

A pleased Van Dyke volunteered some details about his sibling: "As a kid, he was a somnambulist—the world's champion sleepwalker. He could get up, walk and talk to you, and you'd never know he was asleep."

48

That was all Reiner needed to know. He recalls, "About midway through writing the script I told Dick, 'It's getting out of hand. It's too long.' He said, 'Make a two-parter.' Very few shows had done two-parters in those days." The result was "I Am My Brother's Keeper" and "The Sleeping Brother," in which Jerry displays two personalities—an introvert while awake and an extrovert when he is sleepwalking. A sleepwalking performance with his banjo results in an audition for *The Alan Brady Show.*

It then occurred to Reiner to ask Dick if his brother could act. "Oh, sure he can act," Dick assured him. "How do you know?" queried Carl. "Because if he can't," retorted Dick, "I'll *kill* him!"

Reiner was more than pleased. "Jerry was sensational," he recalls, "a natural."

Jerry Van Dyke appeared in another two-parter during the 1964–65 season, "Stacey Petrie, Parts I and II," also written by Carl Reiner, in which, when he comes back to town to open his own coffee house, he must confess to his army buddy's girl friend that he, not his friend, has been writing her love letters.

Jerry was just one of a group of semiregular players that emerged as the series progressed. Some were even called upon to appear in a variety of roles in addition to their recurring characters. For example, Isabel Randolph appeared in several roles before being permanently cast as Rob's mother, Clara Petrie; J. Pat O'Malley played Sam, Rob's father, before Tom Tully took over the role.

Laura had only one set of parents—Mr. and Mrs. Meehan were Carl Benton Reid and Geraldine Wall.

Pickles, the often-discussed but seldom seen wife of Buddy Sorrell, was originally played by Barbara Perry in "Sally Is a Girl." Subsequently, Joan Shawlee assumed the role for the remainder of the series.

Jerry and Millie Helper had two children, also talked about but rarely seen: Ellen was played by Ann Marie Hediger; and the role of Freddie featured two actors, Peter Oliphant and David Fresco. Gavin MacLeod (who years later would play Murray Slaughter on *The Mary Tyler Moore Show*) almost appeared twice in the series in two different roles. In addition to his part of Maxwell Cooley, in "Empress Carlotta's Necklace," MacLeod was scheduled to be Sally Rogers's ardent suitor in "Ro-

"I Am My Brother's Keeper"
CALVADA PRODUCTIONS

49

Clockwise from bottom left: Grandpa Petrie (Cyril Delevanti), Mrs. Meehan (Geraldine Wall), Mr. Petrie (J. Pat O'Malley), Mrs. Petrie (Isabel Randolph), Mr. Meehan (Carl Benton Reid), Rob Petrie (Dick Van Dyke), and Laura Petrie (Mary Tyler Moore).
CBS PHOTOS

Tom Tully replaces J. Pat O'Malley as Rob's father in "Pink Pills and Purple Parents."
CBS PHOTOS

50

Buddy and wife Pickles #1
(Barbara Perry)
CALVADA PRODUCTIONS

Buddy and wife Pickles #2
(Joan Shawlee)
CALVADA PRODUCTIONS

mance, Roses, and Ryebread." Two days prior to filming, he was stricken with appendicitis and was replaced by Sid Melton.

Al Melvin became a familiar face, turning up in various roles including the recurring character of Sol, Rob's old Army buddy, also played by Marty Ingels.

Veteran actress Jane Dulo appeared in the series a number of times and learned first-hand the wisdom of the show business adage about never appearing with animals or children. Dulo recounts being upstaged in "Never Name a Duck": "My first line to Dick was, 'It's a duck.' The duck suddenly fell in love with my voice, did a take, and went nose-to-nose with me, staring. The audience laughed so long, Dick and I couldn't look at each other or we would have blown the scene!"

The distinction of having the most appearances

Allan Melvin as Sgt. Petrie's old Army buddy.

in the series by a nonregular belongs to Frank Adamo, who had a unique association with *The Dick Van Dyke Show*. Adamo was stand-in, personal secretary, and long-time friend to Van Dyke. In addition to being an actor and dancer, he became a member of *The Dick Van Dyke Show* family. If a walk-on or bit part appeared in the script, Adamo usually was cast. His roles ranged from messenger and delivery boy (replacing Jamie Farr) to the veterinarian's assistant in "Never Name a

Dick Van Dyke and Frank Adamo in "Don't Trip Over the Mountain."

Duck" and the watermelon-wielding beatnik actor in "Romance, Roses, and Ryebread."

Ann Guilbert observed, "We often had actors come in and do a single episode. Every actor in town wanted to be on our show because they heard it was such a congenial set. And they found out it was."

In addition to veteran actors, newcomers who have gone on to achieve greater recognition com-

pleted the stable of players. (A generous sprinkling of familiar names can be found in the episode-by-episode synopsis of *The Dick Van Dyke Show* beginning on page 97.)

Procter & Gamble's sponsorship—and their enormous advertising budget—ensured that *The Dick Van Dyke Show* would become a weekly series, thus forcing CBS president Jim Aubrey to yield and provide a time slot. Sheldon Leonard believes that "the

Familiar face Jamie Farr in "Washington vs. the Bunny" episode.
CALVADA PRODUCTIONS

general flap that surrounded its birth and delivery resulted in Aubrey being cynical" about *The Dick Van Dyke Show.*

Aubrey, therefore, gave the series "a very bad time slot," according to Leonard: Tuesdays at 8:00 P.M. (EST). The competition—*Bachelor Father* and the final half hour of *Laramie*—wasn't particularly fierce. The problem was the *time* the show aired.

Veteran actress Jane Dulo in "Young Man with a Shoehorn," one of her many appearances in the series.
JANE DULO

Smiling for the cameras on a sad occasion: the farewell and "good luck" party following the cancellation after the first season.
CBS PHOTOS

The cast announces their new timeslot.
CBS PHOTOS

Although aired at 8:00 P.M. on the East and West coasts, *The Dick Van Dyke Show* was broadcast at 7:00 P.M. in the Midwest—too close to the dinner hour. So despite Carl Reiner, Sheldon Leonard, the script, the chemistry, the *magic*, *The Dick Van Dyke Show* floundered, struggling to find its audience.

At midseason, CBS pulled it from their Tuesday night lineup and scheduled it for Wednesday

57

nights, 9:30–10:000 P.M. (EST)—up against the very popular musical/variety series, *Perry Como's Kraft Music Hall* on NBC. The switch did nothing to help the series. Procter & Gamble bailed out, and CBS canceled the show.

A feeling of fatality permeated the set, as the cast and crew began to line up other work. A farewell party was planned. Mary reportedly was particularly emotional about the series ending. Danny Thomas remembers her approaching him, saying, "All I want to be is Mrs. Rob Petrie! Please don't let them drop the show!"

"If I were to say to a manufacturer of a product that I could guarantee him that twenty million people would see his product, he would kiss my feet. You get twenty million viewers on television and you're a failure. They don't take that into consideration."

—DANNY THOMAS

Director John Rich also describes Mary as "very tearful. She would say, 'Do you realize this is the *last* reading of the *last* script?' and 'Do you realize this is the *last* run-through of the *last* show . . .?' Finally it became a joke. She'd say, 'Do you realize this is the *last* lunch on the *last* Tuesday we'll be together?' "

Reiner was livid at the cancelation. "Procter & Gamble said to me in the beginning, 'No matter what the ratings are, this is *the* most quality show on the air.' They said we'd be on five years." The situation seemed hopeless. "We were ready to die," Reiner concludes.

Leonard's belief in the series remained undaunted and he decided to take action. At a black tie dinner, Leonard managed to convince Lee Rich (of Benton & Bowles) to accompany him on his mission to save *The Dick Van Dyke Show*. Leonard was so persuasive that Rich flew with him to Cincinnati that very night to meet with "Havvy" Halverstadt, head of television for Procter & Gamble. Leonard recounts their conversation en route to Cincinnati: "I asked him, 'Are you with me or against me, Lee?' He said, 'I don't know.' 'You don't know? What do you mean, you don't know? Your recommendation is the final step. After I make my pitch, Halverstadt

is going to turn to you and ask what Benton & Bowles recommends—and *you* are Benton & Bowles. What are you going to say?' He said, 'I don't know. I'll have to wait and hear what *you* have to say.' "

What Leonard said made all the difference. "We were a strange spectacle," chuckles Leonard, "arriving in Cincinnati at ten A.M., unwashed, unshaven, gaunt, owl-eyed—still in dinner jackets from the night before. We went into the conference room adjoining Halverstadt's office and I said, 'look, Havvy, you *can't* cancel the show—we've just learned what to *do* with it. Carl had written it for himself. It was written for a Bronx Jew actor and who we have playing it is an Indiana Baptist! We got him off on the wrong foot, and it took us a while to learn how to handle him. We are now writing *for* him and showing him off in a true light. In other words, we put a pair of *balls* on him!'

"Halverstadt said, 'Excuse me,' got up from the chair, and walked to the door between the office and the conference room and closed the door. He came back and said, 'There's an unmarried secretary out there. Now, what were you saying about putting *balls* on him?' "

On Lee Rich's recommendation, Halverstadt agreed to continue P&G's sponsorship in spite of the network's opposition. Leonard remembers [CBS president] Jim Aubrey "was furious" at the renewal of the show. But Procter & Gamble, remaining loyal to their successful client, "threatened the withdrawal of their daytime business if the timeslot was not made available."

Once again, *The Dick Van Dyke Show* was alive, thanks to Sheldon Leonard. It had a sponsor, a network, and another chance at building an audience.

But before the new season could begin, the spell Leonard had cast was broken. Halverstadt reevaluated his hasty decision. Procter & Gamble would sponsor only *half* of *The Dick Van Dyke Show*. Leonard, again, was faced with the task of finding an additional sponsor.

The William Morris office informed Leonard that P. Lorillard & Co. (Kent cigarettes) was seeking a show to sponsor. A Lorillard friend maneuvered Leonard into a Kent board meeting in New York. Leonard hypnotized them—as he had Halverstadt in Cincinnati—and convinced them to cosponsor the series.

> *"The more realistic the show, the more honest the characters, the longer it takes to become part of your lifestyle."*
>
> —SHELDON LEONARD

"If it hadn't been for Sheldon Leonard fighting for us," insists Van Dyke, "we would have been off the air."

Opting for the understatement, Leonard concedes: "It is not generally recognized that the show had such a painful adolescence."

Meanwhile, nervous parent Reiner devised an additional plan to save the series. He urged that the show be rebroadcast during the summer months, a programing decision not popular at that time. Reruns could kill the series even faster than replacing it with a summer fill-in, maintained the network. Reiner was adamant and his gamble paid off. "People found us," he explains. "By the time we went back on in the fall, the audience knew who we were."

Down for the count, *The Dick Van Dyke Show* returned a champion.

Back for the second season, more changes occurred. For example, Jerry Paris exercised new creative muscles as he took on additional duties behind the camera. Paris recalls, "Carl said, 'Maybe someday you'll direct.' I said, I don't know how to direct. He looked at me and said, 'I'm producing and I don't know how to produce!' So they threw me a bone and I directed."

Although he was eager for this new experience he admits to being frightened. "The night before I directed for the first time I threw up!"

The battle won, a triumphant Leonard returns.
CARL REINER

*Dick Van Dyke in a publicity
photo announcing yet another of
the several* Dick Van Dyke Show
*timeslots: Oct. 1961–Dec. 1961,
Tues. 8:00–8:30 EST; Jan. 1962–
Sept. 1964, Wed. 9:30–10:00 EST;
Sept. 1964–Sept. 1965, Wed. 9:00–
9:30 EST; Sept. 1965–Sept. 1966,
Wed. 9:30–10:00 EST.*
RICHARD DEACON

He had reason to be nervous—one of his first
directorial assignments was a challenging script—
but the show would become one of the classics of the
series. "It May Look Like a Walnut," written by Carl
Reiner, is remembered for its science fiction plot
about visitors from the planet Twylo who have no
thumbs, a guest appearance by Danny Thomas, and
a nutty gimmick: "I invented the idea of the 1100

pounds of walnuts in the closet," says Paris—an idea
Sheldon Leonard thought had gone too far.

Rose Marie remembers: "Sheldon came in and
we were reading the next week's script ["It May
Look Like a Walnut!"]. We were all enthralled
with it, laughing. Sheldon threw the script down
and said, 'What do you think?' 'I think it's cute. It'll
be a ball—very funny.' He said, 'I don't think it's
funny. Good luck!' And he walked out. He'd never
done that before. We all looked at each other and
somebody said, 'It's *still* a good idea, why don't we
do it?' "

Van Dyke laughs remembering that week: "We
ate so many walnuts, the entire cast and crew got
constipated!"

After viewing the run-through, Rose Marie remembers Leonard addressing the ensemble: "Ladies and gentlemen, this *is* a very funny show. I'm
sorry, I was wrong."

Leonard praises Jerry Paris's skill as a director:
"He worked out very well, largely because the cast
was pulling for him one hundred percent."

Jerry Paris feels, "Acting is reacting and listening, and you can't do anything else. I like directing
better because, when you're a supporting actor, you
have only one color to paint, always blue or gray.
As the director, I had all the colors. I felt like a real
artist—orange, reds, yellows. It was far more exciting."

Paris was so captivated by the story idea of "It
May Look Like a Walnut!" that more than a de-
cade later it inspired him to create alien being
"Mork," first featured on *Happy Days*, and the
spinoff series, *Mork and Mindy*, starring Robin
Williams.

Bill Persky and Sam Denoff began their collab-
oration in the late 1950s at radio station WNEW in
New York. "We did continuity work (scheduling
commercial spots) and the program logs," explains
Persky. "Then we started writing jingles and satire
for the station, and nightclub material for people
you didn't know then and don't know now."

A three-week guarantee as writers on *The Steve
Allen Show* prompted their move to California. In
1962, while working as writers on *The Andy Williams Show*, Persky and Denoff elected to write a
script for *The Dick Van Dyke Show*, entirely on
their own.

Their agent at the William Morris Agency was

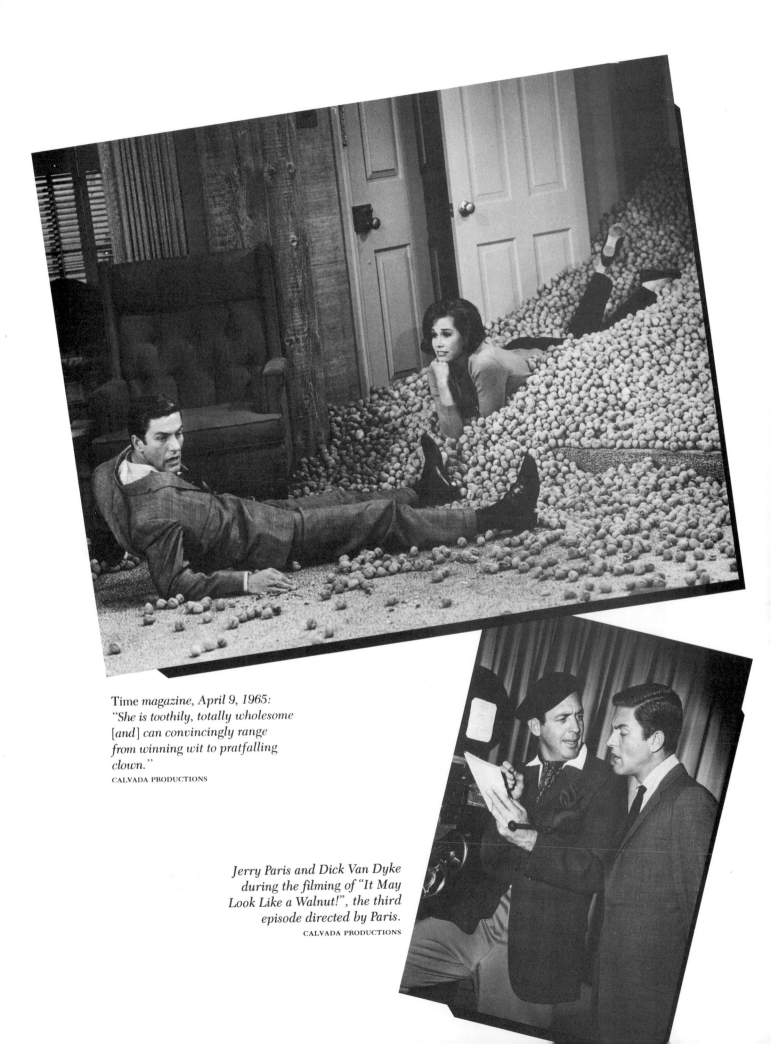

Time *magazine, April 9, 1965:*
"She is toothily, totally wholesome
[and] can convincingly range
from winning wit to pratfalling
clown."
CALVADA PRODUCTIONS

Jerry Paris and Dick Van Dyke
during the filming of "It May
Look Like a Walnut!", the third
episode directed by Paris.
CALVADA PRODUCTIONS

George Shapiro, who coincidentally was also Carl Reiner's agent (and nephew by marriage). Through Shapiro, Persky and Denoff managed to get their script to Reiner. "It was all wrong," Reiner remembers, "so we forgot about it."

Later that year, Shapiro again approached Reiner about Persky and Denoff, arguing that the writers had spent the intervening months studying the series and now understood the characters as well as Carl's philosophy of the show.

At Shapiro's insistence, Reiner agreed to meet with them. Reiner, Persky, Denoff, and Leonard then met to brainstorm story ideas and gauge how closely Persky and Denoff's attitudes meshed with Reiner's own.

> "If I hadn't found Persky and Denoff in the third year, I think I would have had a heart attack!"
>
> —CARL REINER

The outcome of that meeting was twofold: It reassured Reiner that Persky and Denoff had indeed become familiar with the series and resulted in a script idea for a show that would open the third season on September 25, 1963, "That's My Boy??"

Persky and Denoff conjured up a storyline (in flashback) centering on Rob's suspicion that his newborn son may not be his, but rather the result of a mix-up at the hospital where the Petries' baby and the child of a Mr. and Mrs. Peters were born.

Laura Petrie and Mrs. Peters repeatedly receive each other's meals, flowers, and gifts. That confusion, combined with Rob's belief that little Ritchie resembles neither Laura nor himself, leads him to conclude that each couple was given the other's baby. It's not until the last scene, when the Peters call on the Petries, that Rob realizes that it is impossible for them to have the wrong baby—Mr. and Mrs. Peters are black!

According to Bill Persky, it was Sheldon Leonard who suggested the black couple. "We didn't think it would be possible," he recounts.

"That's My Boy??"
CALVADA PRODUCTIONS

Indeed, it very nearly wasn't. "You must remember, it was 1963. There was great unrest in the South and there had been a Civil Rights uproar," emphasizes John Rich, the director of that episode.

Well aware of the ramifications of what he thought was a sensational idea, Reiner nonetheless believed, "you go by the seat of your pants. When

Writers Bill Persky (left) and Sam Denoff
CALVADA PRODUCTIONS

your heart is in the right place, the audience knows it."

Executive producer Leonard dealt less with philosophy and more with forces determined to abort the show. In addition to the standard procedure of providing scripts to CBS, the sponsors, and Benton & Bowles, "That's My Boy??" was submitted to the NAACP. But despite that organization's approval the censorship battle wasn't over. It hadn't even begun.

Leonard received a protest from Procter & Gamble's George Giroux, who told him, "We're frightened of it. You're making fun of the fact that the couple is black." To which Leonard replied, "No, we're not. We're making fun of the fact that Rob is a *dope!*"

Giroux backed down.

Leonard then went to see Lee Rich, "our quarterback who had always protected me." Rich had just

Dick Van Dyke leads a completely surprised John Rich into his farewell party.

been informed that P&G had given the green light to the script, but he surprised Leonard by stating emphatically that Benton & Bowles had no intention of allowing Procter & Gamble to risk its good name and reputation by approving "That's My Boy??"

"I gave him the same speech I gave Procter & Gamble. I implored him to give me the chance to make my point," says Leonard. "I told Rich, 'There will be an audience of three hundred and fifty people—you will be able to tell immediately if anyone is offended.'" Lee Rich accepted Leonard's proposition.

Next Leonard received a phone call from the network categorically rejecting the script. Persuading them with the same argument, Leonard told CBS brass, "If anybody finds this show to be in poor taste or is offended I will personally reshoot the last scene replacing the black couple—at my own expense—with a Chinese, East Indian, American Indian, or Italian couple—anything you want." CBS agreed.

"When my husband passed away [May 1964] I decided that I didn't want to do the show anymore. John Rich called and asked if he could come over that night and see me. I said yes and he came to the house and talked nonstop until two in the morning, and convinced me to stay on the series. Everybody was so marvelous. If there were things in the scripts they thought might upset me, they'd write it out. They were the best in the world. They were family."

—ROSE MARIE

During the summer hiatus, Leonard, Reiner, and John Rich met with Dick Van Dyke on the set of *Mary Poppins.* Director Rich recalls: "We felt the only way the show would work was having Rob give control of the situation to the black man. What scared us was having Rob ask the black man, 'Why didn't you tell me on the phone?'—the exact question the audience would ask. The answer was, 'And miss the expression on your face?' That was the key. It gave control of the moment to the black man."

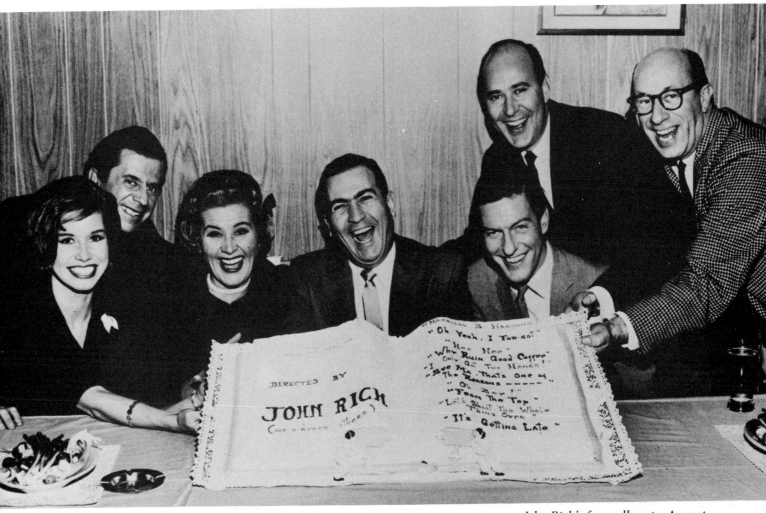

John Rich's farewell party, August 27, 1963, after the filming of "Very Old Shoes, Very Old Rice"
JOHN RICH

Director Rich then was faced with the crucial issue of casting. "I wanted to cast the most handsome black couple I could find." He paired Greg Morris and Mimi Dillard, who as Rich remembers, "were both fairly inexperienced, untrained actors at that time." He instructed Morris and Dillard to "come in and smile—and wait," feeling there would be a moment of shock before the audience fully comprehended the situation.

Mary remembers, "The audience went crazy. It was so gratifying."

Dick insists, "It was the longest laugh of the whole five years," so long, in fact, it had to be trimmed.

If that audience reaction was not enough ammu-

nition to support Reiner's "seat of the pants" philosophy and Leonard's determination to air the episode as originally envisioned, the mail after the telecast began to pour in to CBS "by the satchel," beamed Leonard, "and all applauding."

It was a milestone in television history and led to Leonard being able to cast Bill Cosby in *I Spy*, a series far removed from the stereotypes in *Amos 'n' Andy*.

(The complete script of "That's My Boy??" begins on page 155.)

"Very Old Shoes, Very Old Rice," (in which Rob and Laura find out they are not legally married) was filmed on August 27, 1963. It was the fortieth and final episode of *The Dick Van Dyke Show* directed

65

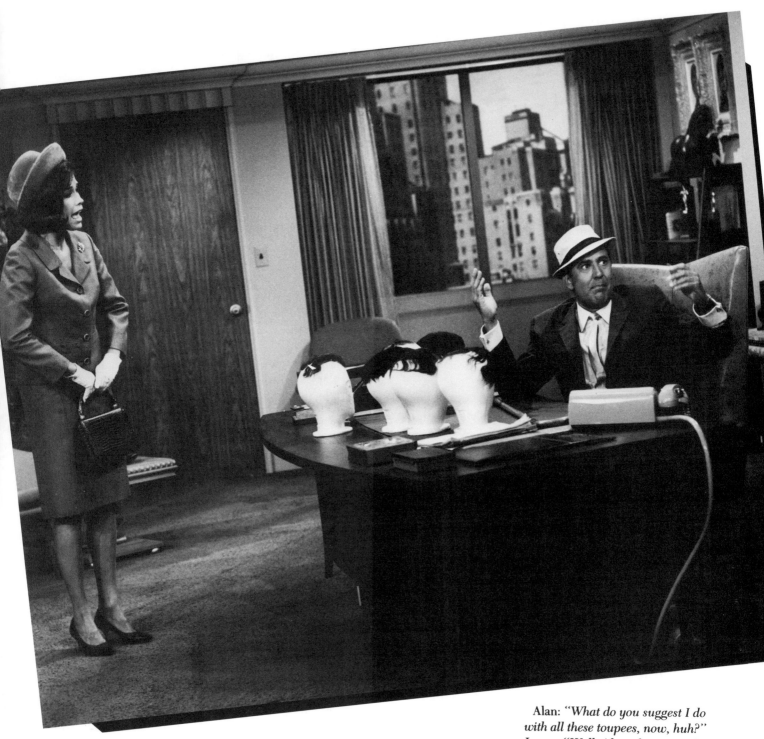

Alan: *"What do you suggest I do with all these toupees, now, huh?"*
Laura: *"Well, Alan, there must be some needy bald people...."*

by John Rich. (He had signed a contract with Paramount requiring him to leave the series to direct a feature film.)

Rich recalls that evening: "I was feeling sentimental, and a little tragic on my last night. One by one, the cast and crew walked by, shook my hand, said good-bye and left. I wondered, Do they hate me, are they embarrassed? I asked if anybody wanted to have a drink but nobody could. It was down to that terribly cold, empty set with me, the director, gathering his things. Dick showed up and I asked him if he wanted to have a drink. He said yes and I thought, Thank God! Dick took me to a place across the street and *everybody* was there. The surprise worked one hundred percent. It was a great night."

After John Rich left there was a period when several new directors were used. The cast wasn't pleased with this continual rotation; they wanted directors, such as Jerry Paris, who knew them and understood their characters. "So we called a meeting," recalls Deacon. "Mary, Rosie, Morey, and I went to Dick to ask him to go tell Sheldon that we didn't want a parade of new directors. Dick said he felt the same way. It was arranged that we all would see Sheldon, with Dick as our spokesman. We went into Sheldon's office and he said, 'Yes, Dick, what do you want?' Dick stammered, 'Well . . . ah, Shel . . . ah . . . the cast feels . . . well . . . how many directors do you plan to use this year?' Sheldon said he didn't know. Dick asked, 'Are you going to have more?' Sheldon said, 'I imagine so.' 'Ah, we feel . . . maybe you could . . . ah,' Dick went on, stammering away for fifteen minutes, and nobody said anything. We came out of Sheldon's office and from then on called Dick 'Old Blood and Guts, our fearless leader!'"

"When you have a boss, it's always a good subject for a show."

—CARL REINER

Carl Reiner created Alan Brady to be talked about, heard from, but not seen.

"I wanted someone who was an important star to appear, but I knew I'd never get an important star to play the small part. So I played him myself, but decided in the beginning never to show him. [The audience] would just see the back of his head, hear his voice. The first year I never appeared, and I think in the second year I kept hidden under a towel in a barbershop."

Script supervisor Marge Mullen speculates: "The first two years, he [Reiner] was so busy, he didn't have time to act, anyway." Alan Brady was seen for the first time in the third season's Christmas show, "The Alan Brady Show Presents." Reiner explains why he decided to appear: "I wrote a show that had such a strong part for him that it would have been unfair to the script not to see the reaction on his face."

From that point on, Alan Brady became a visible character "who appeared four or five times a year," according to Reiner, with one stipulation: "He appeared only when we had a great idea for him." One such idea—and perhaps Alan Brady's most memorable appearance—was in "Coast-to-Coast Big Mouth," written by Persky and Denoff, in which Laura blurts out on national television that her husband's boss wears a toupee; that episode was the season premiere of the 1965–66 season.

"In the beginning, Carl told us: 'Never write anything for Rob Petrie to do that you wouldn't do. I'm taking into consideration that you both are crazy, but never let Rob do anything that you wouldn't do personally.'"

—SAM DENOFF

"I was the story editor, head writer, and producer. It was the hardest single job I ever had in my life," recaps Reiner. "The first year I wrote twenty scripts, the second year, about twenty-two." He estimates that he wrote more than sixty of the one hundred fifty-eight episodes of *The Dick Van Dyke Show*.

Most prolific of the writers Reiner employed were the teams of Bill Persky and Sam Denoff, and Jerry Belson and Garry Marshall.

"Belson and Marshall's scripts were very funny and had less rewrites than most," asserts Marge Mullen. "They were wonderful," praises Reiner. "They always came in with either springboards or whole ideas to develop."

Persky and Denoff were handed a sizable amount

of artistic control when Reiner appointed them story editors in the fourth year of the series. Bill Persky recalls, "In the fifth year we were producing the show [the last thirteen weeks] because Carl was off doing *The Russians Are Coming, The Russians Are Coming*. The first day, we were sitting at the table in the main chairs instead of off to the side. We didn't actually sit in Carl's chair, we were smart enough not to do that. It was a strange, tense moment. The phone rang and I answered it. The lady on the other end said, 'Is this Carl Reiner?' I said, 'No, but I'm doing the best I can!'"

The task of rewriting scripts was also entrusted to Persky and Denoff, which was "a great relief" to Reiner. He explains: "I alone was doing all the rewriting. Writing a show is not as difficult as rewriting; it took me five or six days to write a script of my own and it would take seven, eight, or nine days to rewrite a show."

Rewrite sessions, Bill Persky feels, by their very nature, could sometimes be self-defeating. "After looking for a joke for about an hour, someone would turn a page and say, 'How about this one?' There was always a good joke there, but because it was *already* there, it was not good enough."

The relentless search for the best line had set high standards indeed.

"Very few jokes stood the test of *The Dick Van Dyke Show*," Bill Persky admits. "If you could get [a line] through two readings and three runthroughs and still have it in the show, that was one hell of a joke."

"Carl Reiner. He's a genius. He has tremendous writing ability and an ability to deal with us as people. The flavor, texture, style, and quality he wanted he was able to articulate. He's just one of those people. Everyone worships him, still to this day. I love him dearly, we all do. He's an uncommon human being."

—DICK VAN DYKE

The Dick Van Dyke Show concluded its original network run on June 1, 1966, with the airing of episode 157, entitled "The Last Chapter." It was highlighted by flashback excerpts from several memorable programs as Laura reads Rob's just-completed autobiography. The episode—and the series—ends with the announcement that Rob, Buddy, and Sally will adapt the book for television as a new situation comedy to star Alan Brady.

There was no doubt, as *Life* magazine reported, that CBS was "drooling to continue this consistent entry in the Neilsen Top Twenty," further noting, "Fellow TV tradesmen rewarded it with an Emmy

Richard Deacon, Mary Tyler Moore, Dick Van Dyke, Sheldon Leonard, Bill Persky, Carl Reiner, and Jerry Paris at the Emmy Awards, May 25, 1964
CALVADA PRODUCTIONS

"Why didn't someone tell me? I would have worn my hair!" Carl Reiner accepting his Emmy for Outstanding Writing Achievement in Comedy, May 22, 1962.
CALVADA PRODUCTIONS

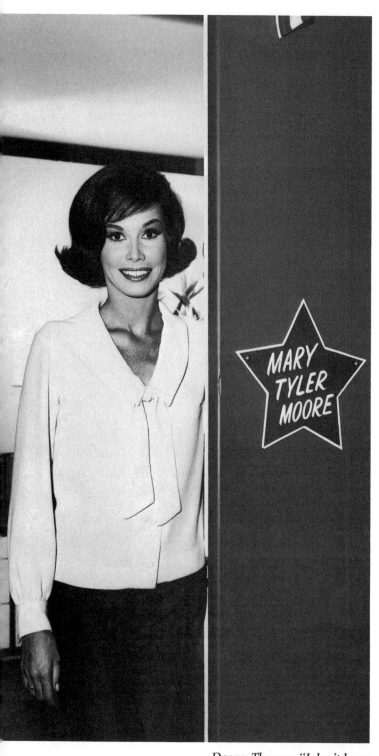

Danny Thomas: "I don't know why it was predestined that it should be Mary Tyler Moore. It was predestined that she is what she is today. Kismet. It happens to all of us."

nomination in every possible category: best show, best direction, best writing, best supporting actress and actor, and best lead actress and actor."

Why would one of the most beloved and acclaimed television programs of all time choose to cease production of its own volition?

Variety speculated: "[it] is doing so . . . ironically because of its success . . . the series has done so well, most everyone connected with it wants to go on to other fields."

According to Dick Van Dyke, however, the decision to halt production had been predetermined not so much by "other challenges" (feature films, Broadway shows, and the like) as by the deliberate effort to maintain a consistent level of quality. "We wanted to quit while we were still proud of it," he states.

Mary Tyler Moore echoes her costar's concern about keeping the series fresh, revealing to Abe Greenburg in his "Voice of Hollywood" column, "The two of us [Dick and Mary] could have spent the rest of our lives getting terribly rich doing the same thing week after week, but Dick and I wanted to quit the series while we were still young and ahead of the game."

Furthermore, Van Dyke maintains, the decision to end the series had been made by Carl Reiner at the outset. "Carl said in the very beginning that we wouldn't go beyond five years."

Reiner supports Van Dyke's contention. "Of course, we had no idea it would become the success it did, but we all had set the clocks in our heads from the beginning to run only five years. We all decided if we went on for a sixth year, we'd be doing more of the same. Good as it was, the quality might suffer. Knowing the fifth year was our last, we worked very hard to keep the quality up so we wouldn't be embarrassed by any of the shows if they were ever rerun. And I think we were right about it."

"I think we quit at the right time," Van Dyke says simply.

Yet not everyone shared that viewpoint, notably associate producer Ron Jacobs ("No one wanted to end the show") and executive producer Sheldon Leonard, who points out that his other television series, such as *The Danny Thomas Show* and *The Andy Griffith Show*, enjoyed extraordinarily long and successful runs (eleven and eight years, respec-

Dick eating his lunch while Carl Reiner and Mary Tyler Moore rehearse "The Gunslinger," the last episode filmed.
CBS PHOTOS

tively) "without ever repeating themselves." Rose Marie contends that if the series had been shot in color it could have, in her estimation, run three years longer.

The demise of *The Dick Van Dyke Show* generated tremendous press coverage, alternately laudatory and atypically sentimental—the media clearly mourned its passing. The usually reserved *TV Guide*

deemed it "one of the most admired comedies ever to grace television."

José M. Ferrer III ended an article on the series in *Life* magazine entitled, "A Good Show Quits While It's Ahead," on this note: "All those laughs you have been hearing are real human being laughs. The only trouble is that the real laughs were so long and loud that the engineers have carefully had to

71

*Richard Deacon, Jerry Paris and
Carl Reiner at the final cast party
after filming of "The Gunslinger"
episode, March 22, 1966.*
RICHARD DEACON

doctor them down . . . the rest of TV should have such a problem."

Veteran television critic Clay Gowran lamented the show's end three years after it ceased its prime-time run, comparing it to subsequent comedies, observing that when the series "went off prime-time air, [it] created a vacuum that never really has been satisfactorily filled . . . nobody comes anywhere close to Van Dyke in gentle, thoroughly funny, happy comedy. And Miss Moore's perfect as a partner."

Amid such fanfare and bouquets was an on-set final cast and crew party with an Hawaiian luau theme, held on March 22, 1966, after "The Gunslinger," a western spoof that was the final episode filmed.

"It was a very sad evening," remembers Rose Marie. Richard Deacon describes that night as "fun—terrible fun." Larry Mathews recalls, "Everybody was crying. I know I was."

Mary Tyler Moore recounts a moment forever etched in her memory: "Glenn [Ross], the prop man—a big bear of a man—asked me to dance. We danced and I put my head on his shoulder and sobbed my face off. He was somehow the embodiment of everything that was tender and loving and sweet on that show."

Expressing the feeling of finality of the last night together as an ensemble, script supervisor Marge Mullen observed: "It was a golden period and we knew it would never happen again, that there would never again be a group of people together who were so compatible and so talented."

One week later, there appeared in the March 30, 1966, edition of the *Ottowa Citizen* an article by Frank Penn entitled, "Goodbye to a Good Show," preserved by many of *The Dick Van Dyke Show* cast:

The studio lights are dark and cold by now, and probably all that remains of *The Dick Van Dyke Show* sets is a few bent nails and scraps of lumber. Maybe in a dark corner a piece of the drapes, torn off during the demolition, hangs in forlorn farewell.

The show is over. And it could be a long while before TV sees its likes again.

How come the heavy drama for what was, after all, just a frothy situation comedy? Hasn't TV got more than enough where that one came from?

No, gentle reader, it hasn't. It hasn't gotten any at all.

The Dick Van Dyke Show was very special. Not because it was funnier, more regularly than most, but because it was lovingly fashioned every week of its long life with honest, painstaking craftsmanship.

Anyway, it's gone now, splintered into a dozen different directions as the actors, writers, and producers go on to other, bigger things.

Maybe, in some future time, when the studios have run out of gimmicks like talking cars, nasal marines, monsters and ghosts and trick photography, someone will put forward a revolutionary idea.

"What d'you say, J.B., we skip the gimmicks. Let's try working with a creative, polished script, real actors and directors."

And, just maybe again, we might see another show as honestly made as *The Dick Van Dyke Show.*

But I fear we've got a lot of trick photography to get through first.

Riding a crest of immeasurable popularity and acclaim, *The Dick Van Dyke Show* family would scatter to meet those "other challenges" they, as artists, were compelled to conquer.

Yet the personal and emotional aspects of their parting could not have made the decision to disband a painless or clear-cut one, no matter how enticing or lucrative the future might be "post-series."

Television veteran Danny Thomas summed up the feelings of many, when he said of *The Dick Van Dyke Show*, "It made you laugh, it made you cry, it made you think. It was one of the best situation comedies ever made."

So despite the conviction to quit while "ahead of the game"—as Mary Tyler Moore had said—the show's end left everyone with bittersweet feelings. "I was heartbroken," Mary reveals. "I wanted it to go on forever."

Mary may get her wish, for, as comic genius Buster Keaton once said, "Only things that one could imagine happening to real people remain in a person's memory."

If that is true, then it is a certainty that *The Dick Van Dyke Show* will be everlasting, for what is both memorable and classic *is* forever—strengthened and all the more valued with the passage of time.

As long as there is laughter, *The Dick Van Dyke Show* will endure.

"I like Mommy's bananas better!"
LARRY MATHEWS

★ 2 ★

The Dick Van Dyke Show Alumni Association

Perhaps a key to explaining *The Dick Van Dyke Show*'s critical acclaim and great popularity (never out of the Neilsen Top Twenty after its struggling first season) lies in the abundant amount of pleasure it gave to its viewers, which derived from a blend of slapstick, sparkling high comedy, and occasional pathos.

An overview of the series' 158 episodes reveals how carefully these comedic foundations were laid from the very beginning. The third episode, "Jealousy," marked the first appearance of neighbors Jerry and Millie Helper; the next installment, "Sally and the Lab Technician," began the practice of showcasing a cast member every several episodes or so, in this case Rose Marie in a touching story of how Sally Rogers's overzealous desire for marriage leads to disaster on a blind date with Laura's shy cousin.

"Oh How We Met the Night That We Danced" introduced the flashback device (that would be used repeatedly throughout the course of the series) in telling the tale of the courtship of Sergeant Robert Petrie and USO dancer Laura Meehan at Camp Crowder, Missouri.

Mary Tyler Moore's strong debut as a comedienne in "My Blonde-Haired Brunette" was soon followed by "The Curious Thing About Women," in which Rob tests his wife's inability to not tamper with his mail by sending himself an inflatable rubber life raft. Finding the mysterious package irre-

sistible, Laura impetuously opens it, causing the raft to quickly swell to mammoth proportions within the confines of the Petries' living room

"Father of the Week" (Carl Reiner's reworking of the *Head of the Family* pilot starring himself) featured Dick Van Dyke in a charming solo turn, performing for Ritchie's classmates, in hopes of impressing his son, who feels his father's occupation is not equal in stature to that of his friends' fathers.

"What's in a Middle Name?" introduced the Petrie and Meehan relatives as well as young Ritchie's

Dick and Mary in a commercial for sponsor Kent cigarettes, the spots airing only within CBS network broadcasts of the program.

SHOKUS VIDEO

"Oh, Rob!"
CALVADA PRODUCTIONS

76

George Neise, Mr. Henderson, and Rose Marie in "Where Have You Been, Fassbinder?"
CALVADA PRODUCTIONS

Rose Marie and Vic Damone in
"Like a Sister"
CALVADA PRODUCTIONS

curious middle name: Rosebud, each letter representing the names of family members—Robert Oscar Samuel Edward Benjamin Ulysses David.

Singer Vic Damone was the only billed guest star to appear on *The Dick Van Dyke Show*. In "Like a Sister," Damone played balladeer Ric Vallone who wooed a very susceptible Sally Rogers while guesting on *The Alan Brady Show*.

Buddy Sorrell's disturbing revelation that his marriage to wife Pickles is over is the storyline of "Divorce," displaying Morey Amsterdam's comedic and less frequently seen dramatic talents.

When Rob agrees to direct the local Parent's Council variety show, he is saddled with "Too Many Stars," including Mel Cooley, who inexplicably performs a wretched ventriloquism act, his partner a dummy bearing an uncanny resemblance to—who else?—Mel Cooley.

"Big Max Calvada" featured an appearance by executive producer Sheldon Leonard in the title role. His gangster character was an inside joke, named after *The Dick Van Dyke Show*'s own company, Calvada Productions, in which he was a partner.

The following week's episode, "The Ballad of the Betty Lou," paired best friends Rob Petrie and Jerry Helper as seamates on their newly acquired boat, the Betty Lou. Rob gets an inkling that Jerry is taking his nautical role as captain a bit too seriously when Jerry admonishes, "Listen, we can hug all you want at home, but on the boat, never touch me!"

"*The Alan Brady Show* Presents" was a delightful Christmas show that also marked Carl Reiner's first appearance as Alan Brady sans towel covering his face in a barbershop. The program was highlighted by a song-and-dance number by Dick and Mary performed in oversized Santa Claus suits, and the "I Am a Fine Musician" musical number, capped by the a capella singing of *The Dick Van Dyke Show* theme music.

"4½" and "*The Alan Brady Show* Goes to Jail" were the titles of a two-part story featuring Don Rickles as petty thief Lyle Delp, who holds up Rob and pregnant Laura in a stalled elevator on the way to her obstetrician (in a flashback). The second half returns to the present, as Rob, Laura, Buddy, and Sally agree to put on a variety show at Delp's prison.

Richard Deacon and friend in
"Too Many Stars"
RICHARD DEACON

"The Alan Brady Show *Presents*"
CALVADA PRODUCTIONS

"I Am a Fine Musician," from
"The Alan Brady Show Presents"
CALVADA PRODUCTIONS

*Rob entertains prisoners Vincent
Barbi, Arthur Batanides, and
Robert Strauss by command
performance.*
CALVADA PRODUCTIONS

Dressed as an inmate for a dance routine with
Laura ("I've Got Your Number") Rob is mistakenly
taken to a cell with actual prisoners, despite his
protests. The group of convicts, who were denied
permission to see the show, spitefully refuse to admit Rob is not one of them until he performs for
them in their cell. At the last minute, he tries to
identify himself by dropping his trousers, revealing
a very unprisonlike pair of striped boxer shorts.

*Rob attempts to escape a stuck
elevator with the help of an
umbrella in "4½."*
CALVADA PRODUCTIONS

82

"The Lady and the Sitter" is noted for the oft-recalled "milk-cake" exchange between Rob and Laura, as he explains what is proper and not proper to drink while eating chocolate cake. (Milk, yes, coffee, *no*.)

Highlights from the last season: "Odd But True," the discovery that the freckles on Rob Petrie's back are in the shape of the Liberty Bell; "Bad Reception in Albany," as a hapless Rob arrives late for Laura's cousin's wedding wearing a "hairy tuxedo" belonging to one of the many Seals, a group of conventioneers, infesting their hotel; Laura's dropping the ugly Petrie family heirloom brooch (in the shape of the continental United States) down the garbage disposal in "The Curse of the Petrie People"; Laura and Millie stacking up tin cans against the Petrie front door as they spend a terror-filled night alone in "Long Night's Journey into Day"; and Millie and Jerry's wedding anniversary party becoming part of the documentary "A Day in the Life of Alan Brady."

The last episode filmed—though not the last broadcast—was a western spoof. "The Gunslinger," written by Bill Persky and Sam Denoff, featured that writing team as well as other writers of the series as extras in "Miss Sally's" saloon.

Blissfully unconscious as dentist Jerry Helper extracts a tooth, Rob dreams he is transported to the days of the old West, as a "gunslinger-turned-singer-turned-dancer-turned-rancher-turned-parson-turned-sheriff." Gunslinger Petrie has a deputy named Sorrell and a friend in Miss Sally, who brings him hot, homemade meals. "Hominy grits!" he exclaims. "Oh, about fifty," replies Miss Sally.

One day, "Killer Cooley" bursts into the saloon, announcing that "Big Bad Brady" will be riding into town shortly and demands a show or Sheriff Petrie must face Brady in a showdown. Wife Laura's attempts to please Brady with her rendition of "I Don't Care" is unsuccessful. She, along with friend Millie and her husband, town "dent" Helper, watch as the showdown commences.

"The Last Chapter" was the final episode written and aired, with the intention of "coming around full circle," according to Carl Reiner.

In it, Rob announces to Laura that he has finally completed his autobiography, which he has toiled over for five years. As Laura curls up on the sofa and reads, flashback excerpts from "The Attempted Marriage" recount Rob's marriage proposal to Laura as they both shiver in an Army jeep, and Rob's hopping to the church after a jeep accident only to find a tearful Laura angry with him for jilting her.

The birth of Ritchie—thanks to the driver of a laundry truck whose motto is "We Pick up and Deliver"—follows in scenes from "Where Did I Come From?" Clips from "That's My Boy??" complete the flashbacks.

The final scene of "The Last Chapter" (and *The Dick Van Dyke Show*, as well) finds the entire company gathered together in the Petrie home waiting for Rob to make an announcement: Alan Brady will produce Rob's book as a new television series to star himself and it will be written by Rob, Buddy, and Sally.

The cast cheers the news as the closing shot frames Rob and Laura kissing.

The Dick Van Dyke Show was complete, indeed "coming around full circle": Carl Reiner (as Alan Brady) would portray Rob Petrie—in essence, himself—in a television situation comedy, as Reiner had done in *Head of the Family* years before, which then became *The Dick Van Dyke Show*.

DICK ON NICK

"*The Dick Van Dyke Show* is bigger now than it's ever been," says Rose Marie. And Dick Van Dyke agrees, "I judge by the fan mail. I am getting a whole bunch from young kids who have just discovered it."

Thanks to syndication, the series has never been off the air since its CBS network premiere in 1961. Now, after twenty-five years in syndication, *The Dick Van Dyke Show* has found an entirely new life and audience on cable as a flagship series in the Nick at Nite primetime lineup.

"We refer to Nickelodeon as a twenty-four-hour network, specializing in children's television. At 8:00 P.M. (E.T./P.S.T., 7:00 P.M. Central) it turns into Nick—an abbreviation for Nickelodeon—at Nite, which we position as more of a family kind of environment," explains Larry Jones, director of marketing for Nick at Nite. "Our position is very much like a museum's as far as collecting the greatest television shows, the classics, that really have withstood the test of time. *The Dick Van Dyke Show* was an obvious choice for our network."

"With a show like this, we realized that Nick at Nite had a real duty to present *The Dick Van Dyke Show* in a respectful, encyclopedic fashion," according to Scott Webb, senior vice president, creative director of Nickelodeon and Nick at Nite, who believes the series deserves the same kind of primetime exposure that it had originally.

The Dick Van Dyke Collection is an example of the grand, "TV Land" Nick at Nite treatment for the series. A record eighty-hour retrospective featured all 158 episodes, back-to-back, over eight "themed" evenings. "The response was phenomenal," notes Larry Jones. "It was a great way to kick off our new mission, our dedication and commitment to preserving our television heritage." *The Dick Van Dyke Collection* was the highest-rated Nick at Nite marathon to date in the history of the cable network.

MY ZAZULA ASSOCIATES

"I keep running into people who know every line in every show and yet they keep watching. I can't figure that out. They know more about it than I do."

—*DICK VAN DYKE*

In April of 1992, Dick Van Dyke was appointed chairman of Nick at Nite. In this newly created position, he has been featured in the network's print advertising campaigns and on-air promotions and serves as an official representative at select television industry functions. His responsibilities include advising and consulting with the network to help increase awareness of the important cultural contributions television has given generations of viewers.

"We had a meeting of the minds on perspectives about television—what it should be, what it is, and what it has been. Nick at Nite has a philosophy about their responsibility to the audience. I just liked their attitude and they liked mine. We ended up cooperating and I ended up with them. And I like the idea," offers Dick.

"Dick Van Dyke is so much responsible for what Nick at Nite is trying to bring to the American public as far as preserving our television heritage," says Larry Jones. "He agreed with it with the same amount of passion that we have for being a place that would provide good television, that is quality television, that isn't violent, that is family oriented. He

believed in all those things, we didn't have to educate him to our points of view. He feels the same way."

Scott Webb adds, "I hope Dick continues to be our chairman and I hope we have *The Dick Van Dyke Show* forever. I know there are the realities of business but I hope he continues to be a key part of our lineup for a long, long time."

And so do the audiences who continue to delight in what more seasoned viewers have known for years. *The Dick Van Dyke Show* is timeless. Thirty years have passed since its network debut yet viewers agree the series does not seem at all dated and remains fresh and funny.

Dick Van Dyke credits Carl Reiner for his foresight: "Carl absolutely tabooed any slang of the day or any mention of current events. It was amazing that he thought of that. He said, 'I don't want any sixties slang in here because it's going to be dated.' You never hear any hip talk and he was careful about the clothes. He wanted everything kind of middle of the road. For that reason, and his writing about human relationships which is timeless, that kind of comedy lasts."

Yet, as Dick notes, bemused, "We had no *idea* that we'd be watching it in our old age!"

Film freezes a moment forever. First syndication and now cable television allows us to enjoy it forever.

Since 1966, each member of *The Dick Van Dyke Show* family has sustained success in a variety of professional endeavors. The following pages chronicle the continuing careers of Dick Van Dyke and company.

DICK VAN DYKE

Dick Van Dyke began his show business career while serving in the Air Force, as announcer of the program *Flight Time*. A detour into his own business—an advertising agency—lasted only one year.

He then teamed with boyhood friend Phillip Ericksen, and formed a pantomime act called "The Merry Mutes." Six years later, Van Dyke settled in Atlanta, where he hosted two local television variety programs. After two years, he moved to New Orleans and starred in a TV variety program prophetically titled *The Dick Van Dyke Show*.

In 1956, Dick got his first network break as emcee of CBS's *Cartoon Theatre*. He subsequently replaced Jack Paar on his morning show, filled in occasionally for Garry Moore, and appeared with Ed Sullivan, Dinah Shore, and Perry Como on their programs.

His 1958 debut on Broadway in *The Girls Against the Boys* won him the lead in *Bye Bye Birdie*.

After *The Dick Van Dyke Show* ended, he moved his family and his three Emmys to Arizona, the location for the first two seasons of *The New Dick Van Dyke Show* costarring Hope Lange. A variety series, *Van Dyke & Company*, followed and won him a fourth Emmy.

Van Dyke also returned to the stage where he starred with Carol Burnett in *Same Time, Next Year* and toured nationally with *Damn Yankees* and *The Music Man*.

He has appeared in numerous films including: *Mary Poppins, Divorce, American Style, Cold Turkey, Chitty, Chitty Bang, Bang,* and *The Comic*.

His critically acclaimed performance in the made-for-TV film *The Morning After* earned him a Emmy nomination for drama.

He starred in a Home Box Office production of *The Country Girl* with Faye Dunaway and *Drop-Out Father*, a CBS-TV movie costarring Mariette Hartley. Other projects include: a one-man revue and a television series with *The Dick Van Dyke Show* writers Sam Denoff and Frank Tarloff; and an NBC-TV movie, *The Psychiatrist*. Dick headlined a national touring company revival of *The Music Man*. In addition to his role as Nick at Nite chairman, he has appeared in a number of made-for-television features and a situation comedy series with his son, Barry. In a character spin-off from the CBS detective series *Jake and the Fatman*, Dick has been seen in a number of comedy-mystery telefilms as "Dr. Sloan," including *Diagnosis for Murder* and *House on Sycamore Street*.

Dick Van Dyke: "They were the five happiest and most enjoyable years of my life. It was gorgeous."

Mary Tyler Moore: "I learned everything from them, especially from Dick. He allowed me to grow."

MARY TYLER MOORE

Mary Tyler Moore has proven herself to be an actress of amazing versatility.

Following *The Dick Van Dyke Show* Mary made several films, including *Thoroughly Modern Millie* and *Change of Habit*. She then was reunited with Dick Van Dyke in his 1969 special, *Dick Van Dyke and the Other Woman*. Her appearance was so well received it led to *The Mary Tyler Moore Show*. During its seven-year run, Mary won Best Leading Actress in a Comedy in 1973, 1974, and 1976 and another Emmy as Actress of the Year in 1974.

Since ending her series in 1977, Mary has met a number of professional challenges. Her performances in *First You Cry* for NBC and *Ordinary People* (earning her an Oscar nomination) were met with critical acclaim. She then appeared on Broadway in *Whose Life Is It Anyway?* and was awarded a special Tony.

In addition to headlining two variety series and a pair of situation comedies (*Mary* and *Annie McGuire*) for CBS following *The Mary Tyler Moore Show*, she has appeared in such theatrical releases as *Six Weeks* and *Just Between Friends*.

Rose Marie: "I'm proud to be associated with a television classic. They were the five happiest years of my life."

ROSE MARIE

Rose Marie, it is estimated, has entertained over a billion people in over one hundred countries since beginning her show business career at the age of three.

"Baby Rose Marie" was a show business phenomenon and star of her own network radio program at the age of seven. When she dropped "Baby," Rose Marie headlined at top nightclubs across the country and costarred in *Top Banana* with Phil Silvers.

Rose Marie then began a still-unbroken association with television, appearing on numerous programs such as *The Ed Sullivan Show, The Bob Cummings Show, Gunsmoke, The Colgate Comedy Hour, Kojak, Love Boat,* and *Honeymoon Suite* with Morey Amsterdam.

On stage, she starred in the national touring companies of *Bye Bye Birdie* and *Call Me Madam.*

After *The Dick Van Dyke Show* (for which she received three Emmy nominations), Rose Marie went on to costar on *The Doris Day Show* and become a resident panelist on *The Hollywood Squares.*

In 1977, she teamed with three other illustrious performers, Margaret Whiting, Helen O'Connell, and Rosemary Clooney. Their musical revue, *4 Girls 4,* was so well received, Rose Marie toured in it for over ten years.

Rose Marie has appeared as Frank Fontana's mother on the CBS situation comedy *Murphy Brown* and also co-starred in the comedy-fantasy series *Scorch.* In addition to headlining an original black-comedy stage vehicle titled *Drop Dead,* she is currently writing her autobiography and developing a new comedy series.

MOREY AMSTERDAM

Morey Amsterdam is a show business institution and a man of unlimited energy. He is a comedian, nightclub performer, writer, concert cellist, producer, director, dramatic actor, and songwriter ("Rum and Coca-Cola" among others).

Morey began his show business career at the age of ten as a boy soprano on a San Francisco radio program. He then joined his older brother's vaudeville act; when his brother quit Morey continued on solo.

Amsterdam also was in demand as a comedy writer for Will Rogers, Jack Benny, Fanny Brice, Milton Berle, and Henny Youngman. He appeared on television and radio with such regularity that Fred Allen once remarked, "The only thing we can turn on in our house without getting Morey Amsterdam is the water faucet!"

His films include *Murder, Inc.* with Peter Falk, Walt Disney's *The Horse in the Grey Flannel Suit*, and *Wholly Moses* with Richard Pryor. On television he was reunited with Rose Marie and Richard Deacon on a *Love Boat* episode.

He is the author of *Keep Laughing* and *Morey Amsterdam's Book for Drinkers or Betty Cooker's Crock Book.*

As always, his nightclub act is in demand in Las Vegas, Lake Tahoe, Reno, London, Hong Kong, New York, Australia, and any place in need of laughter.

Other projects: his autobiography, *I Remember Me.*

Richard Deacon: "Watching the genius of Carl Reiner and Sheldon Leonard was one of the most exciting experiences of my life."

RICHARD DEACON
1922–1984

"Deac," as he is fondly remembered, appeared in hundreds of roles including the feature films *Good Morning, Miss Dove, The Blackboard Jungle, That Darn Cat!, Invasion of the Body Snatchers, The Young Philadelphians,* and *The Solid Gold Cadillac.*

On radio and television, he was seen with Jack Benny, Bob Hope, Red Skelton, Burns and Allen, Phyllis Diller, and Lucille Ball, and on such series (as a guest or a regular) as *Leave It to Beaver, The Life of Riley, The Mothers-in-Law, The Gale Storm Show, My Sister Eileen, Twilight Zone, The Lucille Ball–Desi Arnaz Show* and *The Untouchables.*

He was also the author of *Richard Deacon's Microwave Cookery* and was the host of the syndicated program *Richard Deacon's Micro Magic,* a series featuring Richard, microwave cooking, and celebrity guests.

The beloved and respected Richard Deacon—veteran of more than one thousand television and radio shows as well as one hundred feature films—died of a heart attack at the age of sixty-two on August 8, 1984.

Jerry Paris: "They were all professional and had a great deal of talent to give."

Ann Guilbert: "It wasn't a rumor that everybody got along great. We had a lot of fun, and enjoyed it tremendously."

JERRY PARIS
1925–1986

Most performers work a lifetime before hitting Broadway, but that's where Jerry Paris began, in notable productions such as *Medea* with Dame Judith Anderson, and the revival of *Anna Christie*, starring Celeste Holm.

Paris appeared in more than fifty feature films including *Marty*, *The Wild One* (with Marlon Brando), *The Caine Mutiny*, *The Naked and the Dead*, and *Good Morning, Miss Dove*. His credits on television include dramatic and comedic roles on *Playhouse 90*, *Kraft Theatre*, *Studio One*, *The Lucy Show*, and *The Danny Thomas Show*.

After beginning his career as a director on *The Dick Van Dyke Show* (for which he received two Emmy nominations, one Emmy Award, and a Director's Guild Award), Paris went on to direct the pilot and over thirty-five episodes of *The Odd Couple*, starring Tony Randall and Jack Klugman. He also directed the pilots for *Love, American Style*, *That Girl*, *The Partridge Family*, and *Laverne and Shirley*.

For almost a decade, Jerry Paris produced and directed *Happy Days*, and is credited with creating the character of Mork and the spinoff TV series, *Mork and Mindy*. In addition, he directed many feature films and made-for-TV movies. Jerry Paris passed away in Los Angeles at the age of sixty due to complications of a brain tumor on March 31, 1986.

ANN GUILBERT

Since *The Dick Van Dyke Show*, Ann Morgan Guilbert has done a variety of things—abbreviating her name to Ann Guilbert is one of them.

Following *The Dick Van Dyke Show*, Ann appeared in *The New Andy Griffith Show* and numerous theatrical features and television series, in addition to appearing in regional theatre, often with husband Guy Raymond who can be seen on *Dick Van Dyke* repeats. Ann has also been seen on such series as *Pros and Cons*, *Newhart*, *Seinfeld*, *Empty Nest*, and *Blossom*, as well as starring in the NBC situation comedy series, *The Fanelli Boys*.

"It was a great show," she fondly recalls. "They were funny, witty people, and they helped fill my life with laughter."

LARRY MATHEWS

"I'm still the same person I was then," says Larry Mathews. "Just grown up quite a bit."

Determined to remain a "regular kid," Larry "retired" from show business at the age of ten when *The Dick Van Dyke Show* ended in 1966.

Upon graduation from UCLA in 1976, he resumed his childhood association with Danny Thomas, working for his company, in production, on the TV series *I'm a Big Girl Now*, and for Tony Thomas on the Witt-Thomas-Harris productions of Soap and Benson.

In addition to continuing his acting career, Larry is an account executive at a Hollywood post-production facility. He credits the show for enabling him to avoid the pitfalls most child actors encounter: "People ask me if I was cheated out of money or if I had any bad experiences working on *The Dick Van Dyke Show*—how can you have a bad experience when you work with the kind of people I did?"

Larry Mathews: "I felt very lucky that I was part of a wonderful group of people on such a wonderful show."

John Rich: "The word that comes to mind is love. People were anxious to get to work and didn't want to leave. I can't say that about every show I've done, but that was one of them."

JOHN RICH

John Rich is one of the most respected and in-demand directors in television.

His impressive list of credentials links him with over thirty television series including *Kraft Theater, The Dennis Day Show, I Married Joan, Our Miss Brooks, Gunsmoke, Twilight Zone, Bonanza, Richard Diamond, Private Detective, General Electric Theater, The Danny Thomas Show, I Spy, Hogan's Heroes,* and *Benson.*

Along with Henry Winkler, John Rich was executive producer of the long-running series *MacGyver,* starring Richard Dean Anderson.

Mr. Rich has been honored as the Director's Guild of America Director of the Year in 1972 (for *All in the Family*); Golden Globe Awards in 1973 and 1974 for *All in the Family;* and Emmy Awards for *The Dick Van Dyke Show* in 1963 and *All in the Family* in 1971 and 1972.

Sam Denoff: "We knew it was the best and wanted to write it."

Bill Persky: "The show was never harsh, never vulgar. It showed the best of us."

BILL PERSKY AND SAM DENOFF

The team of Bill Persky and Sam Denoff has left its unique imprint on numerous television shows.

Together they wrote for *The Steve Allen Show* and *The Andy Williams Show* prior to serving as writers and story editors for *The Dick Van Dyke Show.* They created and produced *That Girl*, the long-running series starring Marlo Thomas. Other television credits include: *Good Morning, World* (which introduced Goldie Hawn), *The Funny Side*, and *Lotsa Luck.* They have written specials for Julie Andrews, Bill Cosby, Dick Van Dyke, and Sid Caesar.

To this day, Bill is known to call Sam while watching a rerun of *The Dick Van Dyke Show* to tell him he finally figured out what was wrong with the scene. Sam is known to hang up on him.

Among Bill Persky's television credits is the long-running, award-winning situation comedy *Kate and Allie* starring Jane Curtin and Susan Saint James. Sam Denoff's credits include *Harry and the Hendersons* starring Bruce Davison.

Ronald Jacobs: "We entertained millions of people, and still entertain millions of people."

RONALD JACOBS

Ron Jacobs not only produced the hit film, *On the Right Track*, he *lives* it. The nephew of Danny Thomas, Jacobs began his television career as an assistant to producer Sheldon Leonard on *The Danny Thomas Show.*

He advanced steadily to the post of executive in charge of production, then president of Danny Thomas Productions.

Associated with twenty-two series sold to networks, nineteen comedy/variety specials, and sixteen made-for-TV movies, his credits include: *That Girl, The Mod Squad, I Spy, The Andy Griffith Show, The Over-the-Hill Gang, Satan's Triangle, Three on a Date,* and *The Unbroken Circle.*

Among his other credits is the film *Jimmy the Kid* with *Diff'rent Strokes* and *On the Right Track* star Gary Coleman, a stage production, *Hamlet Two* ("better than the original"), and an upcoming theatrical release to be shot in Russia titled *Russian Roulette.*

Sheldon Leonard: "The Dick Van Dyke Show *cut through all educational and economic levels, which is what we had hoped to do.*"

SHELDON LEONARD

Sheldon Leonard is a quadruple threat in the entertainment industry: actor, director, writer, and producer.

Leonard decided on a show business career, after working at various jobs: "I figured that as long as I couldn't make a living at anything else, I might as well not make a living at something I liked doing."

He appeared on Broadway prior to moving to California in 1939 where he appeared in over 140 films including *After the Thin Man* and *It's a Wonderful Life* (which he did for "two season tickets to the Dodgers ballgames").

He then joined *Make Room for Daddy* as ex-

ecutive producer and director in 1953, thus beginning a successful association with Danny Thomas. Thomas–Leonard Productions brought to television *The Andy Griffith Show, Gomer Pyle USMC, Mayberry RFD,* and *The Real McCoys.*

Mr. Leonard also was executive producer of *I Spy* and the short-lived but critically acclaimed *My World and Welcome to It* that won three Emmy Awards in 1970.

Mr. Leonard is the recipient of sixteen Emmy Award nominations and four Emmy Awards and has been inducted into the Television Hall of Fame by the Academy of Television Arts and Sciences.

Carl Reiner: "It was a totally
nourishing experience."

CARL REINER

Carl Reiner is the Renaissance man of show business.

Renowned as a talented director and prolific writer, Reiner is also remembered for his appearances on the Sid Caesar shows, his recordings with Mel Brooks of *The 2000 Year Old Man*, and his autobiographical novel, *Enter Laughing*.

Reiner has directed Steve Martin in *The Jerk;* Ruth Gordon and George Segal in *Where's Poppa?;* Dick Van Dyke in *The Comic* (which he coauthored); George Burns in *Oh, God!;* and Henry Winkler in *The One and Only*.

In addition, Reiner produced *The New Dick Van Dyke Show*, wrote and directed *Something Different* on Broadway, and has appeared in feature films including *The Gazebo, The Russians Are Coming, The Russians Are Coming, It's a Mad, Mad, Mad, Mad World, Generation,* and *Happy Anniversary*.

In addition to his many television guest appearances, Carl Reiner directed and coauthored *Dead Men Don't Wear Plaid* as well as *The Man with Two Brains*, both starring Steve Martin. Among his other recent theatrical credits are *All of Me* (with Lily Tomlin and Steve Martin), *Sibling Rivalry* (with Kirstie Alley), and *Summer School* with Mark Harmon.

☆ 3 ☆

Flashbacks—158 Synopses

Between Laura Petrie's conviction in the pilot episode that son Ritchie is ill based on the irrefutable evidence that "he turned down his cupcake" to the final show, "The Last Chapter," which featured only a few memorable flashbacks, are 158 episodes of *The Dick Van Dyke Show*—each with its own outstanding moments.

Some viewers may recall Rob Petrie tripping over the ottoman; others will remember him adroitly sidestepping it or occasionally stumbling as he tries to avoid it.

Indelible, too, is Laura's quavering sob, "Oh, Rob!"; Sally Rogers, Mr. Henderson (her cat) and a string of woefully inadequate beaus, including momma's boy Herman Glimcher; Buddy Sorrell's Bar Mitzvah ("I think I'm the only guy to be Bar-Mitzvahed on TV"), his limitless supply of jokes, and his indomitable wife, former showgirl Pickles; Ritchie Petrie's habit of hiding in kitchen cabinets or greeting his father with, "Did you bring me anything, Daddy?"; "Yecch!"—Mel Cooley's contemptuous response to Buddy Sorrell; and Alan Brady barking "Shut up, Mel!" at his inept brother-in-law.

Identifiable characterizations were no accident, contends script supervisor Marge Mullen. "What they were concerned with on the show was building character," she reveals, adding, "and they did build a little bit on everybody's character every single week."

This did not go unnoticed, as *Life* magazine's José M. Ferrer III observed: "The humor comes from the juxtaposition of believable people and absurd events and as an added dividend, it keeps the situations . . . fresh."

★ Concept

448 Bonnie Meadow Road, New Rochelle, New York, looks like an ordinary house, but this is the house where the Petries live: Rob, the head writer of *The Alan Brady Show*, his wife, Laura, and their son, Ritchie. Rob met Laura when he was a sergeant in the army stationed at Camp Crowder in Joplin, Missouri. Laura Meehan was a dancer in a U.S.O. show. After they were married, Laura and Rob struggled through the first years in Ohio. Then Rob landed the job as head writer for *The Alan Brady Show* and they moved to New Rochelle. The Petries became close friends with Jerry and Millie Helper, their neighbors, and Buddy Sorrell and Sally Rogers, Rob's coworkers.

Aired on CBS October 3, 1961–September 7, 1966.

Comedy, 30 minutes, B & W, 158 episodes.

CAST

Rob Petrie	Dick Van Dyke
Laura Petrie	Mary Tyler Moore
Buddy Sorrell	Morey Amsterdam
Sally Rogers	Rose Marie

Millie Helper	Ann Morgan Guilbert
Jerry Helper, a dentist	Jerry Paris
Mel Cooley, the producer	Richard Deacon
Alan Brady, the neurotic star	Carl Reiner
Ritchie Petrie	Larry Mathews
Pickles Sorrell, Buddy's wife,	Joan Shawlee
a former showgirl	Barbara Perry
Freddie Helper, Millie and Jerry's son	Peter Oliphant
	David Fresco
Sam Petrie, Rob's father	Tom Tully, J. Pat O'Malley
Clara Petrie, Rob's mother	Isabel Randolph
Ben Meehan, Laura's father	Carl Benton Reid
Mrs. Meehan, Laura's mother	Geraldine Wall
Stacey Petrie, Rob's brother	Jerry Van Dyke

MUSIC
Earle Hagen

CREATED AND PRODUCED BY:
Carl Reiner

EXECUTIVE PRODUCER
Sheldon Leonard

Calvada Productions • Distributed by Viacom

★ **"The Sick Boy and the Sitter"**
SERIES/EPISODE NUMBER: 7256/0001
Film date: January 19, 1961/Air date: October 3, 1961
Writer: Carl Reiner/Director: Sheldon Leonard

IN BRIEF
Comedy writer Rob Petrie talks wife Laura into leaving their "sick" son Ritchie with a baby sitter while they attend a big party.

CAST
Rob Petrie	Dick Van Dyke
Laura Petrie	Mary Tyler Moore
Buddy Sorrell	Morey Amsterdam
Sally Rogers	Rose Marie
Sam	Michael Keith
Mel Cooley	Richard Deacon
Ritchie Petrie	Larry Mathews
Janie	Mary Lee Dearing
Dr. Miller	Stacey Keach
Dotty	Barbara Eiler

★ **"The Meershatz Pipe"**
SERIES/EPISODE NUMBER: 7256/0002
Film date: June 20, 1961/Air date: November 28, 1961
Writer: Carl Reiner/Director: Sheldon Leonard

IN BRIEF
Television comedy writer Rob Petrie fears he is no longer needed when his cowriters turn out a show without his help.

CAST
Rob Petrie	Dick Van Dyke
Laura Petrie	Mary Tyler Moore
Buddy Sorrell	Morey Amsterdam
Elevator operator	Jon Silo
Mel Cooley	Richard Deacon
Ritchie Petrie	Larry Mathews
Sally Rogers	Rose Marie

★ **"Jealousy!"**
SERIES/EPISODE NUMBER: 7256/0003
Film date: June 27, 1961/Air date: November 7, 1961
Writer: Carl Reiner/Director: Sheldon Leonard

IN BRIEF
Laura begins to worry when Rob has to work nights with a beautiful television star.

CAST
Rob Petrie	Dick Van Dyke
Laura Petrie	Mary Tyler Moore
Buddy Sorrell	Morey Amsterdam
Sally Rogers	Rose Marie
Valerie Blake	Joan Staley
Mel Cooley	Richard Deacon
Ritchie Petrie	Larry Mathews
Jerry Helper	Jerry Paris
Millie Helper	Ann Morgan Guilbert

★ **"Sally and the Lab Technician"**
SERIES/EPISODE NUMBER: 7256/0004
Film date: July 5, 1961/Air date: October 17, 1961
Writer: Carl Reiner/Director: John Rich

IN BRIEF
Laura matches her pharmacist cousin, Thomas, with husband Rob's fireball cowriter, Sally, for a lopsided dinner party.

CAST
Rob Petrie	Dick Van Dyke
Laura Petrie	Mary Tyler Moore
Buddy Sorrell	Morey Amsterdam
Thomas	Eddie Firestone
Sally Rogers	Rose Marie
Delivery boy	Jamie Farr
Ritchie Petrie	Larry Mathews

"Washington vs. the Bunny"
SERIES/EPISODE NUMBER: 7256/0005
Film date: July 11, 1961/Air date: October 24, 1961
Writer: Carl Reiner/Director: John Rich

IN BRIEF
Rob is determined to go on a business trip even though Laura wants him to see their son Ritchie "star" in a school play.

CAST
Rob Petrie	Dick Van Dyke
Laura Petrie	Mary Tyler Moore
Buddy Sorrell	Morey Amsterdam
Sally Rogers	Rose Marie
Mel Cooley	Richard Deacon
Ritchie Petrie	Larry Mathews
Bill	Jesse White
Delivery boy	Jamie Farr

 "Oh How We Met the Night That We Danced"
SERIES/EPISODE NUMBER: 7256/0006
Film date: July 18, 1961/Air date: October 31, 1961
Writer: Carl Reiner/Director: Robert Butler

IN BRIEF
While rummaging through Rob's old Army equipment, Rob and wife Laura recall that he broke her foot on the night they met.

CAST
Rob Petrie	Dick Van Dyke
Laura Petrie	Mary Tyler Moore
Ritchie Petrie	Larry Mathews
Sol Pomeroy	Marty Ingels
Marcia Rochelle	Nancy James
Mark	Glenn Turnbull
Ellen Helper	Jennifer Gillespie
Dancing girl	Pat Tribble

 "The Unwelcome House Guest"
SERIES/EPISODE NUMBER: 7256/0007
Film date: July 25, 1961/Air date: November 21, 1961
Writer: Carl Reiner/Director: Robert Butler

IN BRIEF
Reluctantly, Rob agrees to take care of Buddy's dog for the weekend, and creates a furor when he brings the animal home.

CAST
Rob Petrie	Dick Van Dyke
Laura Petrie	Mary Tyler Moore
Ritchie Petrie	Larry Mathews
Buddy Sorrell	Morey Amsterdam
Sally Rogers	Rose Marie

 "Harrison B. Harding of Camp Crowder, Mo."
SERIES/EPISODE NUMBER: 7256/0008
Film date: August 1, 1961/Air date: November 6, 1961
Writer: Carl Reiner/Director: John Rich

IN BRIEF
After Rob invites an old Army pal home to dinner, he begins to fear that he has a jewel thief on his hands.

CAST
Rob Petrie	Dick Van Dyke
Laura Petrie	Mary Tyler Moore
Buddy Sorrell	Morey Amsterdam
Sally Rogers	Rose Marie
Policeman	Peter Leeds
Ritchie Petrie	Larry Mathews
H.B. Harding	Allan Melvin
Evelyn Harding	June Dayton

 "My Blonde-Haired Brunette"
SERIES/EPISODE NUMBER: 7256/0009
Film date: August 15, 1961/Air date: October 10, 1961
Writer: Carl Reiner/Director: John Rich

IN BRIEF
Laura turns herself into a blond femme fatale when she fears the romance in her marriage is fading.

CAST
Rob Petrie	Dick Van Dyke
Laura Petrie	Mary Tyler Moore
Buddy Sorrell	Morey Amsterdam
Ritchie Petrie	Larry Mathews
Sally Rogers	Rose Marie
Millie Helper	Ann M. Guilbert
Druggist	Benny Rubin

★ **"Forty-Four Tickets"**
SERIES/EPISODE NUMBER: 7256/0010
Film date: August 22, 1961/Air date: December 5, 1961
Writer: Carl Reiner/Director: John Rich

IN BRIEF
Rob invites forty-four fellow PTA members to his television show, but forgets all about it until air time.

CAST

Rob Petrie	Dick Van Dyke
Laura Petrie	Mary Tyler Moore
Buddy Sorrell	Morey Amsterdam
Sally Rogers	Rose Marie
Mrs. Billings	Eleanor Audley
Nice old lady	Opal Euard
Mel Cooley	Richard Deacon
Ritchie Petrie	Larry Mathews
Jerry Helper	Jerry Paris
Millie Helper	Ann M. Guilbert
Shabby man	Joe Devlin
Policeman	Paul Bryar

 "To Tell or Not to Tell"

SERIES/EPISODE NUMBER: 7256/0011

Film date: August 29, 1961/Air date: November 14, 1961
Writer: David Adler (Frank Tarloff)/Director: John Rich

IN BRIEF

Rob and Ritchie find themselves more than a little lost when Laura briefly resumes her dancing career.

CAST

Rob Petrie	Dick Van Dyke
Laura Petrie	Mary Tyler Moore
Buddy Sorrell	Morey Amsterdam
Delivery boy	Jamie Farr
Sally Rogers	Rose Marie
Mel Cooley	Richard Deacon
Ritchie Petrie	Larry Mathews

 "Sally Is a Girl"

SERIES/EPISODE NUMBER: 7256/0012

Film date: September 5, 1961/Air date: December 19, 1961/Writer: David Adler (Frank Tarloff)/Director: John Rich

IN BRIEF

Rob is accused of being a Don Juan when he takes his wife's advice and stops treating cowriter Sally as one of the boys.

CAST

Rob Petrie	Dick Van Dyke
Laura Petrie	Mary Tyler Moore
Buddy Sorrell	Morey Amsterdam
Sally Rogers	Rose Marie
Delivery boy	Jamie Farr
Mel Cooley	Richard Deacon
Ritchie Petrie	Larry Mathews
Pickles Sorrell	Barbara Perry
Ted Harris	Paul Tripp

 "Empress Carlotta's Necklace"

SERIES/EPISODE NUMBER: 7256/0013

Film date: September 12, 1961/Air date: December 12, 1961/Writer: Carl Reiner/Director: James Komack

IN BRIEF

Rob proudly presents Laura with a huge, horrible necklace, but she cannot bring herself to tell him that it is an atrocity.

CAST

Rob Petrie	Dick Van Dyke
Laura Petrie	Mary Tyler Moore
Buddy Sorrell	Morey Amsterdam
Sally Rogers	Rose Marie
Mel Cooley	Richard Deacon
Pa Petrie	Will Wright
Ritchie Petrie	Larry Mathews
Maxwell Cooley	Gavin MacLeod
Jerry Helper	Jerry Paris
Millie Helper	Ann M. Guilbert
Ma Petrie	Carol Veasie

 "Buddy, Can You Spare a Job?"

SERIES/EPISODE NUMBER: 7256/0014

Film date: September 19, 1961/Air date: December 26, 1961/Writer: Walter Kempky/Director: James Komack

IN BRIEF

After Buddy leaves *The Alan Brady Show* for a job that falls through, Rob and Sally conspire to get him his old job back.

CAST

Rob Petrie	Dick Van Dyke
Laura Petrie	Mary Tyler Moore
Buddy Sorrell	Morey Amsterdam
Sally Rogers	Rose Marie
Mel Cooley	Richard Deacon
Jackie Brewster	Len Weinrib

★ **"Who Owes Who What?"**

SERIES/EPISODE NUMBER: 7256/0015

Film date: October 10, 1961/Air date: January 24, 1962
Writer: Carl Reiner/Director: John Rich

IN BRIEF

For comedy writer Rob Petrie, a forgotten loan turns into a forgotten debt and a television script.

CAST

Rob Petrie	Dick Van Dyke
Laura Petrie	Mary Tyler Moore
Buddy Sorrell	Morey Amsterdam
Jerry Helper	Jerry Paris
Sally Rogers	Rose Marie
Mel Cooley	Richard Deacon
Ritchie Petrie	Larry Mathews

 "Sol and the Sponsor"
SERIES/EPISODE NUMBER: 7256/0016
Film date: October 17, 1961/Air date: April 11, 1962
Writer: Walter Kempley/Director: John Rich

IN BRIEF

A fancy dinner party for Rob's television sponsor and his wife is enlivened by the arrival of Rob's old Army buddy.

CAST

Rob Petrie	Dick Van Dyke
Laura Petrie	Mary Tyler Moore
Ritchie Petrie	Larry Mathews
Arlene Johnson	Patti Regan
Henry Bermont	Roy Roberts
Martha Bermont	Isabel Randolph
Sol Pomeroy	Marty Ingels

 "The Curious Thing About Women"
SERIES/EPISODE NUMBER: 7256/0017
Film date: October 24, 1961/Air date: January 10, 1962
Writer: David Adler (Frank Tarloff)/Director: John Rich

IN BRIEF

Rob's sense of humor backfires when he decides to base a television skit on Laura's penchant for opening his mail.

CAST

Rob Petrie	Dick Van Dyke
Laura Petrie	Mary Tyler Moore
Buddy Sorrell	Morey Amsterdam
Millie Helper	Ann M. Guilbert
Sally Rogers	Rose Marie
Jerry Helper	Jerry Paris
Ritchie Petrie	Larry Mathews
Delivery man	Frank Adamo

★ **"Punch Thy Neighbor"**
SERIES/EPISODE NUMBER: 7256/0018
Film date: November 1, 1961/Air date: January 17, 1962
Writer: Carl Reiner/Director: John Rich

IN BRIEF

Rob's dentist pal, Jerry, strains his friendship when he starts knocking Rob's television show in public.

CAST

Rob Petrie	Dick Van Dyke
Laura Petrie	Mary Tyler Moore
Buddy Sorrell	Morey Amsterdam
Sally Rogers	Rose Marie
Mel Cooley	Richard Deacon
Singing messenger	Frank Adamo
Ritchie Petrie	Larry Mathews
Jerry Helper	Jerry Paris
Millie Helper	Ann M. Guilbert
Freddie Helper	Peter Oliphant
Vinnie	Jerry Hausner

 "Where Did I Come From?"
SERIES/EPISODE NUMBER: 7256/0019
Film date: November 8, 1961/Air date: January 3, 1962
Writer: Carl Reiner/Director: John Rich

IN BRIEF

Six-year-old Ritchie Petrie asks his parents the inevitable "Where did I come from?" question.

CAST

Rob Petrie	Dick Van Dyke
Laura Petrie	Mary Tyler Moore
Buddy Sorrell	Morey Amsterdam
Sally Rogers	Rose Marie
Cabbie	Bill Braver
Mel Cooley	Richard Deacon
Ritchie Petrie	Larry Mathews
Millie Helper	Ann M. Guilbert
Willie	Herbie Faye
Laundry man	Jerry Hausner

 "The Boarder Incident"
SERIES/EPISODE NUMBER: 7256/0020
Film date: November 14, 1961/Air date: February 14, 1962/Writer: Norm Liebmann, Ed Haas/Director: John Rich

IN BRIEF

While his wife is away, Buddy accepts Rob's invitation to move in as a house guest, and quickly wears out his welcome.

CAST

Rob Petrie	Dick Van Dyke
Laura Petrie	Mary Tyler Moore

Ritchie Petrie	Larry Mathews
Buddy Sorrell	Morey Amsterdam
Sally Rogers	Rose Marie

 "A Word a Day"

SERIES/EPISODE NUMBER: 7256/0021

Film date: November 29, 1961/Air date: February 7, 1962
Writer: Jack Raymond/Director: John Rich

IN BRIEF

Ritchie's expanding vocabulary starts to branch out in unexpected directions.

CAST

Rob Petrie	Dick Van Dyke
Laura Petrie	Mary Tyler Moore
Buddy Sorrell	Morey Amsterdam
Sally Rogers	Rose Marie
Mel Cooley	Richard Deacon
Ritchie Petrie	Larry Mathews
Rev. Kirk	William Schallert
Mrs. Kirk	Lia Waggner

 "The Talented Neighborhood"

SERIES/EPISODE NUMBER: 7256/0022

Film date: December 6, 1961/Air date: January 31, 1962
Writer: Carl Reiner/Director: John Rich

IN BRIEF

When his show announces a talent contest, Rob finds himself besieged by the parents of neighborhood prodigies.

CAST

Rob Petrie	Dick Van Dyke
Laura Petrie	Mary Tyler Moore
Buddy Sorrell	Morey Amsterdam
Sally Rogers	Rose Marie
Mel Cooley	Richard Deacon
Ritchie Petrie	Larry Mathews
Jerry Helper	Jerry Paris
Ellen Helper	Anne Marie Hediger
Mr. Mathias	Ken Lynch
Florian	Barry Van Dyke
Cynthia	Ilana Dowding
Frankie	Christian Van Dyke
Mrs. Kendell	Doris Singleton
Kenneth Kendell	Jack Davis
Philip Mathias	Barry Livingston
Martin Mathias	Michael Davis
Annie Mathias	Kathleen Green

 "Father of the Week"

SERIES/EPISODE NUMBER: 7256/0023

Film date: December 13, 1961/Air date: February 21, 1962/Writers: Arnold, Lois Peyser/Director: John Rich

IN BRIEF

Rob Petrie's paternal pride suffers a cruel shock when he finds out his six-year-old son is ashamed of him.

CAST

Rob Petrie	Dick Van Dyke
Laura Petrie	Mary Tyler Moore
Buddy Sorrell	Morey Amsterdam
Sally Rogers	Rose Marie
Mel Cooley	Richard Deacon
Ritchie Petrie	Larry Mathews
Mrs. Given	Isabel Randolph
Floyd Harper	Patrick Thompson
Allan	Allan Fielder
Candy	Cornell Chulay

 "The Twizzle"

SERIES/EPISODE NUMBER: 7256/0024

Film date: January 9, 1962/Air date: February 28, 1962
Writer: Carl Reiner/Director: John Rich

IN BRIEF

Sally Rogers drags the entire production staff to a bowling alley where she unveils a new dance and a new song.

CAST

Rob Petrie	Dick Van Dyke
Laura Petrie	Mary Tyler Moore
Buddy Sorrell	Morey Amsterdam
Randy Twizzle	Jerry Lanning
Counter boy	Tony Stag
Sally Rogers	Rose Marie
Mel Cooley	Richard Deacon
Ritchie Petrie	Larry Mathews
Mr. Eisenhower	Jack Albertson
Freddie Blassie	Himself

 "One Angry Man"

SERIES/EPISODE NUMBER: 7256/0025

Film date: January 16, 1962/Air date: March 7, 1962
Writer: Leo Solomon, Ben Gershman/Director: John Rich

Serving on jury duty, Rob finds himself siding with the beautiful blond defendant.

CAST

| Rob Petrie | Dick Van Dyke |

Laura Petrie	Mary Tyler Moore
Buddy Sorrell	Morey Amsterdam
Sally Rogers	Rose Marie
Marla Hendrix	Sue Ane Langdon
Mr. Berger	Dabbs Greer
Mr. Mason	Lee Bergere
Bailiff	Doodles Weaver
Juror	Herb Vigran
Juror	Herbie Faye
Juror	Patsy Kelly
Judge	Howard Wendell

★ "Where You Been, Fassbinder?"
SERIES/EPISODE NUMBER: 7256/0026
Film date: January 23, 1962/Air date: March 14, 1962
Writer: John Whedon/Director: John Rich

IN BRIEF
Romance enters Sally Rogers's life, in the form of an insurance salesman named Leo Fassbinder.

CAST
Rob Petrie	Dick Van Dyke
Laura Petrie	Mary Tyler Moore
Buddy Sorrell	Morey Amsterdam
Sally Rogers	Rose Marie
Mel Cooley	Richard Deacon
Ritchie Petrie	Larry Mathews
Pickles Sorrell	Barbara Perry
Leo Fassbinder	George Neise

★ "The Bad Old Days"
SERIES/EPISODE NUMBER: 7256/0027
Film date: January 30, 1962/Air date: April 4, 1962
Writers: Norm Liebmann, Ed Haas/Director: John Rich

IN BRIEF
Buddy convinces Rob that he, along with all American husbands, is being dominated by a woman.

CAST
Rob Petrie	Dick Van Dyke
Laura Petrie	Mary Tyler Moore
Buddy Sorrell	Morey Amsterdam
Sally Rogers	Rose Marie
Jerry Helper	Jerry Paris
Ritchie Petrie	Larry Mathews

★ "I Am My Brothers's Keeper"
SERIES/EPISODE NUMBER: 7256/0028
WITH GUEST STAR JERRY VAN DYKE
Film date: February 6, 1962/Air date: March 21, 1962
Writer: Carl Reiner/Director: John Rich

IN BRIEF
Rob's bashful brother arrives in town and proves to be confident and outgoing only when he is sleepwalking.

CAST
Rob Petrie	Dick Van Dyke
Laura Petrie	Mary Tyler Moore
Stacey Petrie	Jerry Van Dyke
Buddy Sorrell	Morey Amsterdam
Sally Rogers	Rose Marie
Ritchie Petrie	Larry Mathews

★ "The Sleeping Brother"
SERIES/EPISODE NUMBER: 7256/0029
WITH GUEST STAR JERRY VAN DYKE
Film date: February 13, 1962/Air date: March 28, 1962
Writer: Carl Reiner/Director: John Rich

IN BRIEF
Rob's talented, sleepwalking brother manages to audition successfully for *The Alan Brady Show* even while wide awake.

CAST
Rob Petrie	Dick Van Dyke
Laura Petrie	Mary Tyler Moore
Stacey Petrie	Jerry Van Dyke
Buddy Sorrell	Morey Amsterdam
Alan Brady	Carl Reiner
Sally Rogers	Rose Marie
Mel Cooley	Richard Deacon
Ritchie Petrie	Larry Mathews
Jerry Helper	Jerry Paris

★ "The Return of Happy Spangler"
SERIES/EPISODE NUMBER: 7256/0030
WITH GUEST STAR J.C. FLIPPEN
Film date: February 20, 1962/Air date: April 18, 1962
Writer: Carl Reiner/Director: John Rich

IN BRIEF
Rob tries valiantly to help an old radio comedy writer make a comeback.

CAST
Rob Petrie	Dick Van Dyke
Laura Petrie	Mary Tyler Moore
Happy Spangler	J.C. Flippen
Buddy Sorrell	Morey Amsterdam
Sally Rogers	Rose Marie
Mel Cooley	Richard Deacon

END OF FIRST SEASON

"Never Name a Duck"
SERIES/EPISODE NUMBER: 7256/0031
Film date: August 7, 1962/Air date: September 26, 1962
Writer: Carl Reiner/Director: John Rich

IN BRIEF

When one of Ritchie's two pet ducks dies, it seems as if the Petrie family has lost one of its human members.

CAST

Rob Petrie	Dick Van Dyke
Laura Petrie	Mary Tyler Moore
Buddy Sorrell	Morey Amsterdam
Miss Singleton	Jane Dulo
Miss Glasser	Geraldine Wall
Sally Rogers	Rose Marie
Mel Cooley	Richard Deacon
Ritchie Petrie	Larry Mathews
Mr. Fletcher	Jerry Hausner
Vet's assistant	Frank Adamo

 "The Two Faces of Rob"
SERIES/EPISODE NUMBER: 7256/0032
Film date: August 14, 1962/Air date: October 3, 1962
Writers: Sheldon Keller, Howard Merrill/Director: John Rich

IN BRIEF

To prove that a wife cannot always recognize her husband on the telephone, Rob disguises his voice and asks Laura for a date.

CAST

Rob Petrie	Dick Van Dyke
Laura Petrie	Mary Tyler Moore
Buddy Sorrell	Morey Amsterdam
Sally Rogers	Rose Marie
Mel Cooley	Richard Deacon
Ritchie Petrie	Larry Mathews

 "Bank Book 6565696"
SERIES/EPISODE NUMBER: 7256/0033
Film date: August 21, 1962/Air date: October 17, 1962
Writers: Ray Allan Saffian, Harvey Bullock/Director: John Rich

IN BRIEF

Rob is puzzled and chagrined when he finds that Laura has a secret nest egg of her own.

CAST

Rob Petrie	Dick Van Dyke
Laura Petrie	Mary Tyler Moore
Buddy Sorrell	Morey Amsterdam
Sally Rogers	Rose Marie

Jerry Helper	Jerry Paris
Ritchie Petrie	Larry Mathews

 "The Attempted Marriage"
SERIES/EPISODE NUMBER: 7256/0034
Film date: August 28, 1962/Air date: October 10, 1962
Writer: Carl Reiner/Director: John Rich

IN BRIEF

A crippled jeep and a sprained ankle make Rob two hours late for his own wedding.

CAST

Rob Petrie	Dick Van Dyke
Laura Petrie	Mary Tyler Moore
Ritchie Petrie	Larry Mathews
Doctor	Sandy Kenyon
Orderly	Ray Kellogg
Chaplain	Dabbs Greer

 "Hustling the Hustler"
SERIES/EPISODE NUMBER: 7256/0035
Film date: September 4, 1962/Air date: October 24, 1962
Writer: Carl Reiner/Director: John Rich

IN BRIEF

Rob has an evening of high adventure with a veteran pool shark who pretends he can't play the game.

CAST

Rob Petrie	Dick Van Dyke
Laura Petrie	Mary Tyler Moore
Buddy Sorrell	Morey Amsterdam
Sally Rogers	Rose Marie
Mel Cooley	Richard Deacon
Blackie Sorrell	Phil Leeds

★ **"What's in a Middle Name?"**
SERIES/EPISODE NUMBER: 7256/0036
Film date: September 11, 1962/Air date: November 7, 1962/Writer: Carl Reiner/Director: John Rich

IN BRIEF

Rob has some explaining to do when son Ritchie learns that his middle name is Rosebud.

CAST

Rob Petrie	Dick Van Dyke
Laura Petrie	Mary Tyler Moore
Buddy Sorrell	Morey Amsterdam
Mr. Meehan	Carl Benton Reid

Mrs. Meehan	Geraldine Wall
Grandpa Petrie	Cyril Delevanti
Sally Rogers	Rose Marie
Mel Cooley	Richard Deacon
Ritchie Petrie	Larry Mathews
Sam Petrie	J. Pat O'Malley
Clara Petrie	Isabel Randolph

 "My Husband Is Not a Drunk"
SERIES/EPISODE NUMBER: **7256/0037**
Film date: September 18, 1962/Air date: October 31, 1962
Writer: Carl Reiner/Director: John Rich

IN BRIEF
A posthypnotic suggestion turns Rob Petrie tipsy every time he hears a bell ring.

CAST
Rob Petrie	Dick Van Dyke
Laura Petrie	Mary Tyler Moore
Buddy Sorrell	Morey Amsterdam
Sally Rogers	Rose Marie
Mel Cooley	Richard Deacon
Ritchie Petrie	Larry Mathews
Glen Jameson	Charles Aidman
Millie Helper	Ann M. Guilbert
Jerry Helper	Jerry Paris
Mr. Boland	Roy Roberts

 "Like a Sister"
SERIES/EPISODE NUMBER: **7256/0038**

WITH GUEST STAR VIC DAMONE
Film date: October 2, 1962/Air date: November 14, 1962
Writer: Carl Reiner/Director: Hal Cooper

IN BRIEF
A handsome balladeer brings romance into television comedy writer Sally Rogers's life

CAST
Rob Petrie	Dick Van Dyke
Laura Petrie	Mary Tyler Moore
Ric Vallone	Vic Damone
Buddy Sorrell	Morey Amsterdam
Sally Rogers	Rose Marie
Mel Cooley	Richard Deacon

 "The Night the Roof Fell In"
SERIES/EPISODE NUMBER: **7256/0039**
Film date: October 9, 1962/Air date: November 21, 1962
Writer: John Whedon/Director: Hal Cooper

IN BRIEF
Rob walks out of the house following a spat with Laura after what has been a tiring day for both of them.

CAST
Rob Petrie	Dick Van Dyke
Laura Petrie	Mary Tyler Moore
Buddy Sorrell	Morey Amsterdam
Freddie Helper	Peter Oliphant
Sally Rogers	Rose Marie
Ritchie Petrie	Larry Mathews
Millie Helper	Ann M. Guilbert

 "The Secret Life of Buddy and Sally"
SERIES/EPISODE NUMBER: **7256/0040**
Film date: October 16, 1962/Air date: November 28, 1962
Writer: Lee Erwin/Director: Coby Ruskin

IN BRIEF
Rob suspects cowriters Buddy and Sally of carrying on a clandestine romance.

CAST
Rob Petrie	Dick Van Dyke
Laura Petrie	Mary Tyler Moore
Buddy Sorrell	Morey Amsterdam
Waiter	Phil Arnold
Sally Rogers	Rose Marie
Mel Cooley	Richard Deacon
Ritchie Petrie	Larry Mathews

 "A Bird in the Head Hurts"
SERIES/EPISODE NUMBER: **7256/0041**
Film date: October 23, 1962/Air date: December 5, 1962
Writer: Carl Reiner/Director: John Rich

IN BRIEF
Ritchie runs into the house screaming that he has been pecked on the head by a giant woodpecker.

CAST
Rob Petrie	Dick Van Dyke
Laura Petrie	Mary Tyler Moore
Buddy Sorrell	Morey Amsterdam
Game warden	Cliff Norton
Sally Rogers	Rose Marie

Ritchie Petrie   Larry Mathews
Millie Helper   Ann M. Guilbert

 "Gesundheit Darling"
SERIES/EPISODE NUMBER: 7256/0042
Film date: October 30, 1962/Air date: December 12, 1962
Writer: Carl Reiner/Director: John Rich

IN BRIEF
Rob begins to fear he is allergic to his own family when
proximity to Laura and Ritchie starts him sneezing.

CAST
Rob Petrie   Dick Van Dyke
Laura Petrie   Mary Tyler Moore
Buddy Sorrell   Morey Amsterdam
Sally Rogers   Rose Marie
Millie Helper   Ann M. Guilbert
Mel Cooley   Richard Deacon
Ritchie Petrie   Larry Mathews
Allergist   Sandy Kenyon
Jerry Helper   Jerry Paris

 "A Man's Teeth Are Not His Own"
SERIES/EPISODE NUMBER: 7256/0043
Film date: November 6, 1962/Air date: December 19,
1962/Writer: Carl Reiner/Director: John Rich

IN BRIEF
Rob feels that he has betrayed his long-time dentist
friend, Jerry Helper, when he lets another dentist work
on his teeth.

CAST
Rob Petrie   Dick Van Dyke
Laura Petrie   Mary Tyler Moore
Buddy Sorrell   Morey Amsterdam
Millie Helper   Ann M. Guilbert
Sally Rodgers   Rose Marie
Mel Cooley   Richard Deacon
Jerry Helper   Jerry Paris

 "Somebody Has to Play Cleopatra"
SERIES/EPISODE NUMBER: 7256/0044
Film date: November 13, 1962/Air date: December 26,
1962/Writer: Martin A. Ragaway/Director: John Rich

IN BRIEF
Rob directs an amateur theatrical in which rehearsals are

dogged by controversy over the casting of a key part—
Cleopatra.

CAST
Rob Petrie   Dick Van Dyke
Laura Petrie   Mary Tyler Moore
Jerry Helper   Jerry Paris
Mrs. Billings   Eleanor Audley
Harry Rogers   Bob Crane
Mrs. Rogers   Shirley Mitchell

 "The Cat Burglar"
SERIES/EPISODE NUMBER: 7256/0045
Film date: November 20, 1962/Air date: January 2, 1963
Writer: Carl Reiner/Director: John Rich

IN BRIEF
A phantom burglar pillages the Petrie home, but the police are baffled as to how he did it.

CAST
Rob Petrie   Dick Van Dyke
Laura Petrie   Mary Tyler Moore
Buddy Sorrell   Morey Amsterdam
Sally Rogers   Rose Marie
Mel Cooley   Richard Deacon
Ritchie Petrie   Larry Mathews
Jerry Helper   Jerry Paris
Millie Helper   Ann M. Guilbert
Policeman   Barney Philips
Photographer   Johnny Silver

★ **"The Foul Weather Girl"**
SERIES/EPISODE NUMBER: 7256/0046

WITH GUEST STAR JOAN O'BRIEN
Film date: November 27, 1962/Air date: January 9, 1963
Writer: Carl Reiner/Director: John Rich

IN BRIEF
Laura sees a threat to her marriage in the person of a
singing weather girl.

CAST
Rob Petrie   Dick Van Dyke
Laura Petrie   Mary Tyler Moore
Jane Leighton   Joan O'Brien
Ritchie Petrie   Larry Mathews
Buddy Sorrell   Morey Amsterdam
Sally Rogers   Rose Marie
Mel Cooley   Richard Deacon

★ **"Will You Two Be My Wife?"**
SERIES/EPISODE NUMBER: **7256/0047**
Film date: December 4, 1962/Air date: January 16, 1963
Writer: Carl Reiner/Director: John Rich

IN BRIEF
Rob is slapped, kicked, and screamed at, among other things, by the girl he left behind when he entered the Army.

CAST

Rob Petrie	Dick Van Dyke
Laura Petrie	Mary Tyler Moore
Buddy Sorrell	Morey Amsterdam
Sally Rogers	Rose Marie
Dorothy	Barbara Bain
Millie	Ann M. Guilbert
Sam	Allan Melvin
Captain	Ray Kellogg
Mother	Elizabeth Harrower

★ **"Ray Murdock's X Ray"**
SERIES/EPISODE NUMBER: **7256/0048**
Film date: December 11, 1962/Air date: January 23, 1963
Writer: Carl Reiner/Director: Jerry Paris

IN BRIEF
Rob finds himself in hot water after giving a television interview in which he unwittingly portrays his wife, Laura, as a nut.

CAST

Rob Petrie	Dick Van Dyke
Laura Petrie	Mary Tyler Moore
Buddy Sorrell	Morey Amsterdam
Ray Murdock	Gene Lyons
Sally Rogers	Rose Marie
Mel Cooley	Richard Deacon
Ritchie Petrie	Larry Mathews

★ **"I Was a Teenage Head Writer"**
SERIES/EPISODE NUMBER: **7256/0049**
Film date: December 18, 1962/Air date: January 30, 1963
Writers: Sheldon Keller, Howard Merrill/Director: Jerry Paris

IN BRIEF
An office crisis sets Rob to reminiscing about his hectic early days as a comedy writer.

CAST

Rob Petrie	Dick Van Dyke

Laura Petrie	Mary Tyler Moore
Mel Cooley	Richard Deacon
Buddy Sorrell	Morey Amsterdam
Sally Rogers	Rose Marie

★ **"My Husband Is a Check-Grabber"**
SERIES/EPISODE NUMBER: **7256/0050**
Film date: January 8, 1963/Air date: February 13, 1963
Writer: Carl Reiner/Director: Alan Rafkin

IN BRIEF
Laura tries to break Rob of his expensive habit of picking up the check.

CAST

Rob Petrie	Dick Van Dyke
Laura Petrie	Mary Tyler Moore
Buddy Sorrell	Morey Amsterdam
Sally Rogers	Rose Marie
Jerry Helper	Jerry Paris
Anatole	Phil Arnold
Richie Petrie	Larry Mathews
Herman Glimcher	Bill Idelson
Pickles Sorrell	Joan Shawlee

★ **"It May Look Like a Walnut!"**
SERIES/EPISODE NUMBER: **7256/0051**
Film date: January 15, 1963/Air date: February 6, 1963
Writer: Carl Reiner/Director: Jerry Paris

IN BRIEF
Rob Petrie, under the influence of science fiction, fears that an imported walnut will steal his imagination and his thumbs.

CAST

Rob Petrie	Dick Van Dyke
Laura Petrie	Mary Tyler Moore
Buddy Sorrell	Morey Amsterdam
Sally Rogers	Rose Marie
Mel Cooley	Richard Deacon
Ritchie Petrie	Larry Mathews
Twilo visitor	Danny Thomas

★ **"Don't Trip Over That Mountain"**
SERIES/EPISODE NUMBER: **7256/0052**
Film date: January 22, 1963/Air date: February 20, 1963
Writer: Carl Reiner/Director: Coby Ruskin

IN BRIEF
To his great regret, Rob ignores Laura's warning to stay off the big slopes on his first skiing excursion.

CAST

Rob Petrie	Dick Van Dyke
Laura Petrie	Mary Tyler Moore
Millie Helper	Ann M. Guilbert
Jerry Helper	Jerry Paris
Nurse	Jean Allison
Doctor	Ray Kellogg

 "Give Me Your Walls!"

SERIES/EPISODE NUMBER: 7256/0053

Film date: January 29, 1963/Air date: February 27, 1963
Writer: Carl Reiner/Director: Jerry Paris

IN BRIEF

Rob needs a paint job in the living room, and he hires a colorful master painter of Rome, Florence, and Brooklyn.

CAST

Rob Petrie	Dick Van Dyke
Laura Petrie	Mary Tyler Moore
Richie Petrie	Larry Mathews
Vito Giotto	Vito Scotti

 "The Sam Pomerantz Scandals"

SERIES/EPISODE NUMBER: 7256/0054

Film date: February 5, 1963/Air date: March 6, 1963
Writer: Carl Reiner/Director: Claudio Guzman

IN BRIEF

Rob, Laura, and the office gang put together a variety show to help out an old friend.

CAST

Rob Petrie	Dick Van Dyke
Laura Petrie	Mary Tyler Moore
Buddy Sorrell	Morey Amsterdam
Sally Rogers	Rose Marie
Mel Cooley	Richard Deacon
Sam Pomerantz	Henry Calvin
Danny Bewster	Len Weinrib
Pickles Sorrell	Joan Shawlee

 "I'm No Henry Walden!"

SERIES/EPISODE NUMBER: 7256/0055

Film date: February 12, 1963/Air date: March 13, 1963
Writer: Carl Reiner/Director: Jerry Paris

IN BRIEF

Comedy writer Rob finds himself very out of place at a dinner party for several celebrated literati.

CAST

Rob Petrie	Dick Van Dyke
Laura Petrie	Mary Tyler Moore
Buddy Sorrell	Morey Amsterdam
Sally Rogers	Rose Marie
Mel Cooley	Richard Deacon
Ritchie Petrie	Larry Mathews
Mrs. Huntington	Doris Packer
Miss Evelyn	Rosane Berard
Mrs. Fellows	Betty Lou Gerson
Mr. Thorley	Frank Adamo
Yale Sampson	Carl Reiner
Henry Walden	Everett Sloane

 "The Square Triangle"

SERIES/EPISODE NUMBER: 7256/0056

Film date: February 19, 1963/Air date: March 20, 1963
Writer: Bill Idelson/Director: Jerry Paris

IN BRIEF

French singing idol Jacques Savon, who has played a curious part in both Rob's and Laura's past, suddenly reappears.

CAST

Rob Petrie	Dick Van Dyke
Laura Petrie	Mary Tyler Moore
Buddy Sorrell	Morey Amsterdam
Sally Rogers	Rose Marie
Mel Cooley	Richard Deacon
Richie Petrie	Larry Mathews
Jacques Savon	Jacques Bergerac
Millie Helper	Ann M. Guilbert

 "Racy Tracy Rattigan"

SERIES/EPISODE NUMBER: 7256/0057

Film date: February 26, 1963/Air date: April 3, 1963
Writers: Ronald Alexander, Carl Reiner/Director: Sheldon Leonard

IN BRIEF

A romantic British film star arouses Rob's ire by his attentions to Laura.

CAST

Rob Petrie	Dick Van Dyke
Laura Petrie	Mary Tyler Moore
Buddy Sorrell	Morey Amsterdam
Tracy Rattigan	Richard Dawson
Sally Rogers	Rose Marie
Mel Cooley	Richard Deacon
Ritchie Petrie	Larry Mathews

"Divorce"

SERIES/EPISODE NUMBER: 7256/0058

Film date: March 5, 1963/Air date: April 10, 1963
Writer: Carl Reiner/Director: Jerry Paris

IN BRIEF

Rob finds himself caught in the middle after Buddy announces he is going to divorce Pickles.

CAST

Rob Petrie	Dick Van Dyke
Laura Petrie	Mary Tyler Moore
Buddy Sorrell	Morey Amsterdam
Pickles Sorrell	Joan Shawlee
Sally Rogers	Rose Marie
Bartender	Charles Cantor
Girl	Marian Collier

 "It's a Shame She Married Me"

SERIES/EPISODE NUMBER: 7256/0059

WITH GUEST STAR ROBERT VAUGHN

Film date: March 12, 1963/Air date: April 17, 1963
Writers: Sheldon Keller, Howard Merrill/Director: James Niver

IN BRIEF

Rob suffers pangs of jealousy when Laura meets a successful old flame.

CAST

Rob Petrie	Dick Van Dyke
Laura Petrie	Mary Tyler Moore
Jim Darling	Robert Vaughn
Ritchie Petrie	Larry Mathews
Jerry Helper	Jerry Paris
Buddy Sorrell	Morey Amsterdam
Sally Rogers	Rose Marie
Mel Cooley	Richard Deacon
Millie Helper	Ann M. Guilbert
Edward	Frank Adamo

 "A Surprise Surprise Is a Surprise"

SERIES/EPISODE NUMBER: 7256/0060

Film date: March 19, 1963/Air date: April 24, 1963
Writer: Carl Reiner/Director: Jerry Paris

IN BRIEF

Laura despairs when husband Rob learns of her elaborate plans to throw a surprise party for him.

CAST

Rob Petrie	Dick Van Dyke
Laura Petrie	Mary Tyler Moore
Buddy Sorrell	Morey Amsterdam

Jerry Helper	Jerry Paris
Sally Rogers	Rose Marie
Mel Cooley	Richard Deacon
Ritchie Petrie	Larry Mathews
Millie Helper	Ann M. Guilbert

 "Jilting the Jilter"

SERIES/EPISODE NUMBER: 7256/0061

Film date: March 26, 1963/Air date: May 1, 1963
Writer: Ronald Alexander/Director: Jerry Paris

IN BRIEF

Sally gets a marriage proposal from an opportunistic comedian who wants her to write his material.

CAST

Rob Petrie	Dick Van Dyke
Laura Petrie	Mary Tyler Moore
Buddy Sorrell	Morey Amsterdam
Sally Rogers	Rose Marie
Mel Cooley	Richard Deacon
Fred White	Guy Marks

 "When a Bowling Pin Talks, Listen"

SERIES/EPISODE NUMBER: 7256/0062

Film date: April 2, 1963/Air date: May 8, 1963
Writer: Martin A. Ragaway/Director: Jerry Paris

IN BRIEF

Rob finds himself in hot water after inadvertently lifting a comedy idea from another show.

CAST

Rob Petrie	Dick Van Dyke
Laura Petrie	Mary Tyler Moore
Alan Brady	Carl Reiner
Ritchie Petrie	Larry Mathews
Barber	Jon Silo
Buddy Sorrell	Morey Amsterdam
Sally Rogers	Rose Marie
Mel Cooley	Richard Deacon
Willie	Herbie Faye

 "All About Eavesdropping"

SERIES/EPISODE NUMBER: 7256/0063

Film date: April 9, 1963/Air date: October 23, 1963
Writers: Sheldon Keller, Howard Merrill/Director: Stanley Cherry

IN BRIEF

Through Ritchie's toy intercom, Rob and Laura tune in on a conversation at the Helpers and almost lose two friends.

CAST

Rob Petrie	Dick Van Dyke
Laura Petrie	Mary Tyler Moore
Buddy Sorrell	Morey Amsterdam
Sally Rogers	Rose Marie
Jerry Helper	Jerry Paris
Millie Helper	Ann M. Guilbert

END OF SECOND SEASON

 "That's My Boy??"

SERIES/EPISODE NUMBER: **7256/0064**

Film date: August 6, 1963/Air date: September 25, 1963
Writers: Bill Persky, Sam Denoff/Director: John Rich

IN BRIEF

Rob recalls the hectic days after Ritchie was born, when he was sure the hospital had given him and Laura the wrong baby.

CAST

Rob Petrie	Dick Van Dyke
Laura Petrie	Mary Tyler Moore
Buddy Sorrell	Morey Amsterdam
Sally Rogers	Rose Marie
Nurse	Amzie Strickland
Mel Cooley	Richard Deacon
Millie Helper	Ann M. Guilbert
Jerry Helper	Jerry Paris
Mr. Peters	Greg Morris
Mrs. Peters	Mimi Dillard

 "The Masterpiece"

SERIES/EPISODE NUMBER: **7256/0065**

Film date: August 13, 1963/Air date: October 2, 1963
Writers: Bill Persky, Sam Denoff/Director: John Rich

IN BRIEF

Rob and Laura return home from an auction with two mysterious objets d'art.

CAST

Rob Petrie	Dick Van Dyke
Laura Petrie	Mary Tyler Moore
Buddy Sorrell	Morey Amsterdam
Sally Rogers	Rose Marie
Mr. Holdecker	Howard Morris
Auctioneer	Alan Reed
Woman	Amzie Strickland
Man	Ray Kellogg

 "Laura's Little Lie"

SERIES/EPISODE NUMBER: **7256/0066**

Film date: August 20, 1963/Air date: October 9, 1963
Writers: Carl Reiner, Howard Merrill/Director: John Rich

IN BRIEF

Complications arise when Laura confesses to Rob that she lied about her age on their marriage certificate.

CAST

Rob Petrie	Dick Van Dyke
Laura Petrie	Mary Tyler Moore
Buddy Sorrell	Morey Amsterdam
Sally Rogers	Rose Marie
Ritchie Petrie	Larry Mathews
Ed Ruben	Charles Aidman

 "Very Old Shoes, Very Old Rice"

SERIES/EPISODE NUMBER: **7256/0067**

Film date: August 27, 1963/Air date: October 16, 1963
Writer: Carl Reiner/Director: John Rich

IN BRIEF

Rob and Laura Petrie, having learned they are not legally married, make plans to elope.

CAST

Rob Petrie	Dick Van Dyke
Laura Petrie	Mary Tyler Moore
Buddy Sorrell	Morey Amsterdam
Sally Rogers	Rose Marie
Old man	Burt Mustin
Young man	Frank Adamo
Mel Cooley	Richard Deacon
Ritchie Petrie	Larry Mathews
Judge	Russell Collins
Millie Helper	Ann M. Guilbert
Old woman	Madge Blake

 "Uncle George"

SERIES/EPISODE NUMBER: **7256/0068**

Film date: September 3, 1963/Air date: November 13, 1963/Writer: Bill Idelson/Director: Jerry Paris

IN BRIEF

Rob's Uncle George arrives in town, and asks his nephew to find him a wife.

CAST

Rob Petrie	Dick Van Dyke
Laura Petrie	Mary Tyler Moore
Buddy Sorrell	Morey Amsterdam

Sally Rogers	Rose Marie
Herman Glimsher	Bill Idelson
Mel Cooley	Richard Deacon
Ritchie Petrie	Larry Mathews
Uncle George	Denver Pyle
Mrs. Glimsher	Elvia Allman

★ **"Too Many Stars"**
SERIES/EPISODE NUMBER: 7256/0069
Film date: September 10, 1963/Air date: October 30, 1963/Writers: Sheldon Keller, Howard Merrill/Director: Jerry Paris

IN BRIEF
As usual, Rob finds he has "too many stars" on his hands when he tries to direct this year's show for the Parent's Council.

CAST
Rob Petrie	Dick Van Dyke
Laura Petrie	Mary Tyler Moore
Buddy Sorrell	Morey Amsterdam
Sally Rogers	Rose Marie
Mel Cooley	Richard Deacon
Carmelita Lebost	Sylvia Lewis
Millie Helper	Ann M. Guilbert
Jerry Helper	Jerry Paris
Mrs. Billings	Eleanor Audley
Delivery man	Jerry Hausner
Howard Lebost	Eddie Ryder

★ **"Who and Where Was Antonio Stradivarius?"**
SERIES/EPISODE NUMBER: 7256/0070
Film date: September 17, 1963/Air date: November 6, 1963/Writer: Carl Reiner/Director: Jerry Paris

IN BRIEF
Rob finds himself at a party in a strange town, swaying to the bossa nova with a breathless young woman who adores him.

CAST
Rob Petrie	Dick Van Dyke
Laura Petrie	Mary Tyler Moore
Buddy Sorrell	Morey Amsterdam
Sally Rogers	Rose Marie
Mel Cooley	Richard Deacon
Hostess	Betty Lou Gerson
Ritchie Petrie	Larry Mathews
Aunt Mildred	Amzie Strickland
Uncle Edward	Hal Peary

Graciella	Sallie Janes
Host	Chet Stratton

★ **"Big Max Calvada"**
SERIES/EPISODE NUMBER: 7256/0071
Film date: October 8, 1963/Air date: November 20, 1963
Writers: Bill Persky, Sam Denoff/Director: Jerry Paris

IN BRIEF
An underworld figure involves Rob, Sally, and Buddy in an unusual writing assignment.

CAST
Rob Petrie	Dick Van Dyke
Laura Petrie	Mary Tyler Moore
Buddy Sorrell	Morey Amsterdam
Sally Rogers	Rose Marie
Max Calvada	Sheldon Leonard
Bernard	Art Batanides
Kenneth Dexter	Jack Larson
Clarisse Calvada	Sue Casey
Mr. Parker	Tiny Brauer
Waiter	Johnny Silver

★ **"The Ballad of the Betty Lou"**
SERIES/EPISODE NUMBER: 7256/0072
Film date: October 15, 1963/Air date: November 27, 1963
Writer: Martin A. Ragaway/Director: Danny Scholl

IN BRIEF
Rob and Jerry invest in a sailboat, and find they have embarked on a disastrous venture.

CAST
Rob Petrie	Dick Van Dyke
Laura Petrie	Mary Tyler Moore
Sailor	Danny Scholl
Jerry Helper	Jerry Paris
Millie Helper	Ann M. Guilbert

★ **"Turtles, Ties, and Toreadors"**
SERIES/EPISODE NUMBER: 7256/0073
Film date: October 22, 1963/Air date: December 4, 1963
Writer: John Whedon/Director: Jerry Paris

IN BRIEF
Rob feels very much the hero when he hires a maid for his overworked wife, Laura.

CAST
Rob Petrie	Dick Van Dyke

Laura Petrie	Mary Tyler Moore
Ritchie Petrie	Larry Mathews
Maria	Miriam Colon
Taxi driver	Tiny Brauer
Immigration officer	Alan Dexter

 "The Sound of the Trumpets of Conscience Falls Deafly on a Brain That Holds Its Ears . . . or Something Like That!"
SERIES/EPISODE NUMBER: 7256/0074
Film date: October 29, 1963/Air date: December 11, 1963
Writers: Bill Persky, Sam Denoff/Director: Jerry Paris

IN BRIEF
Rob becomes involved with the police when he thinks he has witnessed two crooks making their getaway from the scene of a crime.

CAST
Rob Petrie	Dick Van Dyke
Laura Petrie	Mary Tyler Moore
Buddy Sorrell	Morey Amsterdam
Sally Rogers	Rose Marie
Ritchie Petrie	Larry Mathews
Witness	Frank Adamo
Patrolman Nelson	Bernie Hamilton
Lt. Yarnell	Ken Lynch
Man	Edward Holmes
Hoodlum	Alan Dexter
Officer	Ray Kellogg

⭐ **"The Third One from the Left"**
SERIES/EPISODE NUMBER: 7256/0075
Film date: November 5, 1963/Air date: January 1, 1964
Writer: John Whedon/Director: Jerry Paris

IN BRIEF
A young chorus girl on *The Alan Brady Show* falls desperately in love with Rob.

CAST
Rob Petrie	Dick Van Dyke
Laura Petrie	Mary Tyler Moore
Buddy Sorrell	Morey Amsterdam
Joan Delroy	Cheryl Holdridge
Sally Rogers	Rose Marie
Mel Cooley	Richard Deacon
Ernie	Jimmy Murphy

 "*The Alan Brady Show* Presents"
SERIES/EPISODE NUMBER: 7256/0076
Film date: November 12, 1963/Air date: December 18, 1963/Writers: Bill Persky, Sam Denoff/Director: Jerry Paris

IN BRIEF
The entire Alan Brady staff presents a Christmas show, instead of the script turned in by the show's writers.

CAST
Rob Petrie	Dick Van Dyke
Laura Petrie	Mary Tyler Moore
Buddy Sorrell	Morey Amsterdam
Sally Rogers	Rose Marie
Alan Brady	Carl Reiner
Mel Cooley	Richard Deacon
Ritchie Petrie	Larry Mathews
Girl	Cornell Chulay
Boy	Brendan Freeman

⭐ **"My Husband Is the Best One"**
SERIES/EPISODE NUMBER: 7256/0077
Film date: November 19, 1963/Air date: January 8, 1964
Writer: Martin A. Ragaway/Director: Jerry Paris

IN BRIEF
Rob finds himself in trouble with his boss and coworkers after Laura interferes in an interview he is giving on Alan Brady.

CAST
Rob Petrie	Dick Van Dyke
Laura Petrie	Mary Tyler Moore
Buddy Sorrell	Morey Amsterdam
Sally Rogers	Rose Marie
Mel Cooley	Richard Deacon
Diane Mosby	Valerie Yerke
Alan Brady	Carl Reiner
Waiter	Frank Adamo

⭐ **"Happy Birthday and Too Many More"**
SERIES/EPISODE NUMBER: 7256/0078
Film date: November 26, 1963/Air date: February 5, 1964
Writers: Bill Persky, Sam Denoff/Director: Jerry Paris

IN BRIEF
Laura and Rob give Ritchie a birthday party and sixty-three screaming moppets make a shambles of the Petrie house.

CAST

Rob Petrie	Dick Van Dyke
Laura Petrie	Mary Tyler Moore
Buddy Sorrell	Morey Amsterdam
Sally Rogers	Rose Marie
Ritchie Petrie	Larry Mathews
lst boy	Michael Chulay
lst girl	Cornell Chulay
2nd boy	Brendan Freeman
3rd boy	Tony Paris
Delivery man	Johnny Silver

★ "The Lady and the Tiger and the Lawyer"
SERIES/EPISODE NUMBER: 7256/0079
Film date: December 3, 1963/Air date: January 15, 1964
Writers: Garry Marshall, Jerry Belson/Director: Jerry Paris

IN BRIEF

When a handsome bachelor, Arthur Stanwyck, moves in next door, Rob and Laura Petrie turn matchmakers.

CAST

Rob Petrie	Dick Van Dyke
Laura Petrie	Mary Tyler Moore
Buddy Sorrell	Morey Amsterdam
Donna Palmer	Lyla Graham
Sally Rogers	Rose Marie
Ritchie Petrie	Larry Mathews
Arthur Stanwyck	Anthony Eisley

★ "The Life and Love of Joe Coogan"
SERIES/EPISODE NUMBER: 7256/0080
Film date: December 10, 1963/Air date: January 22, 1964
Writer: Carl Reiner/Director: Jerry Paris

IN BRIEF

Laura meets her old love, a young man who has entered the priesthood.

CAST

Rob Petrie	Dick Van Dyke
Laura Petrie	Mary Tyler Moore
Sally Rogers	Rose Marie
Buddy Sorrell	Morey Amsterdam
Mel Cooley	Richard Deacon
Millie Helper	Ann M. Guilbert
Joe Coogan	Michael Forest
Waiter	Johnny Silver

★ "A Nice Friendly Game of Cards"
SERIES/EPISODE NUMBER: 7256/0081
Film date: December 17, 1963/Air date: January 29, 1964
Writer: Ernest Chambers/Director: Howard Morris

IN BRIEF

Inadvertently using a deck of marked cards, Rob wins at poker, and almost loses a few friends.

CAST

Rob Petrie	Dick Van Dyke
Laura Petrie	Mary Tyler Moore
Ritchie Petrie	Larry Mathews
Sally Rogers	Rose Marie
Beth Gregory	Shirley Mitchell
Buddy Sorrell	Morey Amsterdam
Jerry Helper	Jerry Paris
Millie Helper	Ann M. Guilbert
Lou Gregory	Edward Platt

★ "The Brave and the Backache"
SERIES/EPISODE NUMBER: 7256/0082
Film date: December 31, 1963/Air date: February 12, 1964/Writers: Sheldon Keller, Howard Merrill/Director: Jerry Paris

IN BRIEF

Rob consults a psychiatrist to determine whether a series of mysterious ailments is psychosomatic.

CAST

Rob Petrie	Dick Van Dyke
Laura Petrie	Mary Tyler Moore
Buddy Sorrell	Morey Amsterdam
Dr. Phillip Nevins	Ross Elliott
Sally Rogers	Rose Marie
Millie Helper	Ann M. Guilbert
Tony Daniels	Ken Berry

★ "The Pen Is Mightier than the Mouth"
SERIES/EPISODE NUMBER: 7256/0083
Film date: January 7, 1964/Air date: February 19, 1964
Writers: Bill Persky, Sam Denoff/Director: Jerry Paris

IN BRIEF

Rob and Buddy find themselves overworked and overwrought when Sally becomes a television personality overnight.

CAST

Rob Petrie	Dick Van Dyke
Laura Petrie	Mary Tyler Moore

Buddy Sorrell	Morey Amsterdam
Sally Rogers	Rose Marie
Mel Cooley	Richard Deacon
Bernie Quinn	Herb Vigran
Dave	Johnny Silver
Stevie Parsons	Dick Patterson

 ### "My Part-Time Wife"
SERIES/EPISODE NUMBER: 7256/0084
Film date: January 14, 1964/Air date: February 26, 1964
Writers: Bill Persky, Sam Denoff/Director: Jerry Paris

IN BRIEF
When Laura fills in for Sally at the office, she does such a perfect job that Rob almost goes out of his mind.

CAST
Rob Petrie	Dick Van Dyke
Laura Petrie	Mary Tyler Moore
Buddy Sorrell	Morey Amsterdam
Sally Rogers	Rose Marie
Millie Helper	Ann M. Guilbert
Jackie	Jackie Joseph

 ### "Honeymoons Are for the Lucky"
SERIES/EPISODE NUMBER: 7256/0085
Film date: January 21, 1964/Air date: March 4, 1964
Writer: Carl Reiner/Director: Jerry Paris

IN BRIEF
Rob recalls the hectic time of his Army marriage to Laura, and the difficulty in obtaining a three-day pass for their honeymoon.

CAST
Rob Petrie	Dick Van Dyke
Laura Petrie	Mary Tyler Moore
Sally Rogers	Rose Marie
Buddy Sorrell	Morey Amsterdam
Mr. Campbell	Johnny Silver
Millie Helper	Ann M. Guilbert
Sam Pomeroy	Allan Melvin
Capt. Lebost	Peter Hobbs
Mrs. Campbell	Kathleen Freeman

"How to Spank a Star"
SERIES/EPISODE NUMBER: 7256/0086
Film date: January 28, 1964/Air date: March 11, 1964
Writers: Nathaniel Curtis, Bill Idelson/Director: Jerry Paris

IN BRIEF
At the insistence of a domineering guest star, head writer

Rob Petrie takes over as producer of *The Alan Brady Show*.

CAST
Rob Petrie	Dick Van Dyke
Laura Petrie	Mary Tyler Moore
Ritchie Petrie	Larry Mathews
Paula Marshall	Lola Albright
Sally Rogers	Rose Marie
Buddy Sorrell	Morey Amsterdam
Mel Cooley	Richard Deacon

 ### "The Plots Thicken"
SERIES/EPISODE NUMBER: 7256/0087
Film date: February 4, 1964/Air date: March 18, 1964
Writers: Carl Reiner, Bill Persky, Sam Denoff/Director: Jerry Paris

IN BRIEF
A family crisis develops when Rob's and Laura's parents compete to get the couple committed to their respective cemetery plots.

CAST
Rob Petrie	Dick Van Dyke
Laura Petrie	Mary Tyler Moore
Ritchie Petrie	Larry Mathews
Mrs. Meehan	Geraldine Wall
Sam Petrie	J. Pat O'Malley
Clara Petrie	Isabel Randolph
Mr. Meehan	Carl Benton Reid

 ### "Scratch My Car and Die"
SERIES/EPISODE NUMBER: 7256/0088
Film date: February 11, 1964/Air date: March 25, 1964
Writer: John Whedon/Director: Howard Morris

IN BRIEF
When a scratch appears on Rob's brand-new car, it brings on a domestic crisis at the Petrie house.

CAST
Rob Petrie	Dick Van Dyke
Laura Petrie	Mary Tyler Moore
Ritchie Petrie	Larry Mathews
Millie Helper	Ann M. Guilbert
Sally Rogers	Rose Marie
Buddy Sorrell	Morey Amsterdam
Mel Cooley	Richard Deacon

"The Return of Edwin Carp"
SERIES/EPISODE NUMBER: 7256/0089
Film date: February 18, 1964/Air date: April 1, 1964
Writer: Carl Reiner/Director: Howard Morris

IN BRIEF
Rob rounds up three notable personalities from the old days of radio for an Alan Brady "special."

CAST
Rob Petrie	Dick Van Dyke
Laura Petrie	Mary Tyler Moore
Buddy Sorrell	Morey Amsterdam
Sally Rogers	Rose Marie
Mel Cooley	Richard Deacon
Arlene Harris	Herself
Bert Gordon	Himself
Edwin Carp	Richard Haydn

 "October Eve"
SERIES/EPISODE NUMBER: 7256/0090
Film date: March 3, 1964/Air date: April 8, 1964
Writers: Bill Persky, Sam Denoff/Director: Jerry Paris

IN BRIEF
A painting of Laura returns to haunt her; although she has posed fully clothed, the artist took the liberty of "undraping" her.

CAST
Rob Petrie	Dick Van Dyke
Laura Petrie	Mary Tyler Moore
Serge Carpetna	Carl Reiner
Man	Howard Wendell
Buddy Sorrell	Morey Amsterdam
Sally Rogers	Rose Marie
Mel Cooley	Richard Deacon
Woman	Genevieve Griffin

 "Dear Mrs. Petrie, Your Husband Is in Jail"
SERIES/EPISODE NUMBER: 7256/0091
Film date: March 10, 1964/Air date: April 15, 1964
Writers: Jerry Belson, Garry Marshall/Director: Jerry Paris

IN BRIEF
When Rob looks up an old Army buddy at a honky-tonk nitery, the result is a confusion-packed night that finally lands him in jail.

CAST
Rob Petrie	Dick Van Dyke
Laura Petrie	Mary Tyler Moore
Benny Joey	Herkie Styles

Maureen Core	Barbara Stuart
Alberta Schweitzer	Jackie Joseph
Nick	Johnny Silver
Arnold	Art Batanides
Policeman	Henry Scott

 "My Neighbor's Husband's Other Life"
SERIES/EPISODE NUMBER: 7256/0092
Film date: March 17, 1964/Air date: April 22, 1964
Writers: Carl Reiner, Bill Persky, Sam Denoff/Director: Jerry Paris

IN BRIEF
Rob and Laura suspect the worst when they spy their friend Jerry Helper dining out with a beautiful blonde.

CAST
Rob Petrie	Dick Van Dyke
Laura Petrie	Mary Tyler Moore
Buddy Sorrell	Morey Amsterdam
Waiter	Johnny Silver
Sally Rogers	Rose Marie
Jerry Helper	Jerry Paris
Millie Helper	Ann M. Guilbert

 "I'd Rather Be Bald than Have No Head at All"
SERIES/EPISODE NUMBER: 7256/0093
Film date: March 24, 1964/Air date: April 29, 1964
Writers: Bill Persky, Sam Denoff/Director: Jerry Paris

IN BRIEF
Rob starts keeping daily count of the hairs he is losing and enters the nightmare world of the bald and nearly bald.

CAST
Rob Petrie	Dick Van Dyke
Laura Petrie	Mary Tyler Moore
Buddy Sorrell	Morey Amsterdam
Sally Rogers	Rose Marie
Mel Cooley	Richard Deacon
Irwin	Ned Glass

 "Teacher's Petrie"
SERIES/EPISODE NUMBER: 7256/0094
Film date: March 31, 1964/Air date: May 13, 1964
Writers: Jerry Belson, Garry Marshall/Director: Jerry Paris

IN BRIEF
Rob Petrie is skeptical when wife Laura's new writing teacher thinks she shows promise.

CAST

Rob Petrie	Dick Van Dyke
Laura Petrie	Mary Tyler Moore
Buddy Sorrell	Morey Amsterdam
Sally Rogers	Rose Marie
Ritchie Petrie	Larry Mathews
Millie Helper	Ann M. Guilbert
Mr. Caldwell	Bernie Fox
Miss Prinder	Cheerio Meredith

 "My Two Showoffs and Me"

SERIES/EPISODE NUMBER: 7256/0095

Film date: April 3, 1964/Air date: December 16, 1964
Writers: Sheldon Keller, Howard Merrill/Director: Jerry
Paris

IN BRIEF

The prospect of being the subjects of a story in a national
magazine brings out the egotistical worst in Rob, Sally,
and Buddy.

CAST

Rob Petrie	Dick Van Dyke
Laura Petrie	Mary Tyler Moore
Buddy Sorrell	Morey Amsterdam
Sally Rogers	Rose Marie
Mel Cooley	Richard Deacon
Lorraine Gilman	Doris Singleton

END OF THIRD SEASON

 "My Mother Can Beat Up My Father"

SERIES/EPISODE NUMBER: 7256/0096

Film date: August 4, 1964/Air date: September 23, 1964
Writers: Bill Persky, Sam Denoff/Director: Jerry Paris

IN BRIEF

Laura proves herself more proficient than Rob in the art
of self-defense.

CAST

Rob Petrie	Dick Van Dyke
Laura Petrie	Mary Tyler Moore
Buddy Sorrell	Morey Amsterdam
Sally Rogers	Rose Marie
Ritchie Petrie	Larry Mathews
Miss Taylor	Imelda de Martin
Drunk	Paul Gilbert
Ed Wilson	Tom Avera
Tony Daniels	Ken Berry
Vinnie	Lou Cutell

 "The Ghost of A. Chantz"

SERIES/EPISODE NUMBER: 7256/0097

Film date: August 11, 1964/Air date: September 30, 1964
Writers: Bill Persky, Sam Denoff/Director: Jerry Paris

IN BRIEF

Rob, Laura, Sally, and Buddy spend a frightening night
in a haunted cabin at a mountain resort.

CAST

Rob Petrie	Dick Van Dyke
Laura Petrie	Mary Tyler Moore
Sally Rogers	Rose Marie
Buddy Sorrell	Morey Amsterdam
Mel Cooley	Richard Deacon
Mr. Little	Maurice Brenner
Man	Milton Parsons
Cameraman	Edward McCready

 "The Lady and the Baby-Sitter"

SERIES/EPISODE NUMBER: 7256/0098

Film date: August 18, 1964/Air date: October 7, 1964
Writers: Bill Persky, Sam Denoff/Director: Jerry Paris

IN BRIEF

Rob and Laura Petrie are unaware that their teenaged
baby sitter has a crush on Laura.

CAST

Rob Petrie	Dick Van Dyke
Laura Petrie	Mary Tyler Moore
Man	Frank Adamo
Ritchie Petrie	Larry Mathews
Roger McChesney	Eddie Hodges

 "The Vigilante Ripped My Sports Coat"

SERIES/EPISODE NUMBER: 7256/0099

Film date: August 25, 1964/Air date: October 14, 1964
Writer: Carl Reiner/Director: Peter Baldwin

IN BRIEF

Rob's friendship with Jerry is almost destroyed in a row
over a neighbor's crab grass lawn.

CAST

Rob Petrie	Dick Van Dyke
Laura Petrie	Mary Tyler Moore
Buddy Sorrell	Morey Amsterdam
Sally Rogers	Rose Marie
Mel Cooley	Richard Deacon
Ritchie Petrie	Larry Mathews
Jerry Helper	Jerry Paris
Millie Helper	Ann M. Guilbert

"The Man from Emperor"
SERIES/EPISODE NUMBER: **7256/0100**
Film date: September 1, 1964/Air date: October 21, 1964
Writers: Bill Persky, Sam Denoff, Carl Reiner/ Director:
Jerry Paris

IN BRIEF

When Rob is offered a job as humor consultant on a magazine for men-about-town, he runs into misgivings from wife Laura.

CAST

Rob Petrie	Dick Van Dyke
Laura Petrie	Mary Tyler Moore
Sally Rogers	Rose Marie
Buddy Sorrell	Morey Amsterdam
Drew Patton	Lee Philips
Slave girl	Gloria Neil
Coffee girl	Nadia Sanders
Florence	Sally Carter
Miss Finland	Tracy Butler
Masseur	Abdullah Abbas

 "Romance, Roses, and Rye Bread"
SERIES/EPISODE NUMBER: **7256/0101**
Film date: September 8, 1964/Air date: October 28, 1964
Writers: Jerry Belson, Garry Marshall/Director:
Jerry Paris

IN BRIEF

Sally Rogers is romanced by her "secret" admirer—the owner of Monker's Delicatessen.

CAST

Rob Petrie	Dick Van Dyke
Laura Petrie	Mary Tyler Moore
Sally Rogers	Rose Marie
Buddy Sorrell	Morey Amsterdam
Mel Cooley	Richard Deacon
Bert Monker	Sid Melton
Usherette	Jeri Lou James
Actor	Frank Adamo

★ **"4 1/2"**

SERIES/EPISODE NUMBER: **7256/0102**
Film date: September 15, 1964/Air date: November 4,
1964

IN BRIEF

Rob and Laura are on their way to see Laura's obstetrician when they are trapped in a stalled elevator with a hold-up man.

CAST

Rob Petrie	Dick Van Dyke
Laura Petrie	Mary Tyler Moore
Buddy Sorrell	Morey Amsterdam
Sally Rogers	Rose Marie
Mel Cooley	Richard Deacon
Lyle Delp	Don Rickles

★ **"The Alan Brady Show Goes to Jail"**
SERIES/EPISODE NUMBER: **7256/0103**
Film date: September 22, 1964/Air date: November 11,
1964/Writers: Bill Persky, Sam Denoff/Director: Jerry
Paris

IN BRIEF

The Alan Brady writers entertain at a prison and Rob gets locked up with the inmates.

CAST

Rob Petrie	Dick Van Dyke
Laura Petrie	Mary Tyler Moore
Buddy Sorrell	Morey Amsterdam
Sally Rogers	Rose Marie
Lyle Delp	Don Rickles
Boxer Morrison	Robert Strauss
Harry Tinker	Arthur Batanides
Warden Jackson	Ken Lynch
Guard Jenkins	Allan Melvin
Ira	Vincent Barbi

★ **"Three Letters from One Wife"**
SERIES/EPISODE NUMBER: **7256/0104**
Film date: September 29, 1964/Air date: November 18,
1964/Writers: Bill Persky, Sam Denoff/Director: Jerry
Paris

IN BRIEF

Rob Petrie risks his job when he convinces Alan Brady to do a cultural documentary program.

CAST

Rob Petrie	Dick Van Dyke
Laura Petrie	Mary Tyler Moore
Buddy Sorrell	Morey Amsterdam
Sally Rogers	Rose Marie
Mel Cooley	Richard Deacon
Millie Helper	Ann M. Guilbert

"It Wouldn't Hurt Them to Give Us a Raise"
SERIES/EPISODE NUMBER: 7256/0105
Film date: October 6, 1964/Air date: December 2, 1964
Writers: Jay Burton, Ernest Chambers/Director: Peter Baldwin

IN BRIEF
The Brady writers pressure for higher salaries and find themselves tangled up in a maze of interlocking corporations.

CAST

Rob Petrie	Dick Van Dyke
Laura Petrie	Mary Tyler Moore
Buddy Sorrell	Morey Amsterdam
Sally Rogers	Rose Marie
Mel Cooley	Richard Deacon
Douglas Wesley	Roger C. Carmel

 "Pink Pills and Purple Parents"
SERIES/EPISODE NUMBER: 7256/0106
Film date: October 20, 1964/Air date: November 25, 1964
Writers: Jerry Belson, Garry Marshall/Director: Alan Rafkin

IN BRIEF
Laura Petrie takes two pink pills and suffers disastrous side effects.

CAST

Rob Petrie	Dick Van Dyke
Laura Petrie	Mary Tyler Moore
Buddy Sorrell	Morey Amsterdam
Clara Petrie	Isabel Randolph
Sally Rogers	Rose Marie
Millie Helper	Ann M. Guilbert
Sam Petrie	Tom Tully

 "The Death of the Party"
SERIES/EPISODE NUMBER: 7256/0107
Film date: October 27, 1964/Air date: December 9, 1964
Writers: Bill Persky, Sam Denoff/Director: Alan Rafkin

IN BRIEF
Rob Petrie struggles through a party for wife Laura's relatives rather than admit he is sick as a dog.

CAST

Rob Petrie	Dick Van Dyke
Laura Petrie	Mary Tyler Moore
Buddy Sorrell	Morey Amsterdam
Sally Rogers	Rose Marie
Millie Helper	Ann M. Guilbert
Uncle Harold	Willard Waterman
Cousin Margaret	Jane Dulo
Cousin Grace	Patti Regan
Paul	Pitt Herbert
Frank	Frank Adamo

★ **"Stretch Petrie vs. Kid Schenk"**
SERIES/EPISODE NUMBER: 7256/0108
WITH GUEST STAR JACK CARTER
Film date: November 3, 1964/Air date: December 30, 1964/Writers: Jerry Belson, Garry Marshall/Director: Jerry Paris

IN BRIEF
Rob Petrie is forced to squelch the scheme of an opportunistic old friend.

CAST

Rob Petrie	Dick Van Dyke
Laura Petrie	Mary Tyler Moore
Buddy Sorrell	Morey Amsterdam
Sally Rogers	Rose Marie
Ritchie Petrie	Larry Mathews
2nd model	Lynn Borden
Neil Schenk	Jack Carter
Head Waiter	Albert Carrier
Bill Sampson	Peter Hobbs
Messenger	Frank Adamo
1st model	Judy Taylor

★ **"The Impractical Joke"**
SERIES/EPISODE NUMBER: 7256/0109
Film date: November 10, 1964/Air date: January 13, 1965
Writers: Bill Persky, Sam Denoff/Director: Jerry Paris

IN BRIEF
Rob Petrie resorts to psychological warfare to get even with a practical joker.

CAST

Rob Petrie	Dick Van Dyke
Laura Petrie	Mary Tyler Moore
Buddy Sorrell	Morey Amsterdam
Sally Rogers	Rose Marie
Mel Cooley	Richard Deacon
Phil Franklin	Lennie Weinrib
William Handlebuck	Alvy Moore
Guest	Johnny Silver

★ **"Brother, Can You Spare $2500?"**
SERIES/EPISODE NUMBER: 7256/0110
Film date: November 17, 1964/Air date: January 6, 1965
Writers: Jerry Belson, Garry Marshall/Director: Jerry Paris

Rob Petrie receives a ransom demand of $2500 for his lost television script.

CAST

Rob Petrie	Dick Van Dyke
Laura Petrie	Mary Tyler Moore
Buddy Sorrell	Morey Amsterdam
Sally Rogers	Rose Marie
Mel Cooley	Richard Deacon
Harry Keen	Herbie Faye
lst bum	Gene Baylos
2nd bum	Tiny Brauer
Warren	Brian Nash
Cop	Larry Blake

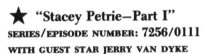

★ "Stacey Petrie—Part I"
SERIES/EPISODE NUMBER: 7256/0111
WITH GUEST STAR JERRY VAN DYKE

Film date: November 24, 1964/Air date: January 20, 1965
Writer: Carl Reiner/Director: Jerry Paris

IN BRIEF

Rob Petrie's younger brother involves Sally Rogers in a romantic Waterloo.

CAST

Rob Petrie	Dick Van Dyke
Laura Petrie	Mary Tyler Moore
Stacey Petrie	Jerry Van Dyke
Buddy Sorrell	Morey Amsterdam
Sally Rogers	Rose Marie
Ritchie Petrie	Larry Mathews
Dr. Lemler	Howard Wendell

★ "Stacey Petrie—Part II"
SERIES/EPISODE NUMBER: 7256/0112
WITH GUEST STAR JERRY VAN DYKE

Film date: December 1, 1964/Air date: January 27, 1965
Writer: Carl Reiner/Director: Jerry Paris

IN BRIEF

Stacey Petrie manages to save his new coffee house from closing and his romance from ending before they get started.

CAST

Rob Petrie	Dick Van Dyke
Laura Petrie	Mary Tyler Moore
Stacey Petrie	Jerry Van Dyke
Millie Helper	Ann M.Guilbert

Julie Kincaid	Jane Wald
Tinker	Kendrick Huxham
Lou Temple	Herbie Faye
Willie Cooke	Carl Reiner

★ "The Redcoats Are Coming"
SERIES/EPISODE NUMBER: 7256/0113

Film date: December 8, 1964/Air date: February 10, 1965
Writers: Bill Persky, Sam Denoff/Director: Jerry Paris

IN BRIEF

The Petries are invaded by a horde of teenagers when they entertain two British rock-and-roll idols.

CAST

Rob Petrie	Dick Van Dyke
Laura Petrie	Mary Tyler Moore
Buddy Sorrell	Morey Amsterdam
Sally Rogers	Rose Marie
Mel Cooley	Richard Deacon
Millie Helper	Ann M. Guilbert
Phoebe	Mollie Howerton
Ernie	Chad Stuart
Freddie	Jeremy Clyde
Richard Karp	Bill Beckley
Janie	Wendy Wilson
Estelle	Ellie Sommers
Margie	Trudi Ames

★ "Boy #1 Versus Boy #2"
SERIES/EPISODE NUMBER: 7256/0114

Film date: December 15, 1964/Air date: February 3, 1965
Writer: Martin A. Ragaway/Director: Jerry Paris

IN BRIEF

Laura Petrie and Millie Helper become unbearable stage mothers when their sons are cast in a television commercial.

CAST

Rob Petrie	Dick Van Dyke
Larua Petrie	Mary Tyler Moore
Ritchie Petrie	Larry Mathews
Sally Rogers	Rose Marie
Buddy Sorrell	Morey Amsterdam
Mel Cooley	Richard Deacon
Millie Helper	Ann M. Guilbert
Freddie Helper	Peter Oliphant
Jerry Helper	Jerry Paris
Announcer	Colin Male

★ "The Case of the Pillow"
SERIES/EPISODE NUMBER: 7256/0115
Film date: December 22, 1964/Air date: February 17, 1965/Writers: Bill Persky, Sam Denoff/Director: Howard Morris

IN BRIEF

Rob Petrie becomes a trial lawyer to prosecute a shifty salesman.

CAST

Rob Petrie	Dick Van Dyke
Laura Petrie	Mary Tyler Moore
Buddy Sorrell	Morey Amsterdam
Sally Rogers	Rose Marie
Jerry Helper	Jerry Paris
Bailiff	Joel Fluellen
Millie Helper	Ann M. Guilbert
Wiley	Alvy Moore
May Wiley	Amzie Strickland
Judge	Ed Begley
Man	Frank Adamo

★ "Young Man with a Shoehorn"
SERIES/EPISODE NUMBER: 7256/0116
Film date: January 12, 1965/Air date: February 24, 1965
Writers: Jerry Belson, Garry Marshall/Director: Jerry Paris

IN BRIEF

Rob Petrie learns that a shoe clerk's lot is not always a happy one when he invests in a shoe store.

CAST

Rob Petrie	Dick Van Dyke
Laura Petrie	Mary Tyler Moore
Sally Rogers	Rose Marie
Buddy Sorrell	Morey Amsterdam
Mel Cooley	Richard Deacon
Sexy girl	Larue Farlow
Millie Helper	Ann M. Guilbert
Lou Sorrell	Lou Jacobi
Sid	Milton Frome
Laughing woman	Amzie Strickland
Customer	Jane Dulo

★ "Girls Will Be Boys"
SERIES/EPISODE NUMBER: 7256/0117
Film date: January 19, 1965/Air date: March 3, 1965
Writers: Jerry Belson, Garry Marshall/Director: Jerry Paris

IN BRIEF

The Petries face a problem when Ritchie is beaten up by a pretty little girl who loves him.

CAST

Rob Petrie	Dick Van Dyke
Laura Petrie	Mary Tyler Moore
Ritchie Petrie	Larry Mathews
Sally Rogers	Rose Marie
Doris Darwell	Doris Singleton
Buddy Sorrell	Morey Amsterdam
Millie Helper	Ann M. Guilbert
Ogden Darwell	Bernard Fox
Priscilla Darwell	Tracy Stratford

★ "Bupkiss"
SERIES/EPISODE NUMBER: 7256/0118
Film date: January 26, 1965/Air date: March 10, 1965
Writers: Bill Persky, Sam Denoff/Director: Lee Phillips

IN BRIEF

Rob learns a song he wrote with an old buddy is about to be a hit, and he starts a fight over authorship rights.

CAST

Rob Petrie	Dick Van Dyke
Laura Petrie	Mary Tyler Moore
Buddy Sorrell	Morey Amsterdam
Sally Rogers	Rose Marie
Ritchie Petrie	Larry Mathews
Buzzy Potter	Robert Ball
Secretary	Patti Regan
Songwriter	Tim Herbert
Mr. Doldan	Charlie Dugdale
Frank Mandalay	Greg Morris

★ "Your Home Sweet Home Is My Home"
SERIES/EPISODE NUMBER: 7256/0119
Film date: February 2, 1965/Air date: March 17, 1965
Writers: Howard Ostroff, Joan Darling/Director: Lee Phillips

IN BRIEF

Rob Petrie recalls the time he and his best friend tried to buy the same house.

CAST

Rob Petrie	Dick Van Dyke
Laura Petrie	Mary Tyler Moore
Jerry Helper	Jerry Paris
Millie Helper	Ann M. Guilbert
Bert Steele	Eddie Ryder
Jack Parkly	Stanley Adams

★ "Not Now Anthony Stone"
SERIES/EPISODE NUMBER: 7256/0120
Film date: February 9, 1965/Air date: March 24, 1965
Writer: Joseph C. Cavella/Director: Jerry Paris

IN BRIEF
Sally's new tall, dark, and handsome boyfriend is mysterious about what he does for a living.

CAST
Rob Petrie	Dick Van Dyke
Laura Petrie	Mary Tyler Moore
Buddy Sorrell	Morey Amsterdam
Sally Rogers	Rose Marie
Anthony Stone	Richard Angarola
Delivery boy	Frank Adamo

 ## "Never Bathe on Saturday"
SERIES/EPISODE NUMBER: 7256/0121
Film date: February 16, 1965/Air date: March 31, 1965
Writer: Carl Reiner/Director: Jerry Paris

IN BRIEF
The Petries' romantic second honeymoon becomes their Waterloo when Laura's toe gets caught in a bath spout.

CAST
Rob Petrie	Dick Van Dyke
Laura Petrie	Mary Tyler Moore
Millie Helper	Ann M. Guilbert
Bellboy	Bill Idelson
Maid	Kathleen Freeman
Waiter	Johnny Silver
Detective	Bernard Fox
Engineer	Arthur Malet

"100 Terrible Hours"
SERIES/EPISODE NUMBER: 7256/0122
Film date: March 2, 1965/Air date: May 5, 1965
Writers: Bill Persky, Sam Denoff/Director: Theodore J. Flicker

IN BRIEF
Rob Petrie recalls his job interview with Alan Brady near the end of an ardous keep-awake marathon.

CAST
Rob Petrie	Dick Van Dyke
Laura Petrie	Mary Tyler Moore
Mel Cooley	Richard Deacon
Alan Brady	Carl Reiner
Waring	Dabbs Greer
William Van Buren	Fred Clark
Arley Chambers	Howard Wendell
Photographer	Johnny Silver
Dr. Gage	Harry Stanton
Dr. Adamo	Frank Adamo

 ## "A Show of Hands"
SERIES/EPISODE NUMBER: 7256/0123
Film date: March 9, 1965/Air date: April 14, 1965
Writer: Joseph C. Cavella/Director: Theodore J. Flicker

IN BRIEF
Just before they are due at a formal banquet, Rob and Laura accidentally dye their hands an indelible black.

CAST
Rob Petrie	Dick Van Dyke
Laura Petrie	Mary Tyler Moore
Buddy Sorrell	Morey Amsterdam
Sally Rogers	Rose Marie
Mel Cooley	Richard Deacon
Ritchie Petrie	Larry Mathews
Millie Helper	Ann M.Guilbert
Roger Johnson	Joel Fluellen
Joe Clark	Henry Scott
Delivery Man	Herkie Styles

 ## "Baby Fat"
SERIES/EPISODE NUMBER: 7256/0124
Film date: March 16, 1965/Air date: April 21, 1965
Writers: Jerry Belson, Garry Marshall/Director: Jerry Paris

IN BRIEF
Rob Petrie helps his boss, Alan Brady, by rewriting a play starring the comic.

CAST
Rob Petrie	Dick Van Dyke
Laura Petrie	Mary Tyler Moore
Buddy Sorrell	Morey Amsterdam
Sally Rogers	Rose Marie
Lionel Dann	Sandy Kenyon
Mel Cooley	Richard Deacon
Alan Brady	Carl Reiner
H.W. Yates	Strother Martin
Buck Brown	Richard Erdman

 ## "Br-room, Br-room"
SERIES/EPISODE NUMBER: 7256/0125
Film date: March 23, 1965/Air date: May 12, 1965
Writers: Dale McRaven, Carl Kleinschmitt/Director: Jerry Paris

IN BRIEF
Rob Petrie buys a motorcycle and is arrested as a joy-riding delinquent the first time out.

CAST
Rob Petrie	Dick Van Dyke
Laura Petrie	Mary Tyler Moore

Buddy Sorrell	Morey Amsterdam
Sally Rogers	Rose Marie
Mel Cooley	Richard Deacon
Policeman	Sandy Kenyon
Counter man	Johnny Silver
Jolly	Jimmy Murphy
Mouse	Bob Random
Gus	Carl Reindel
Doris	Linda Marshall

 "There's No Sale Like Wholesale"

SERIES/EPISODE NUMBER: 7256/0126
Film date: March 30, 1965/Air date: May 26, 1965
Writers: Jerry Belson, Garry Marshall/Director: Jerry Paris

IN BRIEF

Rob and Laura Petrie learn that buying a fur coat wholesale can be nothing but trouble when their "connection" is Buddy Sorrell.

CAST
Rob Petrie	Dick Van Dyke
Laura Petrie	Mary Tyler Moore
Buddy Sorrell	Morey Amsterdam
Sally Rogers	Rose Marie
Millie Helper	Ann M. Guilbert
Nunzio Vallani	Lou Krugman
Opal Levinger	Jane Dulo
Emil	Peter Brocco
Mr. Garnett	A.G. Vitanza
Angeleo	Abdulla Abbas

★ **"A Farewell to Writing"**

SERIES/EPISODE NUMBER: 7256/0127
Film date: April 2, 1965/Air date: September 22, 1965
Writers: Fred Freeman, Lawrence J. Cohen/Director: Jerry Paris

IN BRIEF

Rob Petrie sets out to write a book during his vacation, but has trouble getting started.

CAST
Rob Petrie	Dick Van Dyke
Laura Petrie	Mary Tyler Moore
Horace	Guy Raymond
Ritchie Petrie	Larry Mathews
Millie Helper	Ann M. Guilbert

END OF FOURTH SEASON

★ **"Coast-to-Coast Big Mouth"**

SERIES/EPISODE NUMBER: 7256/0128
Film date: August 3, 1965/Air date: September 15, 1965
Writers: Bill Persky, Sam Denoff/Director: Jerry Paris

IN BRIEF

Laura Petrie blurts out a top secret on a national television quiz show—that comedian Alan Brady wears a toupee.

CAST
Rob Petrie	Dick Van Dyke
Laura Petrie	Mary Tyler Moore
Buddy Sorrell	Morey Amsterdam
Sally Rogers	Rose Marie
Mel Cooley	Richard Deacon
Alan Brady	Carl Reiner
Millie Helper	Ann M. Guilbert
Johnny Patrick	Dick Curtis

 "Uhny Uftz"

SERIES/EPISODE NUMBER: 7256/0129
Film date: August 10, 1965/Air date: September 29, 1965
Writers: Dale McRaven, Carl Kleinschmitt/Director: Jerry Paris

IN BRIEF

Rob Petrie sees a flying saucer and succeeds in tracking it to its lair—the office above his own.

CAST
Rob Petrie	Dick Van Dyke
Laura Petrie	Mary Tyler Moore
Buddy Sorrell	Morey Amsterdam
Sally Rogers	Rose Marie
Hugo	Karl Lukas
Mel Cooley	Richard Deacon
Dr. Phil Ridley	Ross Elliott
Lady	Madge Blake
Karl	John Mylong

★ **"The Ugliest Dog in the World"**

SERIES/EPISODE NUMBER: 7256/0130
WITH GUEST STAR BILLY DE WOLFE
Film date: August 17, 1965/Air date: October 6, 1965
Writers: Bill Persky, Sam Denoff/Director: Lee Phillips

IN BRIEF

Rob and Laura Petrie try to find a permanent home for an ugly little mutt from the dog pound.

CAST
| Rob Petrie | Dick Van Dyke |
| Laura Petrie | Mary Tyler Moore |

Buddy Sorrell	Morey Amsterdam
Sally Rogers	Rose Marie
Mel Cooley	Richard Deacon
Rex Spaulding	Billy De Wolfe
Ritchie Petrie	Larry Mathews
Mr. Berkowitz	George Tyne
Mack	Michael Conrad
Mrs. Spaulding	Florence Halop
Customer	Barbara Dodd

★ "No Rice at My Wedding"

SERIES/EPISODE NUMBER: 7256/0131

Film date: August 24, 1965/Air date: October 13, 1965
Writers: Bill Persky, Sam Denoff/Director: Lee Phillips

IN BRIEF

Rob and Laura Petrie recall their courtship days when
Rob almost lost Laura to another man.

CAST

Rob Petrie	Dick Van Dyke
Laura Petrie	Mary Tyler Moore
Millie Helper	Ann M. Guilbert
Humphrey Dundee	Johnny Silver
Sam Pomerantz	Allan Melvin
Clark Rice	Van Williams
Heckler	Bert Remsen

★ "Draw Me a Pear"

SERIES/EPISODE NUMBER: 7256/0132

Film date: August 31, 1965/Air date: October 20, 1965
Writers: Art Baer, Ben Joelson/Director: Jerry Paris

IN BRIEF

Soon after Rob and Laura Petrie enroll in an art class, the
beautiful instructress has designs on Rob.

CAST

Rob Petrie	Dick Van Dyke
Laura Petrie	Mary Tyler Moore
Millie Helper	Ann M. Guilbert
Valerie Ware	Ina Balin
Agnes	Jody Gilbert
Doris	Dorothy Neumann
Missy	Jackie Joseph
Sebastian	Frank Adamo

★ "The Great Petrie Fortune"

SERIES/EPISODE NUMBER: 7256/0133

Film date: September 9, 1965/Air date: October 27, 1965
Writers: Jerry Belson, Garry Marshall/Director: Jerry
Paris

IN BRIEF

Rob's dreams of inheriting a fortune are dashed until Rob
realizes the intangible worth of an old photograph.

CAST

Rob Petrie	Dick Van Dyke
Laura Petrie	Mary Tyler Moore
Buddy Sorrell	Morey Amsterdam
Sally Rogers	Rose Marie
Luthuella	Elvia Allman
Alfred	Herb Vigran
Rebecca	Amzie Strickland
Ezra	Howard Wendell
Leland Ferguson	Dan Tobin
Ike Balinger	Tiny Brauer
Hezekiah	Dick Van Dyke
Mr. Harlow	Forrest Lewis

★ "Odd but True"

SERIES/EPISODE NUMBER: 7256/0134

Film date: September 21, 1965/Air date: November 3,
1965/Writers: Jerry Belson, Garry Marshall/Director:
Jerry Paris

IN BRIEF

Rob Petrie almost earns $500 because the freckles on his
back are in the shape of the Liberty Bell.

CAST

Rob Petrie	Dick Van Dyke
Laura Petrie	Mary Tyler Moore
Buddy Sorrell	Morey Amsterdam
Sally Rogers	Rose Marie
Mel Cooley	Richard Deacon
Ritchie Petrie	Larry Mathews
Millie Helper	Ann M. Guilbert
Freddie Helper	Peter Oliphant
Potato man	David Fresco
Lady	Hope Summers
Upside-down man	Bert May
Tetlow	James Millhollin

★ "Viva Petrie"

SERIES/EPISODE NUMBER: 7256/0135

Film date: September 28, 1965/Air date: November 10,
1965/Writer: John Whedon/Director: Jerry Paris

IN BRIEF

Rob and Laura have an unusual house guest, a bullfighter
named Manuel who installs himself as a handyman.

CAST

Rob Petrie	Dick Van Dyke
Laura Petrie	Mary Tyler Moore
Buddy Sorrell	Morey Amsterdam
Sally Rogers	Rose Marie
Manuel	Joby Baker
Doctor	Jack Bernardi

 "Go Tell the Birds and the Bees"

SERIES/EPISODE NUMBER: 7256/0136

Film date: October 5, 1965/Air date: November 17, 1965
Writer: Rick Mittleman/Director: Jerry Paris

IN BRIEF

After Ritchie spins a few fantastic stories for his friends, his parents wind up in the school psychologist's office.

CAST

Rob Petrie	Dick Van Dyke
Laura Petrie	Mary Tyler Moore
Buddy Sorrell	Morey Amsterdam
Dr. Gormsley	Peter Hobbs
Sally Rogers	Rose Marie
Ritchie Petrie	Larry Mathews
Miss Reshovsky	Alberta Nelson

 "Body and Sol"

SERIES/EPISODE NUMBER: 7256/0137

Film date: October 12, 1965/Air date: November 24, 1965
Writers: Dale McRaven, Carl Kleinschmitt/Director: Jerry Paris

IN BRIEF

Rob Petrie recalls the time he defended his title as middle-weight champion of an Army camp.

CAST

Rob Petrie	Dick Van Dyke
Laura Petrie	Mary Tyler Moore
Buddy Sorrell	Morey Amsterdam
Sally Rogers	Rose Marie
Sol Pomerantz	Allan Melvin
Referee	Garry Marshall
Bernie Stern	Michael Conrad
Norma	Barbara Dodd
Capt. Worwick	Ed Peck
Boom Boom Bailey	Paul Stader

 "See Rob Write, Write Rob, Write"

SERIES/EPISODE NUMBER: 7256/0138

WITH GUEST STAR JOHN McGIVER

Film date: October 19, 1965/Air date: December 8, 1965
Writers: Lawrence J. Cohen, Fred Freeman/Director: Jerry Paris

IN BRIEF

Rob and Laura Petrie become rivals when each writes a story for children.

CAST

Rob Petrie	Dick Van Dyke
Laura Petrie	Mary Tyler Moore
Lenny Burns	John McGiver
Buddy Sorrell	Morey Amsterdam
Sally Rogers	Rose Marie
Ritchie Petrie	Larry Mathews
Kid	Casey Morgan

 "You're Under Arrest"

SERIES/EPISODE NUMBER: 7256/0139

Film date: October 26, 1965/Air date: December 15, 1965
Writer: Joseph C. Cavella/Director: Jerry Paris

IN BRIEF

Rob goes out to cool off after a quarrel with Laura and winds up in trouble with the law.

CAST

Rob Petrie	Dick Van Dyke
Laura Petrie	Mary Tyler Moore
Buddy Sorrell	Morey Amsterdam
Sally Rogers	Rose Marie
Millie Helper	Ann M. Guilbert
Man	Tiny Brauer
Norton	Phillip Pine
Cox	Sandy Kenyon
Policeman	Ed McCready
Taxey	Johnny Silver
Mrs. Fieldhouse	Bella Bruck
Bartender	Lee Krieger

 "Fifty-two Forty-five or Work"

SERIES/EPISODE NUMBER: 7256/0140

Film date: November 2, 1965/Air date: December 29, 1965/Writer: Rick Mittleman/Director: Jerry Paris

IN BRIEF

Rob Petrie recalls the time he was out of work with a new home, no furniture, and Laura expecting Ritchie.

CAST

Rob Petrie	Dick Van Dyke
Laura Petrie	Mary Tyler Moore
Buddy Sorrell	Morey Amsterdam

Sally Rogers	Rose Marie
Mel Cooley	Richard Deacon
Johnson	Al Ward
Dawn McCracken	Reta Shaw
Truck driver	John Chulay
Herbie Finkel	Jerry Hausner
Brumley	Dabbs Greer
Joe Galardi	James Frawley

★ "Who Stole My Watch?"
SERIES/EPISODE NUMBER: 7256/0141

Film date: November 9, 1965/Air date: January 5, 1966
Writer: Joseph Bonaduce/Director: Jerry Paris

IN BRIEF

Rob loses his friends as well as his watch when the friends learn they're all under suspicion.

CAST

Rob Petrie	Dick Van Dyke
Laura Petrie	Mary Tyler Moore
Buddy Sorrell	Morey Amsterdam
Sally Rogers	Rose Marie
Mel Cooley	Richard Deacon
Millie Helper	Ann M. Guilbert
Jerry Helper	Jerry Paris
Mr. Evans	Milton Frome

★ "Bad Reception in Albany"
SERIES/EPISODE NUMBER: 7256/0142

Film date: November 23, 1965/Air date: March 9, 1966
Writers: Jerry Belson, Garry Marshall/Director: Jerry Paris

IN BRIEF

While out of town for a cousin's wedding, Rob has to locate a television set to watch a special show.

CAST

Rob Petrie	Dick Van Dyke
Laura Petrie	Mary Tyler Moore
Forrest Gilly	Tom D'Andrea
Bartender	Bert Remsen
Fred	Joseph Mell
Sam	John Haymer
Wendell	Robert Nichols
Sugar	Chanin Hale
Chambermaid	Bella Bruck
Edabeth	Lorraine Bendix
Organist	Joyce Wellington
Lou	Tiny Brauer

★ "I Do Not Choose to Run"
SERIES/EPISODE NUMBER: 7256/0143

Film date: November 30, 1965/Air date: January 19, 1966
Writers: Dale McRaven, Carl Kleinschmitt/Director: Jerry Paris

IN BRIEF

Rob can't make up his mind when asked to be a candidate for the city council.

CAST

Rob Petrie	Dick Van Dyke
Laura Petrie	Mary Tyler Moore
Buddy Sorrell	Morey Amsterdam
Sally Rogers	Rose Marie
Voter	Peter Brocco
Doug	George Tyne
Mr. Howard	Philip Ober
Bill Schermerhorn	Artie Johnson
John Gerber	Howard Wendell

★ "The Making of a Councilman"
SERIES/EPISODE NUMBER: 7256/0144
WITH GUEST STAR WALLY COX

Film date: December 7, 1965/Air date: January 26, 1966
Writers: Dale McRaven, Carl Kleinschmitt/Director: Jerry Paris

IN BRIEF

Rob Petrie agrees to run for office but realizes he'd prefer to vote for his brainy opponent.

CAST

Rob Petrie	Dick Van Dyke
Laura Petrie	Mary Tyler Moore
Lincoln Goodheart	Wally Cox
Buddy Sorrell	Morey Amsterdam
Sally Rogers	Rose Marie
Millie Helper	Ann M. Guilbert
Doug	George Tyne
Mrs. Birdwell	Margret Muse
Martha Goodheart	Lia Waggner
First lady	Kay Stewart
Second lady	Holly Harris
Third lady	Marilyn Hare
Herb	Arthur Adams
Samantha	Lorna Thayer
Duke	Remo Pisani
Booth	James Henaghan, Jr.

★ "The Curse of the Petrie People"
SERIES/EPISODE NUMBER: 7256/0145

Film date: December 14, 1965/Air date: February 2, 1966
Writers: Dale McRaven, Carl Kleinschmitt/Director: Jerry Paris

IN BRIEF

Rob's parents give a family heirloom piece of jewelry to Laura who accidentally drops it in the garbage disposal.

CAST

Rob Petrie	Dick Van Dyke
Laura Petrie	Mary Tyler Moore
Buddy Sorrell	Morey Amsterdam
Sally Rogers	Rose Marie
Millie Helper	Ann M. Guilbert
Sam Petrie	Tom Tully
Clara Petrie	Isabel Randolph
Jeweler	Leon Belasco

 "The Bottom of Mel Cooley's Heart"

SERIES/EPISODE NUMBER: 7256/0146

Film date: December 21, 1965/Air date: February 9, 1966
Writer: John Whedon/Director: Jerry Paris

IN BRIEF

Mel Cooley takes Rob Petrie's advice and stands up to Alan Brady—and is promptly fired.

CAST

Rob Petrie	Dick Van Dyke
Laura Petrie	Mary Tyler Moore
Buddy Sorrell	Morey Amsterdam
Sally Rogers	Rose Marie
Mel Cooley	Richard Deacon
Alan Brady	Carl Reiner

 "Remember the Alimony"

SERIES/EPISODE NUMBER: 7256/0147

Film date: January 4, 1966/Air date: February 16, 1966
Writers: Dale McRaven, Carl Kleinschmitt/Director: Jerry Paris

IN BRIEF

Rob and Laura Petrie recall the time they filled in an application for a $10 divorce.

CAST

Rob Petrie	Dick Van Dyke
Laura Petrie	Mary Tyler Moore
Buddy Sorrell	Morey Amsterdam
Sally Rogers	Rose Marie
Ritchie Petrie	Larry Mathews
Sol	Allan Melvin
Bernie	Lee Krieger
Gonzales	Don Diamond
Juan	Bernie Kopell
Maxine	Shelah Hackett

★ "Dear Sally Rogers"

SERIES/EPISODE NUMBER: 7256/0148

Film date: January 11, 1966/Air date: May 18, 1966
Writer: Ronald Axe/Director: Richard Erdman

IN BRIEF

As a gag, Sally Rogers advertises for a husband on a national television show and is flooded with fan mail.

CAST

Rob Petrie	Dick Van Dyke
Laura Petrie	Mary Tyler Moore
Buddy Sorrell	Morey Amsterdam
Sally Rogers	Rose Marie
Mel Cooley	Richard Deacon
Stevie Parsons	Dick Schaal
Herman Glimcher	Bill Idelson
Announcer	Bert Remsen

★ "Buddy Sorrell—Man and Boy"

SERIES/EPISODE NUMBER: 7256/0149

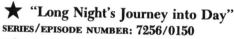 WITH GUEST STAR PIPPA SCOTT

Film date: January 18, 1966/Air date: March 2, 1966
Writers: Art Baer, Ben Joelson/Director: Richard Erdman

IN BRIEF

Symptoms and evidence indicate that Buddy Sorrell is either seeing a psychiatrist or having an affair.

CAST

Rob Petrie	Dick Van Dyke
Laura Petrie	Mary Tyler Moore
Dorothy	Pippa Scott
Buddy Sorrell	Morey Amsterdam
Cantor	Arthur Ross Jones
Sally Rogers	Rose Marie
Mel Cooley	Richard Deacon
Leon	Ed Peck
David	Sheldon Golomb

★ "Long Night's Journey into Day"

SERIES/EPISODE NUMBER: 7256/0150

Film date: January 25, 1966/Air date: May 11, 1966
Writers: Jerry Belson, Garry Marshall/Director: Jerry Paris

IN BRIEF

Laura Petrie spends a harrowing night alone in the house when the rest of the family goes off on a fishing trip.

CAST

Rob Petrie	Dick Van Dyke
Laura Petrie	Mary Tyler Moore
Artie	Ogden Talbot

| Jerry Helper | Jerry Paris |
| Millie Helper | Ann M. Guilbert |

 ### "Talk to the Snail"
SERIES/EPISODE NUMBER: 7256/0151
WITH GUEST STAR PAUL WINCHELL
Film date: February 1, 1966/Air date: March 23, 1966
Writers: Jerry Belson, Garry Marshall/Director: Jerry
Paris

IN BRIEF
Believing that comedian Alan Brady plans to cut down
his writing staff, Rob applies for a job with a ventriloquist.

CAST
Rob Petrie	Dick Van Dyke
Laura Petrie	Mary Tyler Moore
Claude Wilbur	Paul Winchell
Buddy Sorrell	Morey Amsterdam
Sally Rogers	Rose Marie
Mel Cooley	Richard Deacon
Alan Brady	Carl Reiner
Doug Bedlork	Henry Gibson

"A Day in the Life of Alan Brady"
SERIES/EPISODE NUMBER: 7256/0152
Film date: February 8, 1966/Air date: April 6, 1966
Writer: Joseph Bonaduce/Director: Jerry Paris

IN BRIEF
The Petries' anniversary party for the Helpers turns into
a television documentary for Alan Brady.

CAST
Rob Petrie	Dick Van Dyke
Laura Petrie	Mary Tyler Moore
Buddy Sorrell	Morey Amsterdam
Sally Rogers	Rose Marie
Mel Cooley	Richard Deacon
Alan Brady	Carl Reiner
Millie Helper	Ann M. Guilbert
Jerry Helper	Jerry Paris
Blanche	Joyce Jameson
Hi	Lou Wills

"Obnoxious, Offensive, Egomaniac, Etc."
SERIES/EPISODE NUMBER: 7256/0153
Film date: February 22, 1966/Air date: April 13, 1966
Writers: Dale McRaven, Carl Kleinschmitt/Director:
Jerry Paris

IN BRIEF
Rob Petrie and his writers are in big trouble for adding
insults to an Alan Brady script—when the target is Brady
himself.

CAST
Rob Petrie	Dick Van Dyke
Laura Petrie	Mary Tyler Moore
Buddy Sorrell	Morey Amsterdam
Mac, the watchman	Forrest Lewis
Sally Rogers	Rose Marie
Mel Cooley	Richard Deacon
Alan Brady	Carl Reiner

"The Man from My Uncle"
SERIES/EPISODE NUMBER: 7256/0154
WITH GUEST STAR GODFREY CAMBRIDGE
Film date: March 1, 1966/Air date: April 20, 1966
Writers: Jerry Belson, Garry Marshall/Director: Jerry
Paris

IN BRIEF
The Petrie home becomes a command post when government agents put a neighbor's home under surveillance.

CAST
Rob Petrie	Dick Van Dyke
Laura Petrie	Mary Tyler Moore
Mr. Girard	Steve Goney
Harry Bond	Godfrey Cambridge
Mr. Phillips	Biff Elliott

"You Ought to Be in Pictures"
SERIES/EPISODE NUMBER: 7256/0155
Film date: March 8, 1966/Air date: April 27, 1966
Writer: Jack Winter/Director: Jerry Paris

IN BRIEF
Rob is cast opposite a gorgeous Italian actress in a low-
budget film and turns out to be the screen's worst lover.

CAST
Rob Petrie	Dick Van Dyke
Laura Petrie	Mary Tyler Moore
Buddy Sorrell	Morey Amsterdam
Leslie Merkle	Michael Constantine
Sally Rogers	Rose Marie
Lucianna	Jayne Massey
Headwaiter	Frank Adamo

"Love Thy Other Neighbor"
SERIES/EPISODE NUMBER: 7256/0156
Film date: March 15, 1966/Air date: May 4, 1966
Writers: Dale McRaven, Carl Kleinschmitt/Director:
Jerry Paris

Rob and Laura Petrie are dismayed by Millie Helper's jealousy of their new neighbors.

CAST

Rob Petrie	Dick Van Dyke
Laura Petrie	Mary Tyler Moore
Millie Helper	Ann M. Guilbert
Jerry Helper	Jerry Paris
Mary Jane Stagg	Sue Taylor
Fred Stagg	Joby Baker

 ## "The Last Chapter"

SERIES/EPISODE NUMBER: 7256/0157

Film date: March 15, 1966/Air date: June 1, 1966
Writers: Carl Reiner, Bill Persky, Sam Denoff/Director: Jerry Paris, John Rich

IN BRIEF

Rob Petrie's autobiography conjures up scenes from the past and leads Alan Brady to buy the book for a television series.

CAST

Rob Petrie	Dick Van Dyke
Laura Petrie	Mary Tyler Moore
Buddy Sorrell	Morey Amsterdam
Sally Rogers	Rose Marie
Jerry Helper	Jerry Paris
Mel Cooley	Richard Deacon
Ritchie Petrie	Larry Mathews
Alan Brady	Carl Reiner
Millie Helper	Ann M. Guilbert

"The Gunslinger"

SERIES/EPISODE NUMBER: 7256/0158

Film date: March 22, 1966/Air date: May 25, 1966
Writers: Bill Persky, Sam Denoff/Director: Jerry Paris

IN BRIEF

The Petries and their friends are transported to the Wild West when Rob dreams he is a frontier sheriff.

CAST

Rob Petrie	Dick Van Dyke
Laura Petrie	Mary Tyler Moore
Buddy Sorrell	Morey Amsterdam
Sally Rogers	Rose Marie
Mel Cooley	Richard Deacon
Ritchie Petrie	Larry Mathews
Millie Helper	Ann M. Guilbert
Jerry Helper	Jerry Paris
Alan Brady	Carl Reiner
Gun Salesman	Allan Melvin

☆ 4 ☆

The Dick Van Dyke 500

TRIVIA QUESTIONS

1. Rob and Laura once lived in Ohio. True or false?
2. Where did Rob find his brother after his first sleepwalking attack?
3. In "Punch Thy Neighbor," where did Rob accidentally slug Laura?
4. What one-time British host of the popular game show "Family Feud" once appeared on the series as a very flirtatious star?
5. What was the name of Rob's fiancée before he met Laura?
6. Who was Henry Walden?
   a. a poet
   b. a playwright
   c. a one-time writer on *The Alan Brady Show*
   d. a beau of Sally's
7. Why did Laura spend "A Long Night's Journey into Day"? Where was Rob?
   a. on a fishing trip
   b. on a business trip
   c. with Jerry on a boat
   d. in a cabin writing a book
8. Who played the peculiar ventriloquist Claude Wilbur?
9. What was missing from the inscription on the watch given to Rob by his Army buddies?
10. Who were the two child actors who played Millie's sons?
11. What actor who years later would play Murray Slaughter on *The Mary Tyler Moore Show* appeared as Maxwell Cooley?

12. In "Viva Petrie," Rob and Laura's houseguest vainly attempted to work for them as what?
    a. a tutor for Ritchie
    b. a house painter
    c. a handyman
    d. a valet
13. In "The Two Faces of Rob," who did Rob say he was when he phoned Laura and disguised his voice?
14. What prompted Rob to get in trouble with the law in "You're Under Arrest"?
15. What did Rob suspect his friends of stealing after his birthday party?
16. In "There's No Sale Like Wholesale," Laura surprised Rob with a movie projector as a present. True or false?

17. In "A Show of Hands," Rob and Laura were invited to accept an award for Alan Brady presented by what organization?
18. The Petrie living room always featured the same furnishings. True or false?
19. In how many episodes was the character of Pickles actually seen?
20. What was the name of the crook who held up Rob and Laura in a stalled elevator in "4½"?
21. How and where did Rob and Laura first meet?
22. Laura had one maiden name at the show's beginning and it was later changed. What were her two maiden names?
23. Carl Reiner played several other roles in the series besides his semiregular appearances as Rob's egomaniacal boss. True or false?
24. What was the name of the drunk Laura decked in a bar?
    a. Stanley
    b. Cavendish
    c. Jacobson
    d. Blackburn

25. Rob and Laura discovered that they were not legally married. True or false?
26. Who was the talk-show host who grilled Rob into revealing intimate secrets about Laura?
    a. Stevie Parsons
    b. Johnny Davis
    c. Ray Murdock
    d. Ed Lester
27. Why did Rob, Laura, Buddy, and Sally go to jail?
28. Who was *The Alan Brady Show* switchboard operator?
29. Who was Willie, who often barged into *The Alan Brady Show* offices?
    a. deli man
    b. shoeshine man
    c. dry cleaner
    d. pizza man
30. What did Mel Cooley usually say to Buddy after being the brunt of an insult?
31. Though featured in "When a Bowling Pin Talks, Listen," Alan Brady's face was never actually seen in that episode. True or false?
32. What was Laura's occupation before becoming "Mrs. Robert Petrie"?
33. What was Ritchie ashamed of in "Father of the Week"?

34. Who invented "The Twizzle"?
35. What was unusual about Rob and Laura's first married kiss?
36. What was Rob's first job after leaving the armed forces?
37. Laura and Millie played cards in "Three Letters from One Wife"—what did they play?
    a. hearts
    b. gin rummy
    c. poker
    d. old maid
38. Rob and Laura once watched a program called "Camera on Culture"—what was the featured act?
39. How was jokester Buddy Sorrell billed?
40. What "Love Boat" star played Juan in "Remember the Alimony"?
41. How much had Laura put away in her secret little nest egg bank account?
    a. $294.12
    b. $451.02
    c. $378.16
    d. $398.26

42. Why did Buddy sneak around in "Buddy Sorrell—Man and Boy"?

43. Stacey Petrie auditioned for *The Alan Brady Show* playing his guitar. True or false?

44. Dick Van Dyke won three Emmy Awards for his role as Rob Petrie. True or false?

45. Where were the offices of *The Alan Brady Show*?

46. *The Alan Brady Show* was aired live, not taped. True or false?

47. Ritchie was attacked by what kind of bird?
    a. woodpecker
    b. whooping crane
    c. a pigeon
    d. a yellow-bellied sap sucker

48. What was discovered by the Petries and the Helpers in the basement of "Your Sweet Home Is My Sweet Home"?
    a. termites
    b. a valuable rolltop desk
    c. a giant rock
    d. a rare photograph of Abraham Lincoln

49. Laura hated the jewelry Rob brought her home in "Empress Carlotta's Necklace"—true or false?

50. Who was "The Unwelcome House Guest"?
    a. Rob's mother-in-law
    b. Buddy Sorrell
    c. Uncle Ezzie
    d. Larry Sorrell

51. Rob's art teacher told him he had great potential after seeing his painting of a pear. True or false?

52. Who played Kolack?

53. Stacey Petrie was finally able to audition for *The Alan Brady Show* while fully awake. True or false?

54. What did Ritchie wear to protect himself from a bird attack?

55. In "Divorce," what did Buddy go home to get after storming out?
    a. his cello
    b. his dog
    c. his lucky sports coat
    d. his car

56. Laura warned Rob not to ski, but it was *she* who broke her leg while Rob went away in "Don't Trip Over the Mountain." True or false?

57. In "A Farewell to Writing," Rob tried vainly to complete his unfinished novel. True or false?

58. What did Laura notice about Rob when her back was turned in "It May Look Like a Walnut"?

59. Where did Rob practice his skiing?

60. What did the cast sing at the conclusion of the Christmas episode?

61. In "Remember the Alimony," Rob and Laura filed for divorce. How much did it cost?
    a. $2.00
    b. $5.00
    c. $10.00
    d. $25.00

62. The pilot on which the Van Dyke series was later based was titled:
    a. "Head of the Family"
    b. "Double Trouble"
    c. "All in a Day's Work"
    d. "Love and Marriage"

63. *The Dick Van Dyke Show* was filmed in front of a live audience. True or false?

64. Where did Sally take the gang to see "The Twizzle"?

65. Where did Rob escape to finally write his "masterpiece"?

66. In "Romance, Roses and Rye Bread," who was Sally's secret admirer?

67. The last episode of the series was filmed in color. True or false?

68. Who was Ezikiah Petrie?

69. Millie was pregnant at the same time Laura was expecting Ritchie. True or false?

70. On what program did Laura reveal Alan Brady's secret in "Coast to Coast Big Mouth"?

71. What kind of TV dinner did Rob make for himself and Ritchie when Laura was away in "To Tell or Not to Tell"?

72. Where did Rob leave the only copy of a script in "Buddy, Can You Spare $2,500?"?
   a. on the train
   b. in a cab
   c. in Grand Central Station
   d. in an elevator

73. What special dinner did Sally make for her date in "Where Have You Been, Fassbinder?"?

74. What well-known comic played opportunist Neil Schenk?
   a. Guy Marks
   b. Don Rickles
   c. Frank Fontaine
   d. Jack Carter

75. From what planet did the aliens come to take over the world in "It May Look Like a Walnut"?

76. Rob was once convinced that Sally and Buddy were having a love affair. True or false?

77. In "Boy #1 Versus Boy #2," Laura and Millie became unbearable stage mothers. Why?

78. When Rob played paddleball to avoid writing in "A Farewell to Writing," what was his all-time high score?
   a. 298
   b. 374
   c. 392
   d. 407

79. What was Laura's alien name?

80. Why did Laura give Rob the silent treatment in the car on the ride home from a restaurant where they ran into Buddy, Sally, Pickles, and Herman Glimscher?
   a. Rob insulted her cousin
   b. Rob arrived late for dinner
   c. Rob's drunken behavior
   d. Rob's check-grabbing

81. With whom did Rob go skiing in "Don't Trip Over That Mountain"?
   a. no one
   b. Laura
   c. Buddy
   d. Jerry

82. In "Stacey Petrie—Part Two," Rob and Laura both told Stacey they understood how he felt. What did Stacey reply over and over?

83. Before Laura's maid arrived for the first time, Laura quickly cleaned the house. True or false?

84. How did Rob and Laura overhear Jerry and Millie's conversations in "All About Eavesdropping"?

85. Who gave Rob the idea for a talking bowling-pin sketch?

86. Why did the writing staff get in big trouble with the boss in "Obnoxious, Offensive, Egomaniac, Etc."?

87. In "Gesundheit, Darling," Rob feared he was allergic to whom because of his sneezing?
   a. Laura
   b. Ritchie
   c. the Helpers
   d. all of the above

88. Who did Rob refer to when telling Ritchie about the facts of life?

89. Where was Freddie Helper born?

90. What actor played more bit parts on the series than any other?

91. What did Rob and Laura eat at home after a dinner party at the Helpers' in "All About Eavesdropping"?
   a. Crummy Buttons candy
   b. breakfast cereal
   c. stale pretzels
   d. chocolate cake and coffee

92. In "One Angry Man," Rob gets into hot water for siding with whom?

93. Who was Mister Henderson?

94. In "Romance, Roses and Rye Bread," Bert

was confused when who showed up in the seat he thought was Sally's?

    a. Rob
    b. Buddy
    c. Laura
    d. Mel

95. Buddy promised Rob he could get a fur coat for Laura wholesale for how much?

    a. $150
    b. $250
    c. $325
    d. $375

96. How did Laura fight off a drunk, causing Rob great embarrassment?

97. What was Sally's favorite deli sandwich?

98. What was the present Alan gave to Mel in "Three Letters from One Wife"?

99. How much did Laura Petrie weigh?

100. Laura bid on an unusual art object in "The Masterpiece"—how much was her winning bid?

    a. $30
    b. $45
    c. $50
    d. $75

101. What was "Baby Fat"?

102. Rob came out of an amnesia fog at a party. Where was it held?

103. Where did Mel Cooley go to college?

    a. Harvard
    b. Yale
    c. Princeton
    d. Bennington

104. Which was Jerry Van Dyke's first appearance on *The Dick Van Dyke Show*?

    a. "Stacey Petrie, Part One"
    b. "Odd but True"
    c. "The Sleeping Brother"
    d. "I Am My Brother's Keeper"

105. What was the *official* address of the Petrie home?

106. What did Alan want Rob to do with his "Baby Fat"?

107. Before making his real full-faced debut, how was Alan Brady usually seen on-camera?

108. Dick Van Dyke directed the final episode of the series. True or false?

109. Name the writing team who next to Carl Reiner wrote the most scripts for the series?

110. In what episode was Millie's daughter named Patty?

    a. "Jealousy"
    b. "Love Thy Other Neighbor"
    c. "Punch Thy Neighbor"
    d. "Boy #1 Versus Boy #2"

111. How did Rob describe his imagined hair loss from his comb?

112. What kind of attire did Mary Tyler Moore make popular as Laura?

113. When did *The Dick Van Dyke Show* end its CBS prime time network run?

114. Who took the home movies of Rob and Laura's wedding?

    a. Sam
    b. Sol
    c. Millie
    d. Harrison B. Harding

115. Who was the script supervisor whose name appeared in the credits on most episodes?

116. Who was Dick Van Dyke's leading competitor for the role of Rob Petrie?

117. How many seasons of *The Dick Van Dyke Show* were there?

    a. four
    b. five
    c. six
    d. seven

118. Laura believed that Rob's habit of check-grabbing would keep "Ritchie out of college"—true or false?

119. What were the names of Millie and Jerry's kids?

120. In the original pilot which later became *The Dick Van Dyke Show*, what Andy Warhol film star had the role of Sally Rogers?

121. Who was the first director of the series?

122. What was Buddy's real first name?

123. In "Too Many Stars," what did Mel do to audition for a part in the talent show?

    a. soft shoe
    b. sang "More" (Theme from Mondo Conde)
    c. played "Antony" to Millie's Cleopatra
    d. ventriloquist act

124. In "The Night the Roof Fell In," Laura complained that Rob should be graceful and charming like what great dancer?

125. What college did Rob attend, and what was his major?
126. What was Laura's code name in "There's No Sale Like Wholesale"?
127. Laura stumped Rob by throwing him a surprise party on a Saturday morning. True or false?
128. In "Stacey Petrie—Part One and Part Two," Stacey pretended to be James Garner. True or false?
129. Rob's father's first name was:
    a. Oscar
    b. Sam
    c. Edward
    d. Benjamin
130. Who was the creator of the series?
131. What secret about Alan Brady did Rob blurt out to Laura in their kitchen?
132. What was the pilot episode?
    a. "Jealousy"
    b. "Sally Is a Girl"
    c. "Sick Boy and the Sitter"
    d. "That's My Boy??"

133. H. W. Yates had a pet which was at his side constantly. What was it, and what was its name?
134. How many Emmy Awards did *The Dick Van Dyke Show* win?
    a. five
    b. twelve
    c. eighteen
    d. twenty
135. How did Laura get to the hospital to deliver her son?
136. Larry Mathews became a regular on *The Doris Day Show* following *The Dick Van Dyke Show*—true or false?
137. How many episodes of the series were there?
138. In "A Surprise Surprise Is a Surprise," Laura had all the guests wear to Rob's surprise party:
    a. formal attire
    b. prison outfits
    c. pajamas
    d. Roaring Twenties costumes
139. Who played Big Max Calvada?
140. What was the name of Jerry and Rob's co-owned boat?
141. In what season did Persky and Denoff become story editors?
    a. two
    b. four
    c. five
    d. never were story editors
142. Who was Rob and Laura's odd houseguest in "Viva Petrie"?
143. In "Where Did I Come From?" what did Rob borrow of Buddy's in order to take Laura to the hospital?
144. What was the question Laura was asked on television which tricked her into revealing a secret about Alan Brady?
145. Jerry once gave Rob a roll of quarters as a birthday present. True or false?
146. Sally once received a red rose which smelled distinctly like pastrami. True or false?
147. What was the name of the guest-star crooner in "Like a Sister"?
148. "Divorce" was an episode in which Buddy planned to divorce his wife. True or false?
149. Who did Mel's dummy look like in "Too Many Stars"?

150. What was Ritchie's unusual middle name?

151. In "Will You Two Be My Wife?" which actress who later would star in a long-running spy series appeared as Rob's jilted fiancée?
    a. Barbara Bain
    b. Julie Newmar
    c. Diana Rigg
    d. Stephanie Powers

152. What was Rob's hometown?

153. Why did Rob feel he betrayed dentist friend Jerry?

154. In "4½," with what did Rob try to escape from a stalled elevator?

155. In what episode did Rob and Laura have the famous "milk-cake" talk about what should and should not be drunk with chocolate cake?

156. Richard Deacon was one of two actors to play Mel Cooley. True or false?

157. What was Laura's favorite food?

158. What was the piece of furniture that Ezikiah Petrie left to Rob?

159. Rob's most common pet name for his wife was:
    a. Laurie
    b. honey
    c. sweetheart
    d. darling

160. What did Laura usually say in a quivering voice to her husband?

161. Who was the composer of *The Dick Van Dyke Show* theme?
    a. Henry Mancini
    b. Earle Hagen
    c. Johnny Mercer
    d. Wilbur Hatch

162. Stacey Petrie was older than Rob. True or false?

163. Rob's mother's first name was Clara. True or false?

164. What did Rob pour over Tracy Rattigan's head when he flirted with Laura?
    a. champagne
    b. iced tea
    c. ketchup
    d. black ink

165. Rob was an investor in his brother's club. True or false?

166. In "Where Did I Come From?" how did Rob get a black eye?

167. What was the name of the dapper visitor from Twylo?

168. Where did Rob and Laura last see his new birthday present in "Who Stole My Watch?"?

169. What did Sally Rogers collect?

170. What did Rob bring Buddy to eat as a peace offering in "The Impractical Joke"?

171. What episode introduced the use of the flashback device?
    a. "Where Did I Come From?"
    b. "Go Tell the Birds and the Bees"
    c. "Oh, How We Met the Night That We Danced"
    d. "The Bad Old Days"

172. What was the missing ingredient Rob told Big Max Calvada was missing from his nephew's performance?

173. Was Rob left- or right-handed?

174. What was the last episode *aired*?

175. In what episode did neighbors Millie and Jerry first appear?
    a. "Jealousy"
    b. "Sick Boy and the Sitter"
    c. "All About Eavesdropping"
    d. "The Talented Neighborhood"

176. In "The Curious Thing About Women," Rob sent Laura a package to see whether she could resist opening his mail. What did he send her?

177. Who furnished Dick Van Dyke's wardrobe for the series?

178. Which episode introduced the Petrie and Meehan parents?
    a. "The Plot Thickens"
    b. "Pink Pills and Purple Parents"
    c. "The Sleeping Brother"
    d. "What's in a Middle Name"

179. Where did Happy Spangler work when Rob was reunited with him after many years?

180. Name Rob's 2 P.M. radio program in "One Hundred Terrible Hours."

181. Why did Laura borrow Rob's new car in "Scratch My Car and Die"?

182. How did H. B. Harding know Laura?

183. What did Laura want to serve Rob for breakfast in "It May Look Like a Walnut"?

184. With what did Rob and Laura decorate Stacey's new night spot?
    a. guitars
    b. wax fruit
    c. Chinese lanterns
    d. coffee pots

185. In "Sick Boy and the Sitter," Laura surprised all the party guests by performing a calypso dance. True or false?

186. In "Talk to the Snail," Rob was fired by Alan Brady temporarily and was forced to work for a ventriloquist. True or false?

187. What was the name of the food service that catered in *The Alan Brady Show* offices?

188. What did Rob tell Laura was the reason he stayed out all night in "Who and Where Was Antonio Stradivarius?"?

189. Rob said he had a "sprained body" when he returned from his ski trip, except for one place. Where?

190. Mary Tyler Moore had never played comedy before this series. True or false?

191. What did Rob usually do when he got nervous?

192. What was Ritchie's first nickname?
    a. "Ritch"
    b. "Champ"
    c. "Sport"
    d. "Tiger"

193. What kind of ice cream did Rob mistakenly bring home to be served with Laura's apple pie dessert?

194. Rob hired an inept maid but got her another job where?

195. In "That's My Boy??" Laura mistakenly got some things while in the hospital intended for another patient. What were they?

196. Millie's part-time job was as a receptionist in her husband's office. True or false?

197. Why did Laura suddenly decide to dye her hair blonde?

198. How many tickets to *The Alan Brady Show* did Rob forget to reserve for Mrs. Billings and members of her organization, which was also the title of that episode?

199. What did Laura do which made Rob and Ritchie very unhappy for one week in "To Tell or Not to Tell"?

200. What was the problem in "Sally Is a Girl"?

201. Who unexpectedly showed up for the weekend as Rob was planning a very important dinner party with his sponsor?
    a. Sol Pomeroy
    b. Sol Pomerantz
    c. Sam Pomeroy
    d. Sam Pomerantz

202. Why did Rob "Punch Thy Neighbor," even though it was an accident?

203. Who were the two actors who played talk show host Stevie Parsons?

204. Buddy once used the name "Tony Morello"— true or false?

205. Who subbed for Sally while she was appearing on television as a talk show guest?

206. Danny Thomas financed the pilot of *The Dick Van Dyke Show*. True or false?

207. In *The Alan Brady Show* Goes to Jail," Rob and Laura performed a song-and-dance number in prison outfits. What did they perform?

208. In whose column did Laura's story about decking a drunk appear?
    a. Ed Wilson
    b. Earl Wilson
    c. Tommy Wilson
    d. Tony Wilson

209. How was Rob accidentally hypnotized once?

210. In "Love Thy Other Neighbor," Jerry was instructed by Millie to say she was busy in order to avoid talking to Laura. Where did Jerry say Millie was?

211. Who was Tony Daniels?

212. In *The Alan Brady Show* Presents" Rob and Laura performed a dance number wearing what?

213. Mel Cooley was Alan Brady's brother-in-law. True or false?

214. Why did Rob sneak out of the house at 5 A.M. in "Death of the Party"?
    a. to play golf
    b. to fish
    c. to sail
    d. an early business meeting

215. What did Rob say in order to crash a wild party in "Who and Where Was Antonio Stradivarius?"?

216. What was on the mobile deli cart that catered in the Alan Brady offices to get a customer's attention?
    a. a whistle
    b. a car horn
    c. a bicycle horn
    d. a little gong

217. Who was Joe Coogan?

218. What was Buddy's famous trademark saying when telling a joke?

219. What happened the first time Stacey Petrie had a sleepwalking attack?

220. Who played Alberta Schweitzer?

221. Why did Rob and Laura think Jerry was unfaithful to Millie in "My Neighbor's Husband's Other Life"?

222. Laura saved a lump of sugar as a romantic memory. True or false?

223. In "My Husband Is Not a Drunk," what did Rob do when he heard one bell and then a second bell?

224. Who were "My Two Showoffs and Me"?

225. Sheldon Leonard was the voice of Floyd B. Bariscale. True or false?

226. Rob was thrilled when Laura's creative writing teacher thought she had particular writing talent. True or false?

227. Where do Twyloites have their eyes?

228. What brought out the egotistical worst in Rob, Buddy, and Sally?

229. Laura proved herself completely in acting as a temporary replacement for Sally in "My Part-time Wife." True or false?

230. What did Sally do to make sure that Leo Fassbinder would return for a second date?

231. In what suburb did the Petrie family reside?

232. What did Jane want to knit for Rob as a token of her appreciation in "The Foul Weather Girl"?

233. What was the prize that Laura did *not* win as a game show contestant on "Coast to Coast Big Mouth"?
    a. hair dryer
    b. hi-fi
    c. movie projector
    d. vacuum

234. What was Sally's fiancé's nickname for her?

235. Laura and Rob discovered an original Grant Wood painting while at an art auction in "The Masterpiece"—true or false?

236. Buddy threatened to "Divorce" his wife when he discovered she was:
    a. cheating on him
    b. writing checks to another man
    c. lying to him about her past
    d. previously married
237. What did Rob have to decide to reveal to Laura in "To Tell or Not to Tell"?
238. Where was *The Dick Van Dyke Show* filmed?
239. How long did Rob have to hop on one foot in order to meet Laura to get married?
    a. 1 hour
    b. 2 hours
    c. 2½ hours
    d. 3½ hours
240. What was "October Eve"?
241. What was the audition song of "The Foul Weather Girl"?
    a. "Stormy Weather"
    b. "Day In, Day Out"
    c. "Come Rain or Come Shine"
    d. "Just in Time"
242. What special meal did Laura cook for Rob in "The Two Faces of Rob"?
243. Rob did not come home all night, causing Laura to be frantic in "The Night the Roof Fell In"—true or false?
244. What was the musical number Rob, Laura, Buddy, and Sally performed as toy soldiers in the Christmas episode?

245. What solo number did Ritchie sing in the same episode?
246. Buddy once assumed Rob and Pickles were having an affair and he socked Rob in the eye. True or false?
247. For his birthday, Sally gave Rob:
    a. dinner at Nunzio's
    b. a roll of quarters
    c. round-trip limousine service
    d. two theater tickets
248. What was the program on which Sally made several guest appearances making her a local celebrity?
249. What was Laura's most-often used term of affection for Rob?
250. What was the name of Stacey Petrie's new club?
    a. The Point After
    b. Stacey's
    c. The Coffee Pot
    d. Burford's
251. What was the title of the final episode of the series?
252. Buddy made a mess out of the Petrie kitchen when as "The Border Incident," he attempts to make what for breakfast?
253. In "When a Bowling Pin Talks, Listen," what did Buddy put up in the office with a replica of Mel's face on it?
    a. a dart board
    b. a paddle board
    c. a pillow
    d. a punching bag
254. Mel often called Buddy "It"—true or false?
255. In its original pilot, who was the very first actor to play the part of Rob Petrie?
    a. Peter Lawford
    b. Carl Reiner
    c. Johnny Carson
    d. Ray Walston
256. Who was Harper Worthington Yates?
257. In "My Blonde-haired Brunette," Rob returned home and is shocked to discover Laura has a full head of bleached blonde hair. True or false?
258. In "The Cat Burglar" what did Ritchie hide under his pillow?
259. What gave Mel the courage to finally tell off Alan Brady after lunch with Buddy, Sally, and

Rob in "From the Bottom of Mel Cooley's Heart"?

260. Why did Laura gulp down a pitcher of water in "It May Look Like a Walnut"?

261. To what song did Rob and Laura dreamily dance at the end of "The Square Triangle" episode?

262. When did Rob sleep with the telephone under his blanket and his hat over the bed?

263. What did Rob do when he entered his living room for the final scene of "The Last Chapter"?

264. Who were the boys in "Boy #1 Versus Boy #2"?

265. Where did Laura buy her favorite, most sexy nightgown that was made of black lace?

266. Who was Edwin Carp?

267. Where had Buddy's black-sheep brother been living before visiting Buddy in New York?

268. What was Rob smelling to test his allergy in "Gesundheit, Darling," as Millie and Jerry walked into their living room?

269. Where was the bird that kept attacking Ritchie?
    a. school playground
    b. Petrie front yard
    c. Petrie back yard
    d. Helper's front lawn tree

270. In "The Boarder Incident," what special dinner did Laura cook in honor of Buddy's first evening as their guest?

271. What did Sally quote, usually out of the blue?

272. Who invariably was cast as the female lead in the local variety shows Rob produced and directed?

273. "Divorce" revealed Barton Nelson's profession and current residence. What were they?

274. Who played Ellen Helper?

275. What did Rob try unsuccessfully to obtain in "Will You Two Be My Wife?"?

276. Mr. Caldwell was Laura's amorous creative writing teacher. True or false?

277. Where were Rob and Laura married?

278. What was often seen on the Petrie dining room table before and after meals?

279. What was Laura saving up to buy in "Bank Book 6565696"?

280. How did Laura always know when Ritchie stayed in the bathtub too long?

281. What strange bridge bid did Rob make when distracted about "Forty-four Tickets"?

282. What did Mrs. Billings not like about *The Alan Brady Show*?

283. In "Punch Thy Neighbor," Rob accidentally spilled coffee on Jerry's pants. What then did Millie do?

284. What "Laugh-In" regular appeared as Doug Bedlock in "Talk to the Snail"?

285. Where did Rob propose to Laura?

286. How much later after they were wed did Laura give birth to Ritchie?

287. In "Hustling the Hustler," what did Sally make Buddy do every time he insulted Mel Cooley?

288. What did Rob think Laura was saving up to buy for him in "Bank Book 6565696"?

289. In "The Redcoats Are Coming," who played the rock 'n' rollers who turned the Petrie household upside down?
    a. The Monkees
    b. Herman's Hermits
    c. Four Seasons
    d. Chad and Jeremy

290. In the confusion in getting Laura to the hospital to deliver her son, Rob hit two cars in the Petrie driveway and locked bumpers. Whose cars were they?

291. What kind of car did Laura drive?

292. What card game did Buddy and Sally play to kill time in the office?
   a. poker
   b. gin rummy
   c. hearts
   d. old maid

293. What did Rob write in the three days he spent away from home in "A Farewell to Writing"?

294. What happened to disrupt "A Nice Friendly Game of Cards"?

295. The star of "F-Troop" and "Mayberry R.F.D." appeared in two episodes as Tony Daniels. Who?

296. What was Ritchie's favorite children's program?

297. What great Harold Arlen song did Sally belt in "The Secret Life of Buddy and Sally"?

298. What did Rob fear he would lose if he became a Twyloite?

299. Where did Ritchie write the dirty words he learned?

300. Who was Rudolph Schmetner?

301. In what episode did Rob appear in traction in a hospital recounting a story in flashback?
   a. "Don't Trip Over That Mountain"
   b. "The Vigilante Ripped My Sports Coat"
   c. "Br-room, Br-room"
   d. "My Mother Can Beat Up My Father"

302. What was the sci-fi themed episode of the series and who directed it?

303. Who was Mister Henderson's girlfriend?

304. Laura Petrie always wore the same hairstyle. True or false?

305. In "Odd But True," when connected, what did Rob's freckles on his back resemble?
   a. the Liberty Bell
   b. the Milky Way
   c. the Leaning Tower of Pisa
   d. the Big Dipper

306. What did Rob wear to Laura's cousin's wedding in "Bad Reception in Albany"?

307. What is the correct pronunciation of the name "Petrie"?

308. How was Rob finally convinced the hospital gave Rob and Laura the right baby?
   a. matching footprints
   b. the other couple was African American
   c. the other couple was Native American
   d. finding the original birth certificate

309. What did terror-stricken Laura and Millie put in front of the door to keep burglars from breaking in during their "Long Night's Journey Into Day"?

310. What was the fortieth and final episode directed by John Rich?
   a. "That's My Boy"
   b. "Coast to Coast Big Mouth"
   c. "The Masterpiece"
   d. "Very Old Shoes, Very Old Rice"

311. Who played the roles of the couple surprising Rob at their doorstep in "That's My Boy??"?

312. Rob thought he was going bald after counting twenty-seven hairs on his comb one morning. True or false?

313. What did the letters of Ritchie's middle name stand for?

314. In "That's My Boy??" what did Rob and Jerry leave in Laura's hospital room?

315. What did maid Maria put in the dryer which shrunk to munchkin size in "Turtles, Ties and Toreadors"?

316. In "Teacher's Petrie," Ritchie needed a photograph of something for a class project which Rob was helping him locate. What was it?
   a. a dinosaur
   b. Alan Brady
   c. a kangaroo
   d. an anteater

317. Peeved at them, how did Rob and Laura refer to Millie and Jerry in "All About Eavesdropping"?

318. Where was Stacey Petrie's club located?

319. In "Buddy, Can You Spare a Job?" Buddy was offered the position of head writer on what television program?
   a. *The Dan Rogers Show*
   b. *The Jackie Kaye Show*
   c. *The Dan Howard Show*
   d. *The Billy Berle Show*

320. What was the play Bert Monker wanted Sally to see with him in "Romance, Roses and Rye Bread"?

321. Rob's horrifying feeling he was part of an alien invasion in "It May Look Like a Walnut," was due to an elaborate gag created by Buddy and Sally. True or false?

322. What was the first episode in which Alan Brady was actually seen full-faced, and not camouflaged?
    a. *The Alan Brady Show* Presents"
    b. "Coast to Coast Big Mouth"
    c. "A Day in the Life of Alan Brady"
    d. "I Was a Teenaged Head Writer"

323. What created office tension between Rob, Buddy, and Sally in "The Pen Is Mightier Than the Mouth"?

324. Who played pickpocket Lyle Delp?

325. Laura discovered a check in which Rob had loaned Buddy how much money in "Who Owes Who What?"?
    a. $25
    b. $35
    c. $75
    d. $100

326. How much was Rob's weekly haircut and lunch allowance?

327. In "Punch Thy Neighbor," Jerry sent Rob a singing telegram. How was it signed?

328. Who was Roger McChesney?

329. What unexpected problem faced Rob and Laura in "A Word a Day"?

330. What unusual combination was Buddy's favorite dinner?

331. "The Talented Neighborhood" featured cameos by the real-life children of:
    a. Dick Van Dyke
    b. Mary Tyler Moore
    c. Rose Marie
    d. Carl Reiner

332. In "Go Tell the Birds and the Bees" where did Ritchie say babies came from?

333. What was the name of the convention group that infested the hotel in "Bad Reception in Albany"?

334. What was "The Curse of the Petrie People"?

335. The character "Marge" was never seen—true or false?

336. What were the shapes of the pillows on the Petrie living-room love seat?

337. On what network did the series originally air?

338. In many episodes, what round object was seen near the phone on Sally's desk?

339. In "100 Terrible Hours," what radio station did Rob work for?

340. What ingredient did Laura leave out of her dip recipe when she gave it to Millie?
    a. sour cream
    b. peanut butter
    c. avocado
    d. mustard

341. What did Uncle Spunky always do to his guest stars each week, which happened to Alan Brady as well?

342. Anthony Stone had an unusual occupation. What was it?

343. Millie and Laura were best friends before becoming next-door neighbors. True or false?

344. What did Alan Brady do to a comedy script if he didn't like it?
    a. burned it
    b. tore it up
    c. squirted seltzer water on it
    d. threw it out the window

345. In "Who Owes Who What?" Rob was frustrated when Laura's talking made him miss what once-in-a-lifetime event on TV?

346. Who played the bearded beatnik in "Romance, Roses and Rye Bread"?
    a. Frank Adamo
    b. Charles Aidman
    c. Ken Berry
    d. Sandy Kenyon

347. Who did Sally call "White Fang"?

348. What was Ritchie's stuffed monkey named?
    a. Killer
    b. Chip
    c. Tarzan
    d. Kong

349. Pickles' mother lived with Buddy and Pickles—true or false?

350. Sally Rogers lived in New York City. True or false?

351. On his practice date with Sally, what did Stacey unravel while sitting on her sofa?
    a. her blouse
    b. his shirt sleeve
    c. Sally's sofa pillow
    d. his pants

352. Rob's twenty-four-hour virus in "Death of the Party" caused him to have a temperature of:
    a. 97
    b. 98.6
    c. 99
    d. 101

353. In "It May Look Like a Walnut," what kind of vision did Laura have?

354. In the dream sequence of "I'd Rather Be Bald Than Have No Head at All," what happened to Rob's hair?

355. In "The Impractical Joke," what was Rob finally told to do with his telephone?

356. What did Rob usually wear to sleep in?
    a. nightshirt
    b. wool underwear
    c. striped pajamas
    d. checkered pajamas

357. In "Buddy, Can You Spare a Job?" Mel was told by Buddy that he was a member of the "FBI"—what did that stand for?

358. Why did Rob tell Jerry kiddingly to take out all his teeth but leave his tongue in "A Man's Teeth Are Not His Own"?

359. Alan Brady intended to hit Rob in the face with a pie while in his office. Who got hit with the pie instead?
    a. Mel
    b. Sally
    c. Buddy
    d. Alan

360. Why did a woodpecker attack Ritchie Petrie?

361. What did Rob and Laura sing in "The Secret Life of Buddy and Sally"?

362. Mel became so agitated in "44 Tickets" that he almost did what?

363. In "Where Did I Come From?" who did Rob kiss good-bye by mistake when leaving for the office instead of Laura?

364. Rob and Laura purchased a painting not unlike Grant Wood's *American Gothic*. How did theirs differ?
    a. positions were reversed
    b. the figures in the painting were smiling
    c. they faced each other
    d. there was no pitchfork

365. What did the framed lithograph in back of Sally's desk read?

366. What unusual thing did Rob and Laura both do when he proposed?

367. What did Stacey bring with him on his date with Sally?

368. Millie once phoned her pharmacy for an emergency delivery for Laura. What did she need sent?

369. What kind of sandwich did Rob put in his attache case in "Baby Fat"?

370. What was the secret answer to the radio quiz in "100 Terrible Hours"?

371. What was the name of the woman Rob believed had fallen for him in "The Square Triangle"?
    a. Mimi
    b. Yvette
    c. Brigette
    d. Anna

372. Who played the lady with the big feet who insisted Rob fit her with tiny shoes in "Young Man with a Shoehorn"?
    a. Kathleen Freeman
    b. Jane Dulo
    c. Mazie Strickland
    d. Jackie Joseph

373. Why did a little girl beat up Ritchie in "Girls Will Be Boys"?

374. Who was Johnny Patrick?

375. What was "Uhny Uftz"?

376. Who was Doctor Phil Ridley?

377. Who was Laura's other ardent suitor while she was courting Rob in "No Rice at My Wedding"?

378. What was "The Great Petrie Fortune"?
    a. a collection of old coins
    b. a rolltop desk
    c. a glass doorknob
    d. an old photograph

379. Who played Rob's old eccentric relative, Ezikiah?

380. What was the premiere date of *The Dick Van Dyke Show*?

381. Where did Sally keep her purse in the office?
    a. under her desk
    b. in the typewriter desk drawer
    c. on the water cooler
    d. in the filing cabinet

382. Who played the put-upon judge in "The Case of the Pillows"?

383. On more than one occasion, Sally did a musical tribute to a beloved and immortal comedian. Who was it?

384. In "Sick Boy and the Sitter," with what musical routine did Rob, Sally, and Buddy begin their entertainment for the party guests?
    a. "Goodbye, Goodbye"
    b. "I Wish I Could Sing Like a Million"
    c. "I've Got the World on a String"
    d. "Hello, Hello"

385. Rob first became aware of "The Secret Life of Buddy and Sally" when they both declined an invitation to what?

386. Laura sang what song to herself so she wouldn't hear Rob describe the cute ducks he brought home?
    a. "Swanee River"
    b. "Shine On, Harvest Moon"
    c. "I Don't Care"
    d. "Toot-Toot, Tootsie"

387. What was the name of the restaurant in which Laura was bothered by a drunk?
    a. Nino's
    b. Rocky Leone's
    c. Nunzio's
    d. La Petite Maison

388. What game did Rob and Sally play to amuse themselves at the office?

389. What drink did Herman Glimscher usually order in a restaurant, much to Sally's displeasure?

390. Rob only took off half a work day to marry Laura. True or false?

391. In "It's a Shame She Married Me," Laura boasted to Rob she made a bargain meal costing only how much:
    a. 39 cents
    b. 72 cents
    c. 87 cents
    d. 94 cents

392. What was Rob's original intention in disguising his voice on the telephone in speaking to Laura?

393. What did Sally give to Rob for his birthday in "Who Stole My Watch?"?

394. Harrison B. Harding bragged to Rob and Laura that he went on a diet and lost much weight. Where did his wife say he lost all of it?

395. How many eyes did Kolack have?
   a. one
   b. three
   c. three and one-half
   d. four

396. What was Millie Helper's maiden name?

397. What was the state and time record Rob was competing against his battle to stay awake in "100 Terrible Hours"?

398. Who broke in on Sally's date with Stacey and ripped her apartment apart?

399. Rob's "secret formula" to retard baldness was made of olive oil, vinegar, and eggs. True or false?

400. Who played Sally's Aunt Agnes?

401. In "Divorce," Buddy insisted on one certain drink. What?

402. In "Honeymoons Are for the Lucky," what did Rob have a great deal of difficulty in obtaining?

403. How many actresses played the part of Pickles Sorrell?

404. What were the first words Rob said to Laura when they met?

405. For Rob and Laura, it was love at first sight. True or false?

406. Where did Rob really sleep after storming out of the house in "The Night the Roof Fell In"?

407. In "To Tell or Not to Tell," Rob did an impression of what?
   a. Sally preparing for a date
   b. Laura opening Rob's mail
   c. a boy's first day at school
   d. Buddy walking his dog

408. What were Stacey Petrie's two major problems?

409. What was Happy Spangler's nickname for Rob?
   a. Stringbean
   b. Stretch
   c. Pitter-Patter Petrie
   d. Sport

410. Who played Rob's mother?

411. Who played Laura's father?

412. Where did Buddy and Sally go on the weekends in "The Secret Life of Buddy and Sally"?

413. How did Rob get into trouble with Laura when he arrived home from work as "The Foul Weather Girl" was visiting?

414. What was Ritchie's favorite thing on a hamburger?

415. In Laura's account of her fight with Rob in "The Night the Roof Fell In," what was she wearing when Rob came home from work?

416. When having his allergic reaction, what *really* made Rob sneeze uncontrollably?

417. What were the names of Ritchie's pet ducks?

418. Why did Rob take to court the man who sold him pillows in "The Case of the Pillows"?

419. In "A Word a Day," Rob demanded to meet the parents of the child whom Rob thought was teaching Ritchie dirty words. Why was Rob shocked when the boy's father came to visit?

420. In "That's My Boy??" Rob was convinced that the Petries were given the wrong baby, in part based on the last name of the couple whom Rob believed actually had Ritchie by mistake. What was their last name?

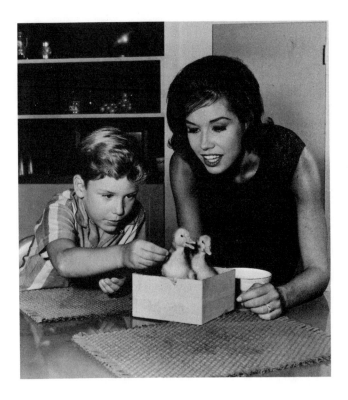

a. Petrie
b. Peters
c. Petroff
d. Peterson

421. Who was "The Death of the Party"?

422. Rob thought "The Secret Life of Buddy and Sally" was a clandestine romance between the two—true or false?

423. What was the key part Rob had to cast for an amateur variety show which caused him no end of grief and jealous wives?

424. What television program triggered the crazy dream in "It May Look Like a Walnut"?

425. In "I'm No Henry Walden," what was the name of the society matron who could never remember Rob and Laura's real names?
   a. Mrs. Allen
   b. Mrs. Walden
   c. Mrs. Billings
   d. Mrs. Huntington

426. What was Rob's fiancée's pet name for him in "Will You Two Be My Wife?"?

427. In "Buddy, Can You Spare a Job?" Buddy accepted a job which had actually been offered to Rob first—true or false?

428. What did Sol bring Rob and Laura as a present in "Sol and the Sponsor"?

429. In "Death of the Party," Rob collapsed while playing charades giving clues to what title?
   a. *The Telltale Heart*
   b. *The Canterbury Tales*
   c. The Gettysburg Address
   d. "Yankee Doodle Dandy"

430. What did Rob discover Laura had hidden away in a glove in their dressing table, causing him to be very upset?

431. In "Hustling the Hustler," who was Rob conned by in a "friendly game of pool"?

432. When Stacey Petrie was in a sleepwalking state, he was:
   a. extremely outgoing
   b. painfully shy
   c. hostile
   d. morose

433. What so impressed Rob and Buddy about the magazine Buddy brought in "The Bad Old Days"?

434. What was Jerry and Rob's regular poker night?
   a. Monday
   b. Tuesday
   c. Wednesday
   d. Saturday

435. Sally and Buddy once performed under another name. What?

436. The role of Pickles was first played by whom?

437. Who were Fred and Mary Jane Stagg?

438. What did Maria paint on Ritchie's turtle in "Turtles, Ties and Toreadors"?

439. Rob did not realize his house was vandalized until he saw that the dining room set was missing. True or false?

440. Who ultimately was the one to decide that the series would end?

441. What individual did Laura reveal she most admired in "My Husband Is Not a Drunk"?

442. Mary Tyler Moore received two Emmy Awards for her role as Laura Petrie—true or false?

443. Who was the second actress to play Pickles Sorrell?

444. What did dieting Sally order for lunch in "To Tell or Not to Tell"?

445. What "Laugh-In" regular made an appearance as Bill Schermerhorn in the "I Do Not Choose to Run" episode?

446. Rob once wore a pair of false eyelashes while in the Army. Who did he say he looked like when he had them on?

447. Rob's boxing opponent in "Body and Sol" was named Boom-Boom Bailey. True or false?

448. What was Rob's nickname as a boxer?

449. What did Edwin Carp need to fortify himself with in order to perform before an audience?

450. In "Very Old Shoes, Very Old Rice," what did Mel use to vent his frustrations about Buddy's insulting him constantly?
    a. saying, "Yecch!"
    b. used a clicker
    c. used a whistle
    d. played with Silly Putty in his hands

451. What handsome actor who was also known as television's "Green Hornet" played Laura's ardent suitor in "No Rice at My Wedding"?

452. Where did Rob and Alan Brady meet for the very first time?

453. How much were Buddy and Sally paid for doing their nightclub act each weekend at a small resort?
    a. $38.50
    b. $42.50
    c. $43.00
    d. $50.00

454. What character actor played Sally's would-be boyfriend in "Romance, Roses and Rye Bread"?

455. Who was the Petrie's original delivery boy who would later go on to star in a hit series where he would often wear women's clothing?

456. What was Ritchie's pay in the dream sequence of "The Bad Old Days"?

457. Who played Sam Pomerantz in "The Sam Pomerantz Scandals"?
    a. Marty Ingels
    b. Bill Idelson
    c. Henry Calvin
    d. Alan Melvin

458. According to Ritchie, when mommies and daddies wanted a boy or a girl to be born, they picked out their choice by selecting a pink or blue what?

459. Who was Harry Bond?

460. What floor was the office of the Alan Brady writing staff on?

461. Who was Kenneth Dexter?

462. What acid-tongued personality guest-starred as a dog groomer in "The Ugliest Dog in the World" episode?

463. The bum in "Brother, Can You Spare $2500?" also offered Rob, Buddy, and Sally the stolen script from what other variety program?

464. Who was the elevator man in Rob's office building?
    a. Pete
    b. Harry
    c. Willie
    d. Johnny

465. Who were Mister and Mrs. Parker?
466. What tune did Laura's jewelry box play?
467. Who was Sol's gum-snapping date in "Sol and the Sponsor"?
    a. Thelma
    b. Betty
    c. Arlene
    d. Lucille
468. Who did Rob call to get advice about at the bird attacking his son?
469. In "The Last Chapter," who had Alan Brady hired to write his new TV series based on Rob's book?
470. What was the reason Jerry insisted caused Rob to sneeze uncontrollably?
471. In "The Gunslinger," Miss Sally brought Rob a plate of hot food. Rob exclaimed, "Hominy grits!" What did Sally reply?
472. What did Ritchie like more when Laura gave it to him and not his dad?
473. Who gave Laura "The Curse of the Petrie People"?
474. Why was Laura asked to dance on *The Alan Brady Show* for a week?
475. On the night Rob and Laura met, what did Rob accidently do to her?
    a. spilled wine on her dress
    b. broke her foot
    c. gave her a black eye
    d. fractured her rib

476. Sol made a wager that Rob would beat his opponent in a boxing match. How much did Sol bet?
    a. $20
    b. $25
    c. $50
    d. $100
477. Rob was in what unit of the Army?
478. In what season did the series have a slightly different opening musical theme?
479. What did Rob face soon after completing "100 Terrible Hours"?
480. What did Rob have to retrieve for Laura after he confronted her teacher in "Teacher's Petrie"?
481. Who was *not* one of the original sponsors of the show during its original primetime network run?
    a. Kent Cigarettes
    b. General Foods
    c. Chevrolet
    d. Procter and Gamble
482. At the beginning of her career, Mary Tyler Moore danced atop kitchen appliances in a series of television commercials. What was she named?
    a. Happy Hotpoint
    b. Amana Annie
    c. Fanny Frigidaire
    d. Wendy Whirlpool
483. What ill-chosen thing did Rob and Jerry invest in together?
    a. a sports car
    b. golf clubs
    c. a sail boat
    d. a pool table
484. What were the two things wrong with the Petrie's maid, Maria?
485. What question did Ritchie ask when he first saw "The Unwelcome House Guest"?
486. What was the name of the book Laura wrote for children?
487. What was Rob's favorite leftover breakfast?
488. What was Rob's middle name?
489. What was the candy Ritchie particularly hated?
490. What did Bupkiss mean?
491. Who was the renowned art expert who once taught Rob?

492. What did Stacey Petrie always wear, except when sleepwalking?

493. The day Rob brought Laura home from the hospital after giving birth, he said he was dizzy because of what he ate. What was it?

494. What surprised Sally about her blind date, Joe Coogan?

495. What terrible thing did Rob inadvertently do in "When a Bowling Pin Talks, Listen"?

496. Rob was asked to run for what public office?
    a. Parent's Council chairman
    b. congressman
    c. city council
    d. mayor of New Rochelle

497. Where did Rob, Laura, Buddy, and Sally stay in "The Ghost of a Chantz"?

498. In "All About Eavesdropping" Laura amazed everyone but Rob when she guessed Rob's bizarre clues to what song title from *My Fair Lady*?

499. What kind of snazzy sports car did Rob buy in "Scratch My Car and Die"?

500. What was the last moment in "The Last Chapter"?
    a. a group shot of the entire cast
    b. Rob and Laura kissing
    c. Rob tripping over the ottoman
    d. Sally playfully slugging Buddy after an insult

The Dick Van Dyke 500

TRIVIA ANSWERS

1. True
2. In a movie theater watching a Laurel and Hardy festival
3. In the nose
4. Richard Dawson
5. Daphne
6. a
7. a
8. Paul Winchell
9. The last "e" in "Petrie"
10. Peter Oliphant and David Fresco
11. Gavin MacLeod
12. c
13. Dr. Rossano
14. Storming out of the house after a fight with Laura
15. His new watch
16. False
17. Committee for Interracial Understanding
18. False
19. Four
20. Lyle Delp
21. Laura was a dancer when Rob was in the Army at Camp Crowder, MO
22. Meeker and Meehan
23. True
24. b
25. True
26. c
27. To put on a variety show for Lyle Delp
28. Marge
29. a
30. Yecch!
31. True
32. A dancer
33. Rob's occupation
34. Randy Twizzle
35. They both wore surgical masks
36. Operating a lemonade stand
37. b
38. Monkeys dancing to *Swan Lake*
39. The human joke machine
40. Bernie Kopell
41. c
42. He was getting instruction to be Bar Mitzvahed
43. False
44. True
45. New York City
46. True
47. a
48. c
49. True
50. b
51. True
52. Danny Thomas
53. True
54. A pith helmet and sunglasses

55. a
56. False
57. True
58. He had a stain on his tie
59. In the living room
60. *The Dick Van Dyke Show* theme song
61. c
62. a
63. True
64. A bowling alley
65. A cabin in Lake Pushneck
66. Bert Monker
67. False
68. Rob's great-uncle
69. True
70. The Johnny Patrick Show or Pay As You Go
71. Ravioli and meatballs
72. c
73. Homemade lasagna
74. d
75. Twylo
76. True
77. Freddie and Ritchie were cast in a TV commercial
78. b
79. Lolack
80. d
81. d
82. "Nobody knows how I feel!"
83. True
84. Ritchie's interplanetary intercom
85. Ritchie
86. Because a gag script with insults directed at Alan was accidently given to him
87. d
88. Dr. Spock
89. New Jersey
90. Frank Adamo
91. b
92. A beautiful blonde defendant

93. Sally's pet cat
94. c
95. b
96. a judo flip
97. Pastrami with mustard
98. His old toupee
99. 112 pounds
100. a
101. A play in which Alan Brady was appearing
102. Red Hook, New Jersey
103. c
104. d
105. 448 Bonnie Meadow Road
106. Add comedy to the script
107. Under a barber's towel or with his back to the camera
108. False
109. Bill Persky and Sam Denoff
110. b
111. "Falling faster than rats off a sinking ship"
112. Capri slacks
113. June 1, 1966 (followed by reruns)
114. b
115. Marge Mullen
116. Johnny Carson
117. b
118. True
119. Freddie and Ellen and/or Patty
120. Sylvia Miles
121. Sheldon Leonard
122. Maurice
123. d
124. Fred Astaire
125. University of Illinois, journalism
126. Nunzio's wife
127. True
128. True
129. b
130. Carl Reiner
131. He had a nose job
132. c
133. A German shepherd named Mr. Ben
134. b
135. In a laundry truck
136. False
137. 158
138. c
139. Sheldon Leonard
140. Betty Lou
141. b
142. A bullfighter named Manuel
143. His pants
144. "Does Alan Brady wear his toupee at home?"
145. True
146. True
147. Ric Vallone played by Vic Damone
148. True
149. Himself
150. Rosebud

151. a
152. Danville, IL
153. Because he went to another dentist in an emergency
154. An umbrella
155. "Lady and the Baby-Sitter"
156. False
157. Moo-goo-guy-pan
158. A rolltop desk
159. b
160. "Oh, Rob!"
161. b
162. False
163. True
164. a
165. True
166. Hitting himself with a telephone
167. Kolack
168. On the bedroom dressing table next to Laura's pink poodles
169. Souvenir ashtrays
170. Three Mrs. Jelly's Donuts
171. c
172. "Talent"
173. Left-handed
174. "The Last Chapter"
175. a
176. An inflatable rubber life raft
177. Botany 500
178. d
179. A men's clothing store
180. Petrie's Party Patter
181. For Ritchie's car pool
182. He operated the spotlight for her USO show
183. Activated walnuts
184. d
185. False
186. False
187. Snappy Service
188. Temporary amnesia
189. The corner of his mouth

190. True
191. Cough
192. d
193. Licorice
194. In a novelty store on Broadway
195. Rice pudding and flowers
196. False
197. She thought Rob was taking her for granted
198. "44 Tickets"
199. Worked as a dancer on Rob's show
200. Sally was always treated as "one of the fellas"
201. a
202. Jerry was always criticizing Rob's writing and program
203. Dick Patterson and Dick Schaal
204. True
205. Laura
206. True
207. "I've Got Your Number"
208. a
209. Listening to Buddy being hypnotized while getting Ritchie water
210. In the shower
211. Choreographer of *The Alan Brady Show*
212. Oversized Santa Claus suits
213. True
214. a
215. He had "a message from Garcia"
216. c
217. An old flame of Laura's
218. "Funny you should ask!"
219. He took a bus to Chicago
220. Jackie Joseph
221. They spotted him dining with a beautiful blonde
222. True
223. Acted drunk, then acted sober
224. Rob, Buddy, and Sally
225. False
226. False
227. Two in front, two in back
228. A national magazine interviewer

229. True
230. Stole his watch
231. New Rochelle, New York
232. A mohair sweater
233. b
234. "Mommy"
235. False
236. b
237. Mel wanted her to be a regular dancer on *The Alan Brady Show*
238. Desilu-Cahuenga Studios in Hollywood, California
239. c
240. A "nude" painting of Laura
241. d
242. An authentic Italian dinner
243. True
244. "I Am a Fine Musician"
245. "Little Drummer Boy"
246. True
247. d
248. *The Stevie Parsons Show*
249. Darling
250. c
251. "The Gunslinger"
252. Eggs Benedict
253. d
254. True
255. b
256. The playwright who wrote "Baby Fat"
257. False
258. His cupcake
259. Several martinis
260. "For a breath of fresh air"
261. "I Only Have Eyes for You"
262. When they were expecting Ritchie to be born
263. Trip over the ottoman
264. Ritchie and Freddie
265. Chicago
266. An old radio performer who appeared on *The Alan Brady Show*
267. South America
268. Laura's fur coat
269. b
270. Corned beef and cabbage
271. Sayings by her Aunt Agnes
272. Laura
273. A forger who was in prison
274. Ann Marie Hediger
275. A pair of three-day passes
276. True
277. In a hospital room at Camp Crowder
278. A chess set
279. A sports car for Rob
280. "His fingers and toes were all pruney"
281. 4 no tickets, 44 no trump
282. Alan told jokes
283. Sprinkle sugar on his lap
284. Henry Gibson

285. In a jeep
286. One year and nine months later
287. Put a quarter in a coffee can for charity
288. A movie projector
289. d
290. Millie's and the cab driver's
291. A station wagon
292. b
293. The dedication
294. It was discovered the cards were marked
295. Ken Berry
296. Uncle Spunky
297. "Come Rain or Come Shine"
298. His thumbs and his imagination
299. On the blackboard at school and his at home
300. The author of Laura's favorite childhood stories
301. d
302. "It May Look Like a Walnut" and Jerry Paris
303. Penelope
304. False
305. a
306. A hairy tuxedo
307. Pet-tree not Pee-tree
308. b
309. Tin cans
310. d
311. Greg Morris and Mimi Dillard
312. True
313. Robert, Oscar, Samuel, Edward, Benjamin Ulysses, David
314. Laura
315. Her favorite red sweater
316. c
317. Mildred and Gerald
318. Greenwich Village
319. c
320. "Waiting for an Armadillo"
321. False
322. d
323. Sally missed work because she became a talk show celebrity

324. Don Rickles
325. a
326. $25
327. The Phantom Neighbor
328. Ritchie's babysitter who had a crush on Laura
329. Ritchie was repeating dirty words
330. Liver and bananas
331. a
332. A baby vegetable garden
333. The seals
334. An ugly brooch in the shape of the continental United States
335. True
336. Round and triangular
337. CBS
338. An eight ball
339. WOFF
340. d
341. Threw a pie in the guest's face
342. Undertaker
343. True
344. c
345. "The punch of the century"
346. a
347. Herman's mother
348. b
349. False
350. True
351. d
352. c
353. 20–20–20–20
354. Mel got it
355. Go on his lawn, swing the phone over his head and scream like a chicken
356. c
357. Fat, Bald and Ignorant

358. So he could curse himself with it
359. a
360. To use his hairs to build a nest
361. "Harmony"
362. "Take an aspirin"
363. Millie
364. b
365. "The Dairy Maids"
366. Shiver
367. His banjo
368. "Number Three Brown Hair Coloring"
369. Sardine
370. "The Battle of Waterloo"
371. b
372. b
373. She loved him
374. The host of Pay As You Go in "Coast to Coast Big Mouth"
375. The sound of a toy flying saucer and the title of an episode
376. The toy inventor in "Uhny Uftz"
377. Clark Rice
378. d
379. Dick Van Dyke
380. October 3, 1961
381. d
382. Ed Begley
383. Jimmy Durante
384. a
385. To his "world-famous barbecue"
386. a
387. b
388. Paddleball
389. Skim milk at body temperature
390. True
391. c
392. To test his theory for a comedy sketch
393. An electric ice crusher
394. In his face
395. d
396. Krumbermacher
397. Texas: 99 hours and 50 minutes
398. Herman Glimcher
399. True
400. She was never seen or heard, only quoted
401. Tomato juice with tabasco, lemon, and pepper
402. A three-day pass
403. Two
404. "Hey, baby, how about a little kiss?"
405. False
406. In the car in their garage
407. d
408. Shyness and sleepwalking
409. a
410. Isabel Randolph
411. Carl Benton Reid
412. Herbie's Hiawatha Lodge
413. He kissed the "Foul Weather Girl" by mistake
414. Tuna fish
415. An evening gown and a tiara

416. A cat Ritchie hid in the garage
417. Stanley and Oliver
418. They smelled like ducks
419. The father was a clergyman
420. b
421. Rob
422. True
423. Cleopatra
424. "Insomnia Theatre"
425. d
426. Robby-Bobby-Boo
427. True
428. A beer opener
429. b
430. A secret bank book
431. Blackie Sorrell, Buddy's brother
432. a
433. "It cost 60 cents and had no girlie pictures"
434. b
435. Gilbert and Solomon
436. Barbara Perry
437. New neighbors of the Helpers and the Petries
438. A sketch of the Petrie family
439. True
440. Carl Reiner
441. Abraham Lincoln
442. True
443. Joan Shawlee
444. A wedge of lettuce and skim milk
445. Arte Johnson
446. Bambi
447. True
448. Pitter-Patter-Petrie
449. An eight-ounce tumbler of elderberry wine
450. b
451. Van Williams
452. In a hotel suite in Chicago
453. b
454. Sid Melton
455. Jamie Farr
456. Nine cents a week
457. c
458. Shopping cart
459. The government agent in "The Man From My Uncle" episode
460. Twenty-eighth
461. The untalented nephew of Big Max Calvada
462. Billy DeWolfe
463. *The Jackie Kaye Show*
464. a
465. Witnesses at Rob and Laura's "remarriage"
466. "The Blue Danube"
467. c
468. Game warden of the Animal Shelter
469. Rob, Buddy, and Sally
470. Hidden hostility
471. "Oh, about fifty"
472. Bananas

473. Rob's parents
474. Because a dancer hurt her foot
475. b
476. c
477. Special Services
478. First
479. A job interview with Alan Brady
480. Her purse
481. c
482. a
483. c
484. She couldn't speak English and she had a broken arm
485. "Who is the wolf driving Daddy's car?"
486. Seven Dreams for Danny
487. Spaghetti
488. Simpson
489. Crummy Buttons
490. Nothing
491. Professor Zimmering
492. His eyeglasses
493. Pretzels, potato chips, and a bottle of sour milk
494. He was a priest
495. Steal an idea from another TV show
496. c
497. A haunted mountain cabin resort
498. "On the Street Where You Live"
499. A Tarantula
500. b

Dick Van Dyke's artwork on a
commemorative ashtray given to
the cast of the show.

RICHARD DEACON

☆ 5 ☆

"That's My Boy??" —A Milestone in Television History

The script "That's My Boy??" (copyright © 1963 by Calvada Productions) was written by Bill Persky and Sam Denoff on May 22, 1963, revised on August 2, 1963, and filmed on August 6, 1963. The production was directed by John Rich.

Fade in:
Int. Petrie living room—evening
Rob, Laura, Millie, Jerry, and Mel are seated around dining table sipping coffee, finished with dinner.

ROB: Come on, everybody, let's sit over here. You can bring your coffee if you like. Mel, you sit right here—lean back.

MEL: Laura, you're a wonderful cook. I don't know when I've had a better meal.

LAURA: I don't either . . . it really pays to fuss.

MEL *(laughs):* As a matter of fact the entire evening has been very pleasant.

LAURA: Why thank you, Mel . . . that's very sweet of you.

ROB: Stop bowing, honey. It's been pleasant for Mel only because Buddy's not here.

MEL: Rob, you promised you wouldn't mention his name. You know everybody's so nice to me, I ought to have my wife leave town more often.

MILLIE: It's your wife's sister who had the baby, isn't it?

MEL: Yes, first one . . . I spoke with my wife earlier and she says our new niece is beautiful. That's a lucky baby.

ROB: Why "lucky"?

MEL: Oh, you've never seen my sister-in-law.

ROB: What does she look like?

MEL: A lot like my brother-in-law.

ROB: Is that the one Buddy calls Godzilla?

MEL: That's the one. But their baby is gorgeous! I highly suspect the hospital gave them the wrong child.

JERRY: The wrong child?

All laugh.

MEL: Did I say something funny?

JERRY: You sure did. You said the hospital gave them the wrong child, but that's impossible, right, Rob?

ROB: Uh, well . . .

LAURA: Oh. Ask Rob . . . He's an expert on the subject.

MEL *(surprised)*: Really?

MILLIE: Oh, sure. Rob, tell Mel what happened when you brought Ritchie home from the hospital.

ROB: Nah, nobody wants to hear that again.

All ad lib "yes we do," etc.

MEL: Come on—what happened?

ROB: It was just a silly mistake . . . it was nothing.

JERRY: Nothing? He just decided they had the wrong baby, that's all!

MEL (shocked): He didn't!

LAURA: He did.

MEL (to Rob): You didn't?

ROB: I did.

Dissolve to:
Int. Petrie living room—seconds later
Petries, Helpers, and Mel are still seated, eating cake and drinking coffee.

ROB: Now wait a minute, Mel . . . if you'd been there and been in my position and collected all the evidence I did, you'd have come to the conclusion that the hospital gave you the wrong baby, too.

MEL: I never knew anybody who got the wrong baby. What was all this evidence?

ROB: Well . . . first of all, there was the blue foot . . . you remember that, Jerry?

JERRY: I'll never forget it.

ROB: And then there was the . . .

LAURA: Darling, why don't you start at the beginning.

ROB: Okay. You see, Jerry and I went to the hospital to bring Laura and Ritchie home. You know how hectic that first day can be.

MEL: Uh-huh . . .

Close-up of Laura. Camera dollies in on Laura's reflective face.

ROB (V.O.): Well, I was like any other new father . . . no more nervous . . . no less nervous . . .

Oil dissolve to:
Flashback—1956
Int. hospital room—day
Rob is seated on a chair with his head between his knees. Laura and Jerry are leaning over him. On various tables and stands are flowers, stuffed animals, and other typical maternity gifts. Rob is in a semi-stupor.

LAURA: Rob, are you all right?

ROB (sitting up): I'm fine . . . fine! Let's not sit around gabbing. Honey, sit down, you shouldn't be standing up!

LAURA: Well you . . .

ROB: Please! There's a lot to do!

He stands and wobbles into Jerry's arms.

JERRY: Yeah, there's a lot to do . . . Like fainting again?

ROB: I did not faint! I'm just a little dizzy from that elevator ride up here.

JERRY: Rob, we're only on the second floor.

ROB: I know, but I went up to the tenth.

JERRY: Why?

ROB: I got stuck with an emergency appendectomy and they wouldn't let me off. Let's see now . . . Jerry starts grabbing things—we've gotta get going.

LAURA (solicitously): Rob, did you eat today?

ROB: Of course I ate!

LAURA: What did you eat?

ROB: Potato chips. . . pretzels. . . and a bottle of sour milk.

LAURA: Where on earth do you buy sour milk?

ROB: You don't buy it. There's twelve bottles of it on the back porch.

LAURA: Oh, Rob, why don't you eat an apple for my sake?

ROB (takes one and pockets it): Later. . . don't worry . . . I'm fine. (taking charge) Are we ready to go? Jerry, take the bag. (notices fruit) Didn't I pack that?

LAURA: Yes, you did.

ROB: Oh, well, I'll take it. . . and the giraffe—put his neck under my neck.

He takes fruit and Laura puts giraffe under his chin.

LAURA: Did you pay the bill?

ROB: I paid the bill. All right—that's just about everything.

LAURA: How about the baby?

ROB (points): Only a mother would think of that.

Knock on door

ROB (cont'd): Come in!

Door opens and nurse's aide enters with fresh linens. Rob starts over toward her, expecting to see the baby.

156

ROB (cont'd): Aahh . . . there he is! Look at that cute . . . bunch of linen!

A nurse enters pushing a wheelchair, and says to aide:

NURSE: Edna, make up this room right away.

Aide starts changing bed linens.

ROB (noting chair): What's that for?
NURSE: Hospital rules . . . patients have to ride out.

She exits.

ROB: Good rule, good rule. Let me help you, honey. Take my finger.

He crosses over to Laura and holds out a finger to "help" her into chair. The nurse returns carrying a blanket-wrapped baby.

NURSE: Here's your baby, Mrs. Petrie. Watch the head.
LAURA (taking baby): Thank you, Miss Ransom.
ROB (leaning over to see baby): Let me see . . . let me see . . . aahh . . . look at my son . . . hi, there, boy!
NURSE: I'll be back in a moment with the baby's records and the rest of your things.

The nurse exits.

ROB (to Laura): Honey, you shouldn't exert yourself. You better not carry the baby. (starts to take baby but sees his arms are full) Jerry, put that stuff down.

Jerry does.

LAURA: Rob, I can carry the baby . . .
ROB: No, you just rest. Take this from me . . . (gives Jerry stuff he's been carrying) The giraffe's neck goes under your neck . . . Now I can take the baby. (He takes baby from Laura.) There!
LAURA: Watch his head.
ROB: Honey, get in the chair. Now we're all set. Let's go.

Rob and Jerry exit, leaving Laura alone. Rob returns.

ROB (cont'd): Jer . . .
JERRY: Yeah, Rob?
LAURA: Rob, why don't you give me the baby?
ROB: No! You take the baby! . . . And watch his head. (Gives her baby. His arms are now empty. He looks at stuff on stand, puzzled.) Now, let's see. Oh! Jerry, pick up that stuff. No . . . I'll get that stuff.

Rob picks up things from the stand. The nurse reenters, carrying several manila envelopes.

NURSE: I'm sorry I held you up, but we've had such a busy day . . . so many new babies going home at the same time.
LAURA: I understand.
NURSE (holding up envelopes): Here are the baby's records. Be sure you put them in a safe place.
ROB: Would you put them in my breast pocket, please?

Nurse puts them in Rob's pocket.

NURSE: And here are your valuables. Would you check them, please? (She opens envelope.)
LAURA: All I checked was a watch.
NURSE (looks at envelope marking): Oh, how stupid! This one belongs in 203. Busy, busy, busy! Here's yours. Good-bye, Mr. and Mrs. Petrie, and I wish you a lot of luck with her.

Nurse's aide moves toward the door.

ROB: *Her??*
NURSE (reminding herself): Oh, I'm sorry. *Him.* Baby Boy Peters.
ROB: Petrie.
NURSE: Whatever. (to assistant) Oh, Edna, when you finish here go to Room 203 and make up Mrs. Petrie's room.
ROB: We're the Petries . . .
NURSE: Well, whatever . . . they're checking out, too. I'll be glad when this day is over.

The nurse exits.

ROB (*kiddingly to baby*): How do you like that, tiger—she thought you were a girl. Boy, what a madhouse! We're all set—let's go! (*He starts pushing chair with his foot.*)
LAURA: Rob, the nurse will do it.

As they are leaving the room, the nurse enters with a large basket of flowers.

NURSE: I'm glad I caught you. These just came.
LAURA: Oh . . . they're lovely!

Rob looks around. Sees that everyone's arms are full.

ROB: Put it around here.

Nurse puts basket handle around Rob's head.

ROB: Good . . . thank you!
JERRY: Okay, let's go.

They start to exit.

NURSE: Oh, she's so cute! You're going to be proud of her.
ROB: *Him!*
NURSE: Whatever.

They exit.

Oil dissolve to:
Present
Int. Petrie living room—Laura's face

MEL (*V.O.*): You mean, just because of those little mixups you thought you had the wrong baby?
ROB: No! The things that happened at the hospital were just a preview of things to come.
MEL (*to Laura*): What happened?

Close-up—Rob's face, reflecting

LAURA (*V.O.*): I didn't know what was going on in Rob's feverish mind because when we got home, Millie and I were busy taking care of the baby.

Oil dissolve to:
Flashback—1956

Int. Petrie living room—day
It is the same living room as the present, except for the furnishings. Some of the flowers that were brought home from the hospital are on the tables throughout the room. Jerry is slouched on the couch. Rob, holding the envelope containing the baby's records, is stalking about the room, opening drawers, opening closet doors, looking behind pictures.

JERRY (*watches Rob for a moment*): What are you doing?
ROB: You want to know what I'm doing? I'm looking for a safe place to hide the baby's records. Who'd steal a baby's records? . . .

(*hides them in book*)

ROB (*cont'd*) (*shakes his head to clear it*): Hey, you know something, Jer, this thing is getting to me. I think I'm a premature father.
JERRY: Why don't you eat something?
ROB: Yeah. (*takes out apple*)
JERRY: Sit down, Rob.
ROB (*sighs*): What a day . . . I'm exhausted!
JERRY: That hospital could wear anybody out. I never saw such confusion.
ROB (*eats apple, thinking about that remark; now probing slightly*): Say, Jer, who do you think the baby looks like? Me or Laura?
JERRY: I don't know. How can you tell at this age? Their looks change every day. That first day he looked like you.
ROB (*slowly*): Yeah . . . then he looked a little bit like Laura. And today, in the cab coming home, he looked a lot like Ralph Martoni.
JERRY: Who's Ralph Martoni?
ROB: The cab driver. Didn't you see his picture on the license? Pudgy little bald guy.
JERRY: Rob, all newborn babies look like Ralph Martoni. The hospital could give you any kid and you wouldn't know the difference.
ROB (*worried*): Really? My grandmother warned me about that.

Millie enters from bedroom. She is bubbling.

MILLIE: Rob, you have *some* baby!
ROB: Uh, Millie . . . who do you think he looks like?

MILLIE: Well, the first time I saw him I thought he was the image of you.

ROB (elated): Yeah?

MILLIE: But today . . .

ROB: He looks like Laura?

MILLIE: No, he doesn't look like either one of you.

ROB (mumbles): Ralph Martoni . . .

MILLIE: What?

ROB: Nothing . . . forget it.

MILLIE: Jerry, do you want to give me a hand in the kitchen?

JERRY: Do I have an alternative?

MILLIE: Nope!

JERRY: In that case I'll give you a hand in the kitchen.

He exits to kitchen after Millie. The bedroom door opens. Laura enters in houserobe. Rob sees her and crosses to her.

LAURA (ecstatically): Rob, have we got a baby! Do you know what he's doing?

ROB: What?

LAURA: Nothing! He doesn't cry or anything . . . he's just the best baby! I've just been standing there staring at him. I can't believe he's ours.

ROB: Uh-huh! (drawing back) You can't believe *what*?

LAURA: You know . . . that he's actually home . . . and he's ours.

ROB (relieved): Oh!

LAURA: And he looks so different.

ROB (anxiously): Oh? How?

LAURA: Well . . . away from the hospital . . . in his own bassinet. He just looks like a different baby.

Rob stares over her shoulder at bedroom door. The front doorbell rings.

LAURA (cont'd): I wonder who it is?

ROB (still looking at bedroom door; concerned): So do I.

LAURA: Well, go see.

ROB: I will.

Rob walks to bedroom door and starts to enter.

LAURA: Rob . . . the front door.

Rob stops in his tracks, does a take, and starts for the front door.

ROB: Of course!

Rob crosses to the front door, opens it, ushering in Sally.

SALLY: Hi, Rob. (kisses him) See you later . . . you're only the father. Hey you look terrible . . . you ought to eat something.

She crosses to Laura. They kiss. Rob takes out apple and eats.

LAURA: It's so nice of you to come all the way up here to see us.

SALLY: We couldn't wait to see the baby. Laura, you look marvelous!

LAURA: Thank you, Sally. Sit down.

Offstage sound: bicycle horn. Buddy rides bike in.

BUDDY: Hi, Rob!

ROB: That's not for us, is it?

BUDDY: No, I rode Sally up on the handlebars.

ROB: But he's only a little baby.

BUDDY: So it's a little bike. They'll grow up together.

SALLY (to Bud): How do you like this girl. Doesn't she look great! She's got her old figure back already. Boy, am I jealous.

BUDDY: Not me—I've already got an old figure.

Millie and Jerry enter from kitchen. All ad lib greetings.

ROB: Say, guys, don't you want to see the baby?

BUDDY: Of course we want to see the baby. I've been practicing funny faces all day.

SALLY: The one you're doing now is hysterical.

Laura, Sally, and Buddy start into bedroom.

LAURA: Sally, do you know what he's been doing all day? Nothing! . . . absolutely nothing!

JERRY: Come on, Millie, it's time to go home.

MILLIE: Let's take one more peek.

Millie joins the others going into bedroom. Jerry starts to join them.

ROB: Jerry, hold it a second . . . close the door.

Jerry waits as the others enter bedroom.

JERRY: What is it, Rob?

ROB: Remember we were talking before . . . about Ralph Martoni?

JERRY: Yeah.

ROB: The nurse gave Laura the wrong jewelry . . . she called him "her" . . . She didn't even know our name . . . uh . . . everybody, including me . . . thinks he looks like a different baby.

JERRY: Rob—

ROB: But even Laura said he looked different . . . his own mother . . . I think.

JERRY: Rob . . . things like that don't happen. You do not have the wrong baby.

ROB: Well . . . it's possible.

JERRY: It's not possible . . . and forget it! And don't you dare tell Laura what you've been thinking.

The bedroom door opens. Buddy and Sally enter ad libbing oohs and ahs.

SALLY: Oh, that baby, that baby . . . I gotta get married! Do you know what that baby did?

ROB: What?

SALLY: He woke up!

BUDDY: That's a cute kid. Are you sure you got the right baby?

ROB: What makes you say that?

BUDDY: Well, you're so tall and the kid is . . . *(gestures)*

SALLY: Cut it out, Buddy!

Laura and Millie enter from bedroom.

MILLIE: He's darling! Isn't he darling! I think he's just darling!

JERRY: Come on, honey . . . let's go.

Flashback—1956
Int. Petrie living room—night
Buddy, Sally, Rob, and Laura say goodnights at door.

BUDDY: Good luck with the kid, and if he needs any jokes, call me.

ROB: Goodnight . . . thanks for coming over and thanks for the present.

SALLY: Wait'll you see what's coming from Aunt Sally.

ROB: What?

SALLY: I don't know, but I think I just committed myself to something very expensive.

Buddy and Sally exit . . . Laura and Rob walk down to sofa.

LAURA: After all the excitement today, it's kind of nice to be alone.

ROB: Yeah . . . just the two of us.

LAURA: The *three* of us.

ROB: Oh, yeah . . . *(nodding to bedroom)* The little stranger . . . uh . . . baby!

LAURA: You know, Rob, I didn't realize we had so many friends. Everything . . . the gifts and the flowers were just beautiful. Say, Rob, who sent those?

ROB: Which?

LAURA: The ones we got when we were leaving the hospital. In all the excitement I never even looked at the card.

ROB *(rising):* Neither did I . . . *(Rob crosses to flowers, finds card, reads.)* Congratulations and much love . . . Dick and Betty Carter.

BOTH: Aahh!

ROB *(frowns):* Do we know a Dick and Betty Carter?

LAURA *(thinking):* No. Maybe it's someone from your office.

ROB: No. The only Dick and Betty Carter I know are Phil and Edna Greenbaum. *(takes out apple core)* Do we have any more apples?

LAURA *(she picks up card envelope from table and looks at it):* Oh . . . this explains it. These are for Mrs. Peters in room 203. It's been going on all week. They kept getting us mixed up. You know . . . Peters, 203 . . . Petrie, 208 . . . the names and numbers look alike. One night . . . *(smiles)* . . . I even got her rice pudding!

ROB: What did you say?

LAURA: That I got her rice pudding.

ROB *(meaningfully):* You got her rice pudding!

LAURA: Yes . . . which means she probably got my blueberry tart.

ROB: Among other things.

LAURA: As a matter of fact, that envelope they gave us today . . . that was hers.

ROB: It figures. That's it. That's how it happened! I knew it!

LAURA: Rob, why're you getting so excited . . . it's only flowers. We'll return them.

ROB (mumbles): Yeah—we're not bringing up the wrong flowers.

LAURA: What're you talking about?

ROB (stammering): Uh . . . Laura . . . You must be tired . . . Why don't you take a little nap?

LAURA: I'm going to, but first I have to change the baby.

She exits.

ROB (concerned): She's right. We've gotta change that baby!

Dissolve to:
Present
Int. Petrie living room—night

ROB: Mel, tell me the truth. Wouldn't you be a little suspicious if you got the wrong flowers and wrong envelope? What would you think?

MEL: I might think I had the wrong baby.

ROB: That's what I thought, except I was sure of it, so I made a phone call.

MEL: You called the hospital?

Close-up of Rob's face, reflecting

JERRY (V.O.): No! Unfortunately, he called me!

Oil dissolve to:
Flashback—1956
Int. Petrie living room—night
Rob and Jerry are alone.

JERRY (reading card): So you got flowers from Dick and Betty. What does that prove?

ROB: What does it prove? Did you ever get flowers from Dick and Betty?

JERRY: I don't even know Dick and Betty!

ROB: Well, neither do we! The only one in this house who knows Dick and Betty is the baby! Shhh!

JERRY (trying to convince Rob, also himself): Rob, I don't care how much circumstantial evidence

there is, a mistake like this is practically impossible.

ROB: But it *is* possible.

JERRY: Yeah . . . but in 1 out of 50 million cases!

ROB: And it had to be us! I better tell Laura.

JERRY: Hold it, Rob. Don't say a word to Laura until you're a hundred percent sure. We need more evidence.

ROB: Yeah, yeah . . . hey, I know what I'll do. I'll call the Peters.

JERRY: Rob, it's not fair to get them upset either unless unless you're sure.

ROB: Yeah . . . but I could just hint around.

JERRY: How could you hint about a thing like that?

ROB: Well . . . uh . . . the first thing I'd say is . . . uh . . . my wife . . . and . . . uh . . . by mistake we got her flowers and I'd be happy to bring them over . . . 'cause I was dropping by their house anyway . . . to . . . uh . . . pick up my baby.

JERRY: That's a pretty big hint!

ROB: We've got to do something! We're getting attached to this baby . . . they're getting attached to that one . . . to ours . . . and the longer this drags out, the tougher it's going to be. There must be some way to make sure.

JERRY: Not without upsetting a lot of people.

ROB: Jerry, let me out of here, I've gotta pace! Hey . . . don't dentists help identify criminals by examining their teeth?

JERRY (admonishingly): Rob . . .

ROB (realizing): Yeah—he has no teeth! Can you do anything with gums?

JERRY (snaps fingers): I got it! Footprints! We'll match his footprints against the records.

ROB: Good idea! There's an ink stamp pad and paper in the drawer over there and his records are in *The Magic Mountain.*

JERRY: What?

ROB: The book.

JERRY: Oh—Thomas Mann . . . that's my book.

ROB: Go get them and I'll sneak the baby out here.

JERRY: What?

ROB: Shh! Laura's asleep.

Jerry crosses and looks for paper and ink pad and records. Rob goes into bedroom and immediately re-enters, tiptoeing, pushing the bassinet ahead of him. Jerry meets him in the center of the room. The two of them stare down at the baby. (We do not see the baby.)

ROB (cont'd) (sadly): Boy . . . I hope our baby is as cute as this one!

JERRY: Rob, that's your baby.

ROB (steeling himself): Oh I hope so . . . (leaning into bassinet) Take it easy there, fella, this won't hurt a bit.

JERRY: You smear some ink on his foot and I'll press the paper against it.

ROB: Okay.

Rob leans into bassinet and applies ink pad to the baby's foot.
Sound: baby gurgles.
Jerry awkwardly leans into bassinet to make footprint.

JERRY: I think I got it.

ROB: Good.

Rob takes paper from Jerry.

ROB (staring at footprint on paper): Hey, Jerry, there's something peculiar about this footprint.

Jerry rifles through envelope. Finds sheet with footprint.

JERRY: Here . . . let's compare them!

They hold papers up side by side.

ROB: I was right, there *is* something peculiar about it. This foot has six toes.

JERRY: Let me see. (looks at paper) That's your thumbprint.

ROB: Oh yeah. Well, Jerry, what do you think?

Jerry examines footprints.

JERRY (very professionally): Rob . . . I would say . . . that that footprint and that footprint are from that baby!

ROB (relieved): Let me look. (Takes papers and looks at them. His mood darkens.) You're positive?

JERRY: Yep!

ROB: That's what I was afraid of. (hands Jerry papers from hospital) Read the top line.

JERRY (reads): Sex . . . male . . . name . . . Baby boy . . . Peters!

ROB: Well, I guess that proves it!

JERRY (backtracking): That proves nothing!

ROB: You just said they were the same!

JERRY: What do I know about footprints? I'm a dentist. I know mouthprints!

ROB: What's the use of kidding ourselves. We wanted proof and we got it.

JERRY: It just proves you got another wrong envelope.

ROB: It's no use, Jer . . . I'm going to have to tell Laura.

JERRY: Rob, at least check with the hospital.

ROB (sighs): Okay! I'll check with them . . . but I'm sure.

Rob crosses to phone. As he does it rings.

ROB (cont'd): Hello! Yes, this is Mr. Petrie . . . Who? (Covers phone with hand: To Jerry) It's Mr. Peters!

JERRY: What does he want?

ROB: What do you think? (into phone) Uh, yes Mr. Peters I know we have something of yours . . . and you have something of ours. A basket of dried figs? (to Jerry) They got Laura's aunt's figs, too. (finding it hard to break the news) You don't know then? Uh . . . this is going to be pretty hard to tell you, Mr. Peters, but . . . well how can I put it . . . Um . . . (fresh attack) Mr. Peters, you do know that there is a tremendous similarity between a three and an eight . . . If you close up the open side of a three, you've got a perfect eight . . . What? Yes, this is Robert Petrie . . . Now you know there's a great similarity in our . . . Yes, I am one of the writers of the Alan Brady television show . . . Well, I'm glad you think our show is funny but I really would like to get this thing settled . . . Uh . . . you know there is also a great similarity in our names . . . Petrie and Peters . . . and . . . both our wives did give birth at the same time in the same hospital, and the hospital was very busy . . . What am I getting at? . . . Mr. Peters . . . may I ask you a personal question? . . . Who does your baby look like? . . . Well, our baby doesn't look like either of us neither, not to mention his footprint. I think I'm making myself very clear. We have each other's babies . . . (very seriously) How do you want to handle this? . . . Yes, I am Robert Petrie the comedy writer, but I can't see any humor in this situation . . . Mr. Peters, may I have your address please . . . I see . . . no, that's fine with me as long as we settle it tonight . . . Fine . . . you got my address from the hospital . . . fine . . .

(hangs up)

JERRY: He's coming here?

ROB: Yeah. He said his wife felt like getting some air! They were going to drop off the dried fruit anyway. Boy he's taking this pretty lightly. Some people just don't care whose baby they bring up.

Laura enters from bedroom. She is in robe.

LAURA: Rob . . . who called? Hi, Jerry!

JERRY: Oh, hi . . . Laura! I was just leaving!

LAURA *(sees baby):* Rob, what's the baby doing out here?

ROB: Well, I was checking . . .

JERRY *(starts out):* G'nite, folks and good luck. *(to crib)* 'Bye, son.

He exits.

ROB: Goodnight, Jerry! Laura . . . sit down . . . there's something I have to tell you! That was . . . uh . . . Mr. Peters . . . the flower people! They . . . uh . . . they're coming over here in a few minutes.

LAURA: They are?

ROB: Uh-huh . . . I hate to tell you this . . . but we have the wrong . . . flowers and . . .

LAURA *(stopping him):* Rob, is something bothering you?

ROB: No . . . I just love you very much. Laura . . . uh . . . how much do you like that baby?

LAURA *(tenderly):* There is something bothering you.

ROB: Laura . . . uh . . . how much do you like the baby?

They sit on sofa.

LAURA: How much do I . . . *(thinks . . . smiles)* Rob,

don't tell me you're getting jealous of the baby already . . .

ROB: Honey, I'm not getting . . .

LAURA *(cont'd):* . . . just like Dr. Spock said. He knows everything!

ROB: He doesn't know everything. For instance, he doesn't know that you're 1 in 50 million!

LAURA: Thank you, darling.

ROB: Don't thank me. Laura, do you know that 1 out of every 50 million women has the wrong baby?

LAURA: That's a cute trick. How does she manage it?

ROB: No . . . no. She doesn't have it while she's having it. It's after she has it that she has it.

LAURA *(thinking Rob is crazy):* Rob, are you trying to tell me we have the wrong baby?

Rob nods.

LAURA *(cont'd):* Rob, you're crazy!

ROB: Honey, keep calm!

LAURA: I'm perfectly calm, except that I'm a little worried about you.

ROB: Don't worry, I can take it. Anyway our baby is probably as cute as this one.

LAURA: Rob, will you stop! Where did you ever get a crazy idea like this.

ROB: At the hospital . . . that's where we got it.

LAURA: Rob, we just got the wrong flowers!

ROB: You forgot the rice pudding and the blueberry tart pretty fast, didn't you? Not to mention the dried figs!

LAURA: Dried figs? *(emphatically)* Rob . . . this is our baby and that's all there is to it!

ROB: Laura, he doesn't even look like us.

LAURA *(looking into bassinet, shouts):* Rob!!

ROB: You see?

LAURA: All I see is our baby with a blue foot. What is this blue stuff on his foot?

ROB: Ink.

LAURA: Who put it there?

ROB: Jerry and I.

LAURA: Why?

ROB: Just running a series of tests.

LAURA: Rob, nothing in the whole world will convince me that the baby in that crib is not ours.

ROB: I don't blame you, honey . . . you just can't face the facts . . . poor kid!

The doorbell rings.

ROB *(cont'd):* There are the Peters now. Laura, prepare yourself!

LAURA: Rob, nobody is taking this baby, do you hear . . . nobody!

ROB: Laura, I think you'd better go to your room. I'll handle this.

LAURA: I'm staying right here!

Rob opens front door.

VOICE *(outside):* Hi, we're Mr. and Mrs. Peters.

ROB: Come in.

A young, attractive Negro couple enter . . . Rob, mouth agape, as they enter carrying a basket of figs and smiling broadly.

MR. PETERS: Would you like to swap some figs for some flowers?

LAURA: Mrs. Peters, won't you come in and sit down?

MRS. PETERS: Thank you—I'm still a little wobbly.

LAURA: Me, too, but not as wobbly as my husband.

MRS. PETERS: I know I shouldn't be up and around but I wanted to be in on the fun.

LAURA: I understand.

ROB: Sit down, Mr. Peters. Why didn't you tell me on the phone!

MR. PETERS: And miss the expression on your face?

ROB: Yeah . . . Did I give you a good one?

MR. PETERS: A beaut!

ROB: I'm sorry . . . I haven't been myself lately. We just had a baby. *(Peters points to himself.)* Oh, you did, too. How about some coffee?

Laura starts to get up, but Rob pushes her down and starts to kitchen.

ROB: I'll make it, honey. Do you want to see the baby we tried to pawn off on you?

MR. PETERS: Hey, that's a beautiful baby . . . and he looks exactly like you.

LAURA: You really think so?

MR. PETERS: No, but why start him off again?

They all laugh.
Fade out
Fade in:
Int. Petrie living room—night—the present
Petries, Helpers, and Mel grouped as in first scene.

MEL: Rob, that's a fantastic story. So everything worked out fine!

ROB: Well, things didn't work out as well as we'd expected.

MEL: What do you mean?

LAURA: What are you talking about?

ROB: You know that Peters little boy, Jimmy . . . he's in Ritchie's grade at school?

LAURA: Yes?

ROB: Top of the class . . . straight A's. Our Ritchie . . . *(zoom)* . . . bottom of the heap. I still think we got the wrong kid!

All chuckle, laugh as Laura hits Rob.
Fade out
The end

Awards

★ **Emmy Awards 1961–62:**
Outstanding Writing Achievement in Comedy: Carl Reiner, *The Dick Van Dyke Show*

★ **Emmy Awards 1962–63:**
Outstanding Program Achievement in the Field of Humor: *The Dick Van Dyke Show*
Outstanding Writing Achievement in Comedy: Carl Reiner, *The Dick Van Dyke Show*
Outstanding Directorial Achievement in Comedy: John Rich, *The Dick Van Dyke Show*

★ **Emmy Awards 1963–64:**
Outstanding Program Achievement in the Field of Comedy: *The Dick Van Dyke Show*
Outstanding Continued Performance by an Actor in a Series (Lead): Dick Van Dyke, *The Dick Van Dyke Show*
Outstanding Continued Performance by an Actress in a Series (Lead): Mary Tyler Moore, *The Dick Van Dyke Show*
Outstanding Writing Achievement in Comedy or Variety: Carl Reiner, Sam Denoff, and Bill Persky, *The Dick Van Dyke Show*
Outstanding Directorial Achievement in Comedy: Jerry Paris, *The Dick Van Dyke Show*

★ **Emmy Awards 1964–65:**
Outstanding Program Achievements in Entertainment: *The Dick Van Dyke Show*, Carl Reiner, producer

Outstanding Individual Achievements in Entertainment (actors and performers): Dick Van Dyke, *The Dick Van Dyke Show*

★ **Emmy Awards 1965–66:**
Outstanding Comedy Series: *The Dick Van Dyke Show*, Carl Reiner, producer
Outstanding Continued Performance by an Actor in a Leading Role in a Comedy Series: Dick Van Dyke, *The Dick Van Dyke Show*
Outstanding Continued Performance by an Actress in a Leading Role in a Comedy Series: Mary Tyler Moore, *The Dick Van Dyke Show*
Outstanding Writing Achievement in Comedy: Bill Persky and Sam Denoff, "Coast to Coast Big Mouth," *The Dick Van Dyke Show*

★ **Emmy Awards 1961-62**
(Presented May 22, 1962, for programs telecast between April 16, 1961, and April 14, 1962)

OUTSTANDING WRITING ACHIEVEMENT IN COMEDY
° Carl Reiner, *The Dick Van Dyke Show* (CBS)
Stan Freberg, *Chunking Chow Mein Hour* (ABC)
Nat Hiken, Tony Webster, Terry Ryan, *Car 54, Where Are You?* (NBC)
Roland Kibbee, Bob Newhart, Don Hinkley, Milt

° Indicated winner

Rosen, Ernie Chambers, Dean Hargrove, Robert Kaufman, Norm Liebman, Charles Sherman, Howard Snyder, Larry Siegel, *The Bob Newhart Show* (NBC)

Ed Simmons, David O'Brien, Marty Ragaway, Arthur Phillips, Al Schwarts, Red Skelton, *The Red Skelton Show* (CBS)

OUTSTANDING DIRECTORIAL ACHIEVEMENT IN COMEDY
° Nat Hiken, *Car 54, Where Are You?* (NBC)
Seymour Berns, *The Red Skelton Show* (CBS)
John Rich, *The Dick Van Dyke Show* (CBS)
Bud Yorkin, *Henry Fonda and the Family* (CBS)
Dave Giesel, *Garry Moore Show* (CBS)

★ **Emmy Awards 1962–63**
(Presented May 26, 1963, for programs telecast between April 15, 1962, and April 14, 1963)

OUTSTANDING PROGRAM ACHIEVEMENT IN THE FIELD OF HUMOR
° *The Dick Van Dyke Show* (CBS)
The Beverly Hillbillies (CBS)
The Danny Kaye Show with Lucille Ball (NBC)
McHale's Navy (ABC)

OUTSTANDING CONTINUED PERFORMANCE BY AN ACTOR IN A SERIES (LEAD)
° E.G. Marshall, *The Defenders* (CBS)
Ernest Borgnine, *McHale's Navy* (ABC)
Paul Burke, *Naked City* (ABC)
Vic Morrow, *Combat* (ABC)
Dick Van Dyke, *The Dick Van Dyke Show* (CBS)

OUTSTANDING CONTINUED PERFORMANCE BY AN ACTRESS IN A SERIES (LEAD)
° Shirley Booth, *Hazel* (NBC)
Lucille Ball, *The Lucille Ball Show* (CBS)
Shirl Conway, *The Nurses* (CBS)
Mary Tyler Moore, *The Dick Van Dyke Show* (CBS)
Irene Ryan, *The Beverly Hillbillies* (CBS)

OUTSTANDING PERFORMANCE IN A SUPPORTING ROLE BY AN ACTRESS
° Glenda Farrell, "A Cardinal Act of Mercy," *Ben Casey* (ABC)
Davey Davison, "Of Roses and Nightingales and Other Lovely Things," *The Eleventh Hour* (NBC)
Nancy Malone, *Naked City* (ABC)
Rose Marie, *The Dick Van Dyke Show* (CBS)
Kate Reid, "The Invisible Mr. Disraeli," *Hallmark Hall of Fame* (NBC)

OUTSTANDING WRITING ACHIEVEMENT IN COMEDY
° Carl Reiner, *The Dick Van Dyke Show* (CBS)
Sam Perrin, George Balzer, Hal Goldman, Al Gordon, *The Jack Benny Program* (CBS)
Paul Henning, *The Beverly Hillbillies* (CBS)
Nat Hiken, *Car 54, Where Are You?* (NBC)
Ed Simmons, Dave O'Brien, Martin A. Ragaway, Arthur Phillips, Larry Rhine, Mort Greene, Hugh Wedlock, Red Skelton, Bruce Howard, Rich Mittleman, *The Red Skelton Hour* (CBS)

OUTSTANDING DIRECTORIAL ACHIEVEMENT IN COMEDY
° John Rich, *The Dick Van Dyke Show* (CBS)
Seymour Berns, *The Red Skelton Hour* (CBS)
Frederick De Cordova, *The Jack Benny Program* (CBS)
David Geisel, *The Garry Moore Show* (CBS)
Richard Whorf, *The Beverly Hillbillies* (CBS)

★ **Emmy Awards 1963–64**
(Presented May 25, 1964, for programs telecast between April 15, 1963, and April 12, 1964)

OUTSTANDING PROGRAM ACHIEVEMENT IN THE FIELD OF COMEDY
° *The Dick Van Dyke Show* (CBS)
The Bill Dana Show (NBC)
The Farmer's Daughter (ABC)
McHale's Navy (ABC)
That Was the Week That Was (NBC)

OUTSTANDING CONTINUED PERFORMANCE BY AN ACTOR IN A SERIES (LEAD)
° Dick Van Dyke, *The Dick Van Dyke Show* (CBS)
Richard Boone, *The Richard Boone Show* (NBC)
Dean Jagger, *Mr. Novak* (NBC)
David Janssen, *The Fugitive* (ABC)
George C. Scott, *East Side, West Side* (CBS)

OUTSTANDING CONTINUED PERFORMANCE BY AN ACTRESS IN A SERIES (LEAD)

° Mary Tyler Moore, *The Dick Van Dyke Show* (CBS)

Shirley Booth, *Hazel* (NBC)

Patty Duke, *The Patty Duke Show* (ABC)

Irene Ryan, *The Beverly Hillbillies* (CBS)

Inger Stevens, *The Farmer's Daughter* (ABC)

OUTSTANDING PERFORMANCE IN A SUPPORTING ROLE BY AN ACTRESS

° Ruth White, "Little Moon of Alban," *Hallmark Hall of Fame* (NBC)

Martine Bartlett, "Journey into Darkness," *Arrest and Trial* (ABC)

Anjanette Comer, "Journey into Darkness," *Arrest and Trial* (ABC)

Rose Marie, *The Dick Van Dyke Show* (CBS)

Claudia McNeil, "Express Stop from Lenox Avenue," *The Nurses* (CBS)

OUTSTANDING WRITING ACHIEVEMENT IN COMEDY OR VARIETY

° Carl Reiner, Sam Denoff, Bill Persky, *The Dick Van Dyke Show* (CBS)

Herbert Baker, Mel Tolkin, Ernest Chambers, Saul Ilson, Sheldon Keller, Paul Mazursky, Larry Tucker, Gary Belkin, Larry Gelbart, *The Danny Kaye Show* (CBS)

Robert Emmett, Gerald Gardner, Saul Turtletaub, David Panich, Tony Webster, Thomas Meehan, Ed Sherman, *That Was the Week That Was* (NBC)

Steven Gethers, Jerry Davis, Lee Loeb, John Mc-Greevey, *The Farmer's Daughter* (ABC)

OUTSTANDING DIRECTORIAL ACHIEVEMENT IN COMEDY

° Jerry Paris, *The Dick Van Dyke Show* (CBS)

Sidney Lanfield, *McHale's Navy* (ABC)

Paul Nickell, William Russell, Don Taylor, *The Farmer's Daughter* (ABC)

Richard Whorf, *The Beverly Hillbillies* (CBS)

★ **Emmy Awards 1964-65**

(Presented September 12, 1965, for programs telecast between April 13, 1964, and April 30, 1965)

OUTSTANDING PROGRAM ACHIEVEMENTS IN ENTERTAINMENT

° *The Dick Van Dyke Show* (CBS)

° "The Magnificent Yankee," *Hallmark Hall of Fame* (NBC)

° *My Name Is Barbra* (CBS)

° "What is Sonata Form?" *New York Philharmonic Young People's Concerts with Leonard Bernstein* (CBS)

The Andy Williams Show (NBC)

INDIVIDUAL ACHIEVEMENT AWARDS IN ENTERTAINMENT (ACTORS AND PERFORMERS)

° Leonard Bernstein, *New York Philharmonic Young People's Concerts with Leonard Bernstein* (CBS)

Lynn Fontanne, "The Magnificent Yankee," *Hallmark Hall of Fame* (NBC)

Alfred Lunt, "The Magnificent Yankee," *Hallmark Hall of Fame* (NBC)

Barbra Streisand, *My Name is Barbra* (CBS)

° Dick Van Dyke, *The Dick Van Dyke Show* (CBS)

Julie Andrews, *The Andy Williams Show* (NBC)

Johnny Carson, *The Tonight Show Starring Johnny Carson* (NBC)

Gladys Cooper, *The Rogues* (NBC)

Robert Coote, *The Rogues* (NBC)

Richard Crenna, *Slattery's People* (CBS)

Julie Harris, "The Holy Terror," *Hallmark Hall of Fame* (NBC)

Bob Hope, *Chrysler Presents a Bob Hope Comedy Special* (NBC)

Dean Jagger, *Mr. Novak* (NBC)

Danny Kaye, *The Danny Kaye Show* (CBS)

David McCallum, *The Man from U.N.C.L.E.* (NBC)

Red Skelton, *The Red Skelton Hour* (CBS)

WRITERS

° David Karp, "The 700-Year-Old-Gang," *The Defenders* (CBS)

William Boardman, Dee Caruso, Robert Emmett, David Frost, Gerald Gardner, Buck Henry, Joseph Hurley, Tom Meehan, Herb Sargent, Larry Siegel, Gloria Steinem, Jim Stevenson, Calvin Trillin, Saul Turtletaub, *That Was the Week That Was* (NBC)

Robert Hartung, "The Magnificent Yankee," *Hallmark Hall of Fame* (NBC)

Coleman Jacoby, Arnie Rosen, *The Wonderful World of Burlesque* (NBC)

Carl Reiner, "Never Bathe on Saturday," *The Dick Van Dyke Show* (CBS)

★ Emmy Awards 1965–66

(Presented May 22, 1966, for programs telecast between May 1, 1965, and April 10, 1966)

OUTSTANDING COMEDY SERIES
° *The Dick Van Dyke Show* (CBS)
Batman (ABC)
Bewitched (ABC)
Get Smart (NBC)
Hogan's Heroes (CBS)

OUTSTANDING CONTINUED PERFORMANCE BY AN ACTOR IN A LEADING ROLE IN A COMEDY SERIES
° Dick Van Dyke, *The Dick Van Dyke Show* (CBS)
Don Adams, *Get Smart* (NBC)
Bob Crane, *Hogan's Heroes* (CBS)

OUTSTANDING CONTINUED PERFORMANCE BY AN ACTRESS IN A LEADING ROLE IN A COMEDY SERIES
° Mary Tyler Moore, *The Dick Van Dyke Show* (CBS)
Lucille Ball, *The Lucy Show* (CBS)
Elizabeth Montgomery, *Bewitched* (ABC)

OUTSTANDING PERFORMANCE BY AN ACTOR IN A SUPPORTING ROLE IN A COMEDY
° Don Knotts, "The Return of Barney Fife," *The Andy Griffith Show* (CBS)
Morey Amsterdam, *The Dick Van Dyke Show* (CBS)
Frank Gorshin, "Hi Di-dle Riddle," *Batman* (ABC)
Werner Klemperer, *Hogan's Heroes* (CBS)

OUTSTANDING PERFORMANCE BY AN ACTRESS IN A SUPPORTING ROLE IN A COMEDY
° Alice Pearce, *Bewitched* (ABC)
Agnes Moorehead, *Bewitched* (ABC)
Rose Marie, *The Dick Van Dyke Show* (CBS)

OUTSTANDING WRITING ACHIEVEMENT IN COMEDY
° Bill Persky, Sam Denoff, "Coast to Coast Big Mouth," *The Dick Van Dyke Show* (CBS)
Mel Brooks, Buck Henry, "Mr. Big," *Get Smart* (NBC)
Bill Persky, Sam Denoff, "The Ugliest Dog in the World," *The Dick Van Dyke Show* (CBS)

OUTSTANDING DIRECTORIAL ACHIEVEMENT IN COMEDY
° William Asher, *Bewitched* (ABC)
Paul Bogart, "Diplomat's Daughter," *Get Smart* (NBC)
Jerry Paris, *The Dick Van Dyke Show* (CBS)

TOTAL NUMBER OF EMMY AWARDS WON: 15

★ 1963 Golden Globe Awards

BEST TELEVISION SHOWS:
The Richard Boone Show
The Danny Kaye Show
The Dick Van Dyke Show

★ 1964 Golden Globe Awards

BEST TELEVISION STAR, FEMALE
Mary Tyler Moore

★ Writers Guild of America Awards

1963: BEST COMEDY, EPISODIC
Martin Ragaway, "My Husband Is the Best One," *The Dick Van Dyke Show*

1965: BEST COMEDY, EPISODIC
Dale McRaven, Carl Kleinschmitt, "Br-room Br-room," *The Dick Van Dyke Show*

1966: BEST COMEDY, EPISODIC
Jack Winter, "You Ought to Be in Pictures," *The Dick Van Dyke Show*

Index

recasting of *Head of the Family*
idea by, 6
script editing by, 30–31,34
"Like a Sister" episode, 79
Lorillard & Co. (Kent cigarettes), 58
Lorimar, 17
Love and Marriage, 5

MacLeod, Gavin, 49–51
McRaven, Dale, 142
Make Room for Daddy, 5, 13, 21, 34
Marshall, Garry, as series writer, 67
Mathews, Larry, 72, 74
biographical notes on, 93
Mazzeo family name of, 13
as Ritchie Petrie, 13, 27
Melton, Sid, 51
Melvin, Al, as Sol (Rob's army
buddy), 51
Melvin Cooley character, 2
Calvin Cooley as original name
for, 2, 13
Deacon as, 10
Miles, Sylvia, as Sally Rogers, 5
Millie Helper character, 22, 75
Guilbert as, 25
Molin, Bud, 35
Moore, Mary Tyler:
awards received by, 165–168
biographical notes on, 88
career development as viewed by,
31
on character of Laura, 45
on filming of show, 31–34
as Laura Petrie, 14–17, 29–30
reaction to cancellation of series,
58
reaction to termination of series,
70, 72–73
wardrobe controversy and, 40–43
Morgan, Gary, as Ritchie Petrie, 5
Mork and Mindy, 60
Morris, Greg, 65
Morris, Howard, 1
Morris, William, Agency, 17, 58, 60–
63
Mr. Meehan (Laura's father)
character, Carl Benton Reid as,
49

Mullen, Marge, 6, 17, 97
reaction to termination of series,
73
as script supervisor, 34–35
"My Blonde-Haired Brunette"
episode, 22, 29
"My Husband Is a Check Grabber"
episode, 46
My Sister Eileen, 7

NAACP, 63
"Never Bathe on Saturday" episode,
29–30
"Never Name a Duck" episode, 46,
51, 52
Nickelodeon (Nick at Nite), 84–85,
87

"October Eve" episode, 46
"Odd But True" episode, 85
"Oh How We Met the Night That
We Danced" episode, 75
Oliphant, Peter, as Freddie Helper,
49
O'Malley, J. Pat, as Sam Petrie
(Rob's father), 49

Pantomine Quiz, 7
Paris, Jerry, 23–25, 46
awards received by, 165, 167, 168
biographical notes on, 92
as director, 59–60
as Dr. Jerry Helper, 23
Mork character created by, 60
Parker, Penney, 13
Pearce, Al, 7
Penn, Frank, 73
Perry, Barbara, as Pickles Sorrell, 49
Persky, Bill, 85
awards received by, 165, 167, 168
biographical notes on, 94
Reiner's influence noted by, 39, 45
as series producer, 69
as series writer, 30, 46, 60–63, 67–
69

Pickles Sorrell character:
Perry as, 49
Shawlee as, 49
Proctor & Gamble, 17, 20, 54, 58
censorship issue and, 63–64

Ragaway, Martin, 142
Randolph, Isabel, as Clara Petrie
(Rob's mother), 49
ratings, television, 58
Real McCoys, The, 5
Reid, Carl Benton, as Mr. Meehan
(Laura's father), 49
Reiner, Carl:
as Alan Brady character, 67, 79, 85
awards received by, 1, 69,
165–168
biographical notes on, 96
Caesar and, 1
Calvada and, 21–22
casting of series by, 6–14, 23
cast's appreciation of, 14, 23, 39,
69
censorship and, 39–40
Laura Petrie's character as viewed
by, 43–45
monitoring of character portrayals
by, 25
as producer and writer of series, 6,
67
reaction to cancellation of series,
58
real-life situations as basis for
writing of, 45–49, 67
on rewriting scripts, 69
as Rob Petrie, 5, 85
in script editing with Leonard, 31
summer reruns advised by, 59
termination of series and, 70
Van Dyke as viewed by, 5, 85
Reiner, Estelle, 1
Reiner, Robert, 2
Rich, John, 64–65
awards received by, 140
biographical notes on, 93
departure from series of, 67
as series director, 22, 25
Rich, Lee, 17, 58, 64
Richard Diamond, Private Detective,
14

171